Tahquamenon Tales

Experiences of an Early French Trader and His Native Family

Timothy J. Kent

Front Cover: Silver Fox paddling with his son Red-tailed Hawk and dog Jacques on the Rivière St. Croix.

Back Cover: Sunning Otter plays a native dice game with her sons Golden Eagle and Red-tailed Hawk.

Tahquamenon Tales

*Experiences of an Early French Trader
and His Native Family*

Timothy J. Kent

Silver Fox Enterprises
Ossineke, Michigan
1998

Copyright © 1998 by Timothy J. Kent
Published by Silver Fox Enterprises
P.O. Box 176
11504 U.S. 23 South
Ossineke, Michigan, 49766

All photographs by Timothy and Dorothy Kent
Printed by Gilliland Printing, Arkansas City, Kansas

Publishers Cataloging-in-Publication Data
Kent, Timothy J.
Tahquamenon Tales, Experiences of an
Early French Trader and His Native Family.
225 pp., 8-1/2 x 11 inches.

Contents:
1. Indians/Native Americans, U.S. and Canada.
2. Explorers and Traders, 17 th Century, U.S. and Canada.
3. French Exploration, Trade, and Settlement, U.S. and Canada.
4. Native and European Contact, 17 th Century, U.S. and Canada.
5. Fur Trade. 6. Commerce. 7. North American History.
8. U.S. History. 9. Canadian History.

Library of Congress Catalog Card Number 98-90468
International Standard Book Number 0-9657230-1-1

Other books by Timothy J. Kent:

Birchbark Canoes of the Fur Trade, Volumes I and II

Acknowledgements

Numerous individuals from the previous four centuries assisted me in my efforts to accurately recreate the lifeways of a French trader of the 1600s and his woodland native family. First, credit must be given to the early French explorers, traders, missionaries, military officers, and administrators who penned accounts of their travels, experiences, business transactions, and observations of daily life during the seventeenth century. In addition, I am grateful to the archivists, researchers, and publishers who labored to preserve those early records, as well as to the many librarians who assisted me in acquiring copies of them. I must also express my appreciation to the field archaeologists who have excavated native and French sites dating from that century, particularly those who published detailed reports to disseminate their discoveries.

My thanks are also extended to those individuals who provided raw materials for my recreations of native items, as well as to the artifact dealers and modern craftworkers who supplied many Euro-American items and the birchbark canoe. Finally, I would like to thank my wife Doree and our sons Kevin and Ben, who with good spirit and much enthusiasm joined me in these many years of living history research.

Each of these numerous individuals, in ways large and small, contributed to the results of the project, which has endeavored to shed new light on the daily lives of many of the inhabitants of the northern tier of North America during the seventeenth century.

Timothy J. Kent

For Gary Litherland, a true friend
and an avid colleague in the search for our past.

Upper: Silver Fox on the Rivière Tahquamenon.
Lower: Sunning Otter in full regalia.

Upper: Golden Eagle (R) and Red-tailed Hawk (L) beneath the canvas lean-to.
Lower: Otter crushing dried corn with a stone mortar and pestle, on a buffalo robe.

Upper: Fox demonstrates the use of a wheellock pistol for his sons and Jacques.
Lower: Otter and the boys playing a native dice game, with dried beans as winnings.

Upper: Paddling up the Rivière St. Croix.
Lower: Otter sleeps beneath the canoe with Hawk and Jacques.

Introduction

Like most other historians, I regret that no time machine has ever been invented which could whisk me back to previous eras. With such a vehicle, it would be simple to make on-the-spot observations of how people went about their daily lives long ago. Objects that we now know only as museum artifacts could be seen being used by individuals who thoroughly understood their usage. The reasons for people's thoughts and actions of long ago could be gleaned. Traveling back in time, I could record the small, mundane details of life that are so treasured by those interested in history, those little items that were never written down, since the participants were either illiterate or thought that such details were so commonly known in that era that there was no need to record them.

Lacking a functioning time machine, I decided on the next best thing — I pretended to build one.

For nearly two decades, my studies had focused on the prehistoric lifeways of Native Americans, as well as the era of early European and native contact in North America. This included the study of prehistoric and historic archaeology, European exploration, the development of the fishing and fur trade industries, and early settlement.

I had also conducted detailed research on over 725 of my French and French Canadian direct ancestors, who had originated from over 120 communities in France. Many of them had been involved in the fur trade of North America, from about 1618 to at least 1758. They were engaged in the occupations of fur trade company manager, clerk, trader, interpreter, guide, voyageur, merchant/outfitter/fur buyer, investor, laborer, tradesman (cutler, gunsmith, post carpenter, etc.), birchbark canoe builder, and trans-Atlantic shipping merchant. In addition, other ancestors had served as soldiers in Canada, in the Carignan-Salières Regiment during the 1660s and the Troupes de la Marine in the 1680s and 1690s.

I found the early historic period, the 1500s and 1600s, particularly fascinating. During those two centuries, European and native cultures first made contact with one another, and began sharing material goods, friendships, ideas. These exchanges were made in both directions, with each culture assessing the other's traits, adopting some and rejecting others. Certain adopted items and concepts were altered considerably to suit the needs of a different world; some were even utilized in an entirely different manner than in the originating culture.

Europeans and Indians each had certain items that the other group valued and wanted to acquire. Europeans had objects of metal, fabric, and glass to offer, as well as much technological knowledge in such areas as firearms. Native Americans had an abundant supply of furs, hides, and other natural products. They also had devised highly successful methods of surviving and thriving in the New World, in regions that were virtually unknown to the French. Many of their methods of hunting, fishing, agriculture, transportation, and warfare would be vital to the French if they were to successfully inhabit that new world.

During the first two centuries of the French experience in New France, the material goods, modes of living, ways of thinking, and religious beliefs of their European culture did not dominate the Native American culture. Later, by about the middle of the 18th century, a pan-Indian culture had been adopted across much of North America, with a similar blend of native and European traits appearing in most regions that had been affected by the fur trade. By that time, many native traditions had been abandoned for European ways. Such was not the case in the 1500s and 1600s.

As I carried out my research, I wanted to gain an understanding of the ways of life of both the French and the native populations during that early period of European exploration, fur trade, and initial settlement. I also hoped to surmise how and why each group reacted to various aspects of the other's culture, and to learn how their lives were changed by adopting one another's traits. These questions made me hungry for details of all areas of their lives: clothing, equipment, weapons, foods, medicines, shelters, stories, music, games, religious beliefs, modes of transportation.

The relative scarcity of early documentation pertaining to a number of these subjects, as well as the rarity of excavated sites from this period, made the quest all the more exciting. Over a number of years, my files grew to include hundreds of early documents and the excavation reports from over fifty North American sites dating from the 16th and 17th centuries. These sites included major French forts and trading centers, small posts, and missions, as well as extensive native villages and small seasonal camps.

During the course of this study, I realized that the only way to discover and understand a great many of the small details of daily life in both cultures would be through living history research. This type of research would entail recreating authentic versions of as many of the objects of daily life as possible of the two worlds, and actually living for periods of time within that blend of material culture. The scenario of those periods would be a recreation of the daily lives of a French trader and his woodland Indian family in the interior regions during the 1600s. These reenactments would include my wife Doree and our sons Kevin and Ben.

Our adventures would parallel those of a number of my ancestors. Olivier LeTardif had been sent by Champlain to live among various native groups in the 1620s as a trade ambassador, before becoming the official interpreter at Quebec in Algonkian, Huron, and Montagnais languages. Claude David lived and traded among the Ottawas and Hurons at Chequamegon Bay, near the western end of Lake Superior, from 1660 to 1663. Mathieu Brunet dit Lestang spent the years from 1687 to 1689 as a trading partner of Nicholas Perrot in the upper Mississippi region. There is considerable likelihood that some or all of these men had at least temporary native families during their years in the interior, before they returned to their spouses and children in the St. Lawrence settlements. Such French-and-native families presumaby existed in the northern woodland regions of North America from the second decade of the 1600s on.

After years of gathering reference materials, I began the process of creating the time machine. The original early documents and the excavated artifacts provided a great deal of information, the solid foundation for the project. Recreating the various items of daily life, and then living with those objects, would fill in many additional treasured details.

Building the time machine was a long, complicated process. (It is actually still continuing, with the discovery of additional early documents, the acquisition of reports from newly-excavated sites, and the ongoing recreation of early items.) For years, gifts for each family member for such events as birthdays, holidays, and Mother's Days consisted of handmade items of equipment and clothing. Doree often suspected that not many other women were as fortunate as she was to receive such rare gifts: for her birthday one year, a pouch made from a dried buffalo bladder, filled with dried corn silk to thicken soups, or for Mother's Day a bundle of dried elk leg tendons for producing sinew sewing threads.

To recreate the early ways of life as authentically as possible, that was the goal. Fabricating copies of original items from the correct materials was to be a major part of the learning process. The quest for genuine materials of the native world reached far and wide — hides, bones, teeth, feathers, claws, furs, antlers, tendons, bladders, tails, brains, buffalo wool yarn, porcupine quills, turtle shells, catlinite, black walnut hulls, gourds, clay, hematite, barks, roots, stones, shells, native copper, various woods.

I notified a major fur buyer in the northern Rockies to spread the word among his trapper contacts for certain of my special requests. For instance, to fashion a fire bag I needed a large, good-looking striped skunk pelt which had been removed from the animal in its natural tubular form, with paws and claws intact, rather than being sliced open and flat with the paws removed. In addition, the trapper was to save the skull, which would be later defleshed and restored to its former location in the head after the pelt had been tanned.

Once the appropriate materials were gathered for a given project and the traditional tools had been made or acquired, I then had to learn whatever skills were necessary to recreate the item. These included such tasks as brain-tanning hides, boiling walnut hulls to make dye, pounding and grinding native copper into knife blade and awl, carving wood, antler, and catlinite, finger-weaving garters, stretching and drying bladders, grinding bone and shell, scraping and stretching rawhide, and sewing clothes with an awl and sinew thread. Neighbors sometimes noticed unusual sights, sounds, and smells emanating from our house and yard.

Not having skills as a flint knapper, I chose to use ancient stone artifacts instead of reproductions for stone axe, adzes, knives, scrapers, drills, and graver. We also used two items of original native pottery, a wide-mouthed water bottle and a deep bowl; these pieces date from the Late Woodland period, about 800 to 1500 A. D.

A number of European items were well beyond my manufacturing skills, as well. Not being a blacksmith, I commissioned a number of craftsmen to forge such iron items as trunk hardware, a spanner wrench for the wheellock gun, a harpoon head, fish hooks, spear and arrow points, awls, firesteels, and a lead-melting ladle with a folding handle. These were fashioned to detailed specifications based on excavated examples from 17th century sites.

The Whitney mills in England, which had produced woolen blankets for the North American trade for over three centuries, had run a special order of an early style of blanket for Colonial Williamsburg. By good fortune, two remaining blankets from that order were located for making our *capotes,* or hooded coats. A maker of custom tents built the tarp shelter that I had designed to fit over our canoe, while a potter created a custom copy of an early style of French plate. Exact reproductions of a series of excavated 17th century knife blades were hand forged by a blade maker, who used methods very similar to those of my cutler ancestor Pierre Paradis (1604-1675).

Glass bottles fashioned after excavated examples were acquired from the glass blowers at Colonial Jamestown. An antique copper pot and an early copper skillet, both of appropriate styles and with the interior tinning intact enough for use, were located through artifact dealers. In northern Minnesota, a builder of birchbark canoes created a craft to my detailed specifications in the original early style that was used in the Great Lakes region.

A number of weaponry items were much more difficult to obtain. I wanted to carry authentic versions of a French wheellock pistol and an early flintlock fowler. Instead of searching among the few skilled craftsmen who might reproduce such weapons, I sought out original specimens among the prominent dealers of antique weapons and at the major gun shows across the country. After a number of years of searching, I owned an original wheellock pistol dating from about 1615 to 1640, a French flintlock pistol from about 1720, and a French flintlock carbine from 1733. Through the same channels, I acquired a 17th century cowhorn belt flask for gunpowder and an early hand-forged iron mold for making lead balls.

After about three years of assembling items, there was sufficient material gathered to begin the living history expeditions (the recreation of additional French and native articles would continue for many years thereafter). At that time, Kevin was age ten and Ben was eight. We spent delightful week-long vacations each year carrying out our reenactments in isolated locales in the upper Great Lakes region. The family had been camping since the boys were born, and three years earlier we had begun our family project of paddling each year a long segment of the mainline fur trade canoe route across Canada. However, those expeditions involved modern equipment.

Utilizing gear and clothing from four centuries ago, and paddling and sleeping beneath a birchbark canoe, created an entirely new learning experience, as we had hoped it would. Since these adventures were intended to lead to discoveries, we did bring, in addition to our ancient equipment, a camera, lenses, films, pens, and notebooks, to record our experiences. We also carried a modern first aid kit (which has luckily not yet been needed).

The chapters in this book describe our experiences during each of the first eight years of our living history research, as we traveled via the time machine. In the tales, told in third-person narrative style, I am a French trader, called Silver Fox by the native people. Doree is Sunning Otter, my native (or *Métis,* mixed-blood) wife, while our sons Kevin and Ben are Golden Eagle and Red-tailed Hawk. Jacques is the stage name of our faithful dog Toby.

Each year, we focused on two or three different aspects of life as it was lived by such a family in the interior regions during the 1600s. We sought to understand the old ways of both cultures as deeply as we could. As is apparent in the tales, our living research often focused on the material culture, the actual objects that were used in daily life. However, we also attempted to understand the reactions of the French and native people as they assessed the various offerings of each other's culture.

Traditional objects could sometimes be abandoned and replaced with a newly introduced item very quickly and easily, while ideas and beliefs often changed much more slowly. Thus, technological changes took place much faster than social changes. We have attempted to gain insights into both of these types of cultural changes, which occurred when the two worlds, native and French, met and intermingled.

We have found these adventures to be educational, entertaining, and broadening. We particularly appreciated sharing these experiences during our sons' formative years. In addition to the great deal of historical knowledge we have gained, we have also acquired a broader perspective on our modern lives, and a deeper appreciation of the times and ways of those who came before us. Our predecessors lived in eras of often far greater physical labors and discomforts than ours. However, they also lived in times when many more aspects of life, learned by example and done by hand, could bring satisfactions. It would behoove us all to look back more often at the old ways, and ponder the value of those things which have been abandoned.

Chapter One

The low, reedy shorelines that the family had encountered on several of the islands in Potagannissing Bay were not very hospitable for a week-long campsite. Paddling further to the northwest of Isle Drummond in Lac Huron, the boys spotted a rather small island in the distance which appeared to have an inviting sandy beach. As the canoe approached the shore and its expanse of tan sand, a large fisher, interrupted from his feast of mussels, leaped from the water's edge back into the underbrush. Golden Eagle and Red-tailed Hawk caught glimpses of a large white object set back among the trees.

To avoid damaging the birchbark canoe, the family disembarked offshore in the shallows and carefully beached the craft. The boys' first discovery near the shore was the frame of a small sweat lodge that was lacking its covering. At the center of the bowl-shaped framework of lashed saplings lay several white rocks, the remnants of previous sweating ceremonies. Advancing about fifty paces inland from the lake, Silver Fox and Sunning Otter entered a large grassy clearing. Toward one side stood three traditional birchbark structures of The People (the name that most native groups called themselves). This explained the white color that the family had glimpsed through the trees from offshore.

The first building was a single-family conical *wigiwam,* a temporary shelter which was usually used for traveling. Upright poles placed in a broad circle had been gathered together at their tops and lashed firmly together in a cone form. The covering, made of long overlapping bark panels, was held in position upon this framework by several long cords of basswood inner bark and a few vertical poles that leaned against the exterior of the shelter.

In line with this first structure stood two semi-permanent ones, a single-family oval *wigiwam* and a multi-family longhouse with an elongated oval form. Neither of these stood much taller than Fox, and he was by no means a tall man. The framework of each of these shelters consisted of two rows of upright saplings inserted into the ground. The tops of the rows had been bent downward toward each other, to form a series of arches. The tips of each pair of poles were lashed together with narrow strips of basswood inner bark. The same cordage had also been used to fasten the long birchbark panels to the framework.

Wigiwaman such as these were sometimes covered on the walls with mats made of bulrushes sewn together side by side, reserving the more water-repellent bark sheets for only the roof area. In other instances, part or all of the shelter was covered by large panels of cedar, elm, or black ash bark, mats of woven strips of cedar inner bark, or hides. With the arrival of French trade goods, woolen blankets or tarpaulins of linen canvas were sometimes used in conjunction with or in place of the traditional native coverings over the pole framework.

At first, Fox had considered the native shelters made of a pole framework and a covering as rather flimsy affairs, compared to the solidly built French buildings of wood and stone. He particularly missed the hearty structures along the St. Lawrence when cold winds

Upper: The family's camp beside three birchbark *wigiwaman*.
Lower: Testing the pot of wild rice and jerky.

A mingling of two cultures: Fox has a French pistol, knife, tomahawk, and shirt, plus many adopted articles of native clothing and equipment.

Upper: Otter tends a food-drying rack of lashed saplings.
Lower: Dining with mussel shell spoons from dishes of birchbark and turtle shell.

The boys while away an afternoon with a game of French cards, inside one of the bark shelters.

Upper: Fox helps his boys set a spring pole snare.
Lower: The three hunters admire their completed deadfall trap.

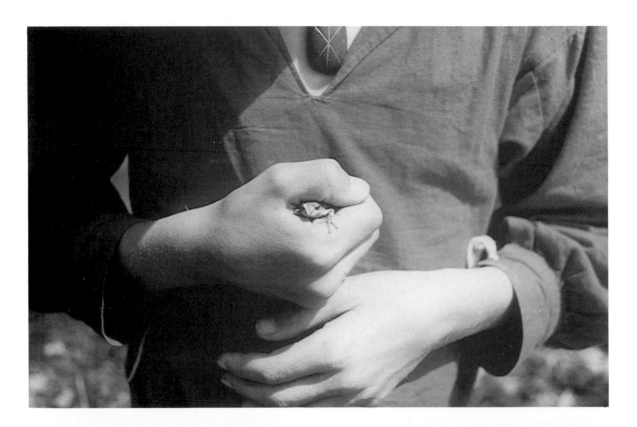

Upper: Hawk shows off his live catch, a tiny green frog.
Lower: Inside a *wigiwam*, the crackling fire dries the family's suspended moccasins and accompanies Eagle's song.

Upper: Hawk fashions a walking stick from a sapling encircled by a vine.
Lower: Eagle molding lead balls for the wheellock pistol.

To ward off the chill, the boys wear deerskin mantles and Otter has donned her *capote*.

drove rain through the smoke hole and the narrow crevices in the walls of his *wigiwam.* However, he was well aware of the seasonal cycles of life in the interior regions. The People moved between various locales that were conducive to successful hunting, fishing, gathering, maple sugar production, gardening, and trading, as they had done for thousands of years. Quickly erecting portable shelters of poles and coverings at each new location certainly made more sense than building permanent log homes at each site. The location where each seasonal activity was carried out sometimes varied from year to year, depending on fluctuating supplies of game, fish, and natural products. Thus, it was often impossible to build permanent structures at a site where the family or group would be certain to return in a given season. However, The People did sometimes erect semi-permanent buildings, made of a pole frame covered with sturdy panels of thick tree bark, at their more usual seasonal locations, such as cleared garden plots, maple sugar groves, and excellent fishing locations. They also often left the lashed framework of their shelters permanently in place at many sites, removing only the covering when they departed.

French travelers in the interior readily adopted the traditional birchbark shelters of The People; only occasionally did they use canvas tents. To cover the pole framework of their temporary shelters, they typically carried a number of *écorces à cabaner;* these were long rolled strips of bark made up of several large panels sewn together end-to-end with split roots. A sapling was usually lashed to each end of the long strip, to facilitate the rolling of the strip for transport and for its attachment to the pole frame at campsites.

When Fox and his family traveled, they utilized a canvas *appentis* (lean-to) erected over their overturned canoe, another common native and French adaptation. A canvas shelter cover was heavier to transport than one made of birchbark strips or sewn rush mats. However, the tightly woven *prélart* or oiled linen tarp, with its individual strips sewn firmly together to form a single large piece, was more waterproof and wind resistant than the series of overlapping bark strips or mats that covered a traditional shelter. In addition, it was extremely durable, over the long term, compared to the native versions. Over time, birchbark strips tended to crack after much rolling and handling, and sewn rush mats could be crushed or broken with repeated usage during long voyages.

Near the three bark structures that Otter and Fox inspected in the clearing, a sturdy frame for hanging items had been built of peeled poles over the fire area, which was outlined with smooth granite rocks. A low food drying platform of slender lashed saplings stood a few steps away, ready for food processing by sun's rays or fire.

Beyond the *wigiwaman,* the land extended gradually upward to the crest of the island, with tall maples and a few birches scattered here and there on the slope. The long, level crest of the land mass stood about fifty feet higher than the shoreline. Halfway up the slope lay an ancient native burial ground, containing nine graves in two irregular rows. Four of the grave sites were covered with white and red granite cobbles gathered from the shoreline. Three were unadorned and sunken, partially filled with rotting leaves. The two at the southern end of the cemetery were each covered with a knee-high grave house built in log-cabin style with a flat roof. These little structures appeared to have been replaced within the last decade or so.

The family was elated to have found such an ideal setting for their camp. But they wondered if any of The People at Sault Ste. Marie might object to their presence at this obviously revered site of the Old Ones. After a consultation, Otter and Fox decided that if anyone saw them on the island, living in the ancient ways, they would understand that the family was respectfully honoring those who had come before. So they unloaded their belongings, and erected the canvas lean-to over the canoe, in line with the three birchbark shelters and handy to the cooking area.

During the following week, Otter spent much time and energy preparing traditional native meals for her family. Breakfasts typically consisted of dried strawberries, walnuts, and wild rice cooked with maple sugar, eaten from birchbark dishes with mussel shell spoons. Midday meals were often of buffalo jerky (dried meat), beans, and grapes, cooked together and eaten from turtle shell bowls. Evening repasts of whitefish-and-cornmeal stew and baked squash were washed down with berry tea from the communal turtle shell cup. What a grand life this was when the food storage trunk was full!

On the first evening, the family walked quietly past the moonlit burial ground and up onto the wooded crest of the island. Beneath the tall maples, they flushed out two deer that had come to investigate the intruders at the south end of their island. Later, back in the canvas shelter, everyone snuggled for the night into beds of woolen blankets and robes of buffalo and black bear.

The morning of the second day, it was time to explore the crest of the island. Running on ahead, Eagle was pleased to discover a very large ancient "sugar bush." This extensive grove of venerable maples had formerly been the scene of innumerable annual maple sugar harvests. The long, angular gashes made at that time in the trees to drain the sap had long since healed into thick, uneven scars. The trees had grown so much since those harvest days that many of the scars were now ten to twelve feet above the ground. Since the dense canopy of the maple tops had shaded the forest floor, no other trees or large underbrush had grown back between the spaced maple trunks since the brush was cleared away long ago for the sugaring operation. These trees had witnessed during many springtime seasons the contented chatter around kettles of boiling sap, and the glee of the youngsters as they feasted — after a long, hungry winter—on candy of maple syrup poured over clean snow.

The introduction of copper and brass kettles and pots had greatly eased the labors of boiling down maple sap into sugar in groves such as this one. With metal containers, The People were able to concentrate the syrup much more effectively than they had formerly done using their traditional containers of wood, pottery, bark, gourd, and hide.

After a midday meal, Otter and her family set out on foot to examine the heavily wooded shoreline all around the perimeter of the island. Tracks and droppings of deer were plentiful nearly everywhere. Upon reaching the windlashed west side, with its long expanses of waterworn cobblestones, it was clear why the Old Ones had decided to place their camp year after year on the lee side of the island. There, it was sheltered from the west and northwest winds, and handy to an excellent canoe landing area, which had a sloping sand bottom free of obstructions.

At the south end of the island, the moist sand at the water's edge was covered with fisher tracks. The entire area was littered with opened mussel shells that glistened white in the sun. Here was where the fisher's feast had been interrupted the day before. Nearby lay a thick tangle of fallen trees and brush, in which he had hidden his den.

The first two days had been spent finding an ideal island, setting up camp, and carrying out a thorough exploration. Much time during the following days would be filled with such tasks as gathering dry limbs for firewood, grinding dried corn with the stone mortar and pestle, and tending the fire and the *marmite de cuivre,* the copper cooking pot. However, Fox and the boys devoted considerable time each day to learning how to construct and set snares, deadfalls, and live pit traps.

These latter activities were of major importance in the continual quest of The People for food and furs. In fact, they hunted and trapped fur-bearing animals a great deal more now than they had previously done. With the increased supply of furs and hides, they traded for many European items which had never before been available in their forest and prairie world before the arrival of the French.

On the first day of trapping practice, Eagle and Hawk began with the most rudimentary type of device, a live pit trap. Using sharpened heavy sticks and antler tines to loosen the soil and a large elk shoulder blade to scoop it out of the hole, they dug a deep pit at the junction of two well-worn game trails in a deep thicket. The soil was placed on a deer hide and dragged a short distance away. Larger tree roots in the hole were cut off with a *petite hache,* a tomahawk.

As they worked, Fox explained to his sons the French tools of iron which were called *pioche* (pickaxe), *houe* (hoe), *beche* or *louchet* (spade), *faucille* (sickle), and *faux* (scythe). He had not brought any of these implements into the interior, even though they would have been of value in digging and gardening tasks in camp. These items would have been rather bulky and heavy within the limited cargo space of his canoe; instead of them, he brought other trade items which were much more highly prized by The People. The larger iron tools were sometimes transported into the interior by other Frenchmen, for use at major posts and mission centers.

The boys dug the pit sufficiently large to hold a raccoon-sized animal, with enough depth and steepness of the walls to prevent the captured prey from escaping. Across the top of the excavation, Hawk laid a number of slender branches; Eagle covered the entire area with a layer of long grasses that grew in the clearing. A piece of jerky was bound to a sapling growing beside the trail as bait.

An animal that might fall into this type of trap, usually unharmed, would be dispatched by a blow to the head with a wooden club or the back side of a tomahawk, or by the stab of a lance. The use of the pit trap was not limited to smaller animals; larger prey only required digging a larger and deeper hole. The boys noted that the only improvement that Fox's trade goods brought to this type of trap was the ease with which the iron tomahawk severed roots within the hole and cut branches to cover the hole.

Since the family was setting traps on the island that week simply for practice purposes, each one was dismantled after being built as a learning experience. Fox therefore dragged the deer hide loaded with soil back to the trap site, and refilled the pit. His trapping lessons would resume the following day.

The next morning was overcast, with a steady breeze off the lake. To ward off the chill, Eagle and Hawk donned their deerskin mantles, while Otter and Fox slipped into their *capotes,* hooded woolen coats. The boys' lessons this day would focus on snares. These traps captured prey by the neck with a noose; as the animal struggled to escape, the noose tightened and caused it to strangle. Snares were used to capture prey that ranged in size from as small as muskrats and ruffed grouse to as large as deer, panthers, and bears.

The People had fashioned snare nooses for thousands of years from native cordage such as twisted inner bark of the basswood tree. The commercial linen cord of various weights (*corde* or *ligne*) that was brought in by the French trade functioned similarly. However, trading for the cordage did eliminate the considerable labor involved in producing the native version by hand. The introduction of *fil de cuivre* and *fil de laiton* (copper and brass wires) improved the effectiveness of many native snares. These metal versions could not be chewed through by inquisitive animals. (Cord nooses were sometimes smeared with lynx or fox droppings to discourage rabbits from chewing them.) In addition, wire nooses could withstand greater forces without breaking as the animal struggled, compared to nooses of cordage.

In advance of the snaring instruction, Fox had twisted together four or five strands of thin brass wire into a strong yet flexible slender cord. Boiling the wire cord in hemlock bark had turned the shiny yellow color to a deep brown and had removed the brassy odor; this would make the wire less noticeable to animals.

Snares were attached to either a fixed anchor such as a bush, spring pole, or balance pole, or to a section of tree limb or small log which the captured animal would drag along the ground or up a tree. These traps were usually positioned along game paths (including fallen logs that were used for crossing streams) or within an enclosure that contained bait.

The boys decided to first make a snare that was attached to a moveable anchor and was set in an enclosure. Pushing short sections of dry limbs into the ground, Eagle created a small V-shaped corral with two walls each about the length of a man's arm. Hawk made a noose by forming a loop at one end of the twisted wire cord and then running the opposite end through the loop. The loose end was then firmly attached to the end of a thick tree branch. This branch was laid across a stump near the enclosure so that the attached wire noose was suspended slightly above the ground in the center of the V-shaped structure.

The boys baited the trap by placing kernels of dried corn in a row leading into the enclosure, as well as a small pile of kernels at the apex of the V. A game bird would be led into the structure by the row of kernels, and into the snare as it attempted to reach the pile of kernels. Struggling to escape from the loop of wire, the prey would tighten the noose and drag the limb, pulling the snare even tighter.

Snares were often mounted to a spring pole or a balance pole. With this method, the captured prey was raised out of reach of other animals that would eat the catch before the trapper could retrieve it. The boys erected a spring pole snare over a well-worn game trail.

The trap consisted of a sturdy sapling bent over as the spring, two slender sections of tree limbs for the bait stick and the trigger, a length of trade cord connecting the trigger to the tip of the spring pole, and a noose made of cord. The snare was arranged so that an animal biting a piece of meat impaled on the end of the bait stick caused that stick to move and dislodge the trigger stick. This freed the sapling to spring back to its upright position, yanking the noose closed around the neck of the prey and hauling it into the air. Standing back at a safe distance, Hawk enjoyed nudging the bait with a long stick to set off the trap.

Fox afterward explained that a straight balance pole was often utilized instead of a bent sapling, since a spring pole would sometimes lose its spring and remain in its set bent position when released, especially when a living or green sapling was used. A balance pole was positioned upon a crotched stick pedistal in such a way that when the trigger was released, the heavy base of the pole suddenly sank to the ground while its light tip rose upward with the attached noose.

After a busy morning constructing snares, the two sons convinced their mother to while away part of the afternoon with them, playing with French cards on the robes in the conical *wigiwam.* Inside, sheltered from the wind, they were warm enough without a fire. By the end of the afternoon, each of them had accumulated a generous pile of dried beans, each bean representing an individual round that the player had won.

On each of the warmer days, the boys spent plenty of time playing at the canoe landing area. Stripped down to just a breechclout and a narrow waist belt, they kicked off their moccasins and curled their feet into the delicious warmth of the sand. Eagle enjoyed following various sets of animal and bird tracks along the wet soil by the water's edge, while Hawk dug and trenched with a large shoulder blade of an elk.

Each evening, Otter kindled a cheery fire with flint and steel in the firepit of one of the *wigiwaman,* while the boys each gathered an armload of small sticks for firewood. Damp moosehide moccasins were suspended on upright sticks around the blaze, where they gave off wisps of steam as they dried. Smoke and occasional sparks wafted upward, escaping through an opening in the bark cover at the center of the roof. Eyes stared into the flames or watched the patterns of yellow light dancing on the brownish tan bark of the walls and ceiling.

The family passed the evening hours sharing native legends, singing French songs, and discussing customs such as the vision quest. This native custom, carried out at the coming-of-age stage of life, involved dreams which were induced by isolation, fasting, and sleep deprivation. Through these dreams, each individual discovered which spirit force would be his or her personal guardian throughout life. For instance, if a young man saw a vision of an elk during his quest, he might thereafter wear an elk hoof or some other body part, secreted in a tiny hide pouch. In times of duress, he would touch the pouch and call upon the spirit of the elk for guidance or assistance. In much the same manner, Fox thought, some Frenchmen wore a brass crucifix or saint's medal, and through it sought aid in times of need. This and other traditions of growing up in the world of The People were compared to the customs of the French way of life. These talks led to quiet, restful sleep.

The last major type of native trap that the boys wanted to master was the deadfall. This device could be used to capture the full range of animal sizes, from weasel to bear. It operated by releasing a log which fell atop the head or upper body of the prey.

Fox helped the boys drag a heavy fallen log to the base of a pair of large maples. They then built a miniature shelter of limbs and brush at the base of the two trees. The large limbless log was laid on the ground so that it stretched across the entrance of the shelter. Two pairs of sturdy limbs were driven into the ground on each side of the log, to serve as guide posts. To set the trap, Fox and Hawk lifted one end of the log, while Hawk positioned a triggering device beneath the raised end to hold it up. The device was made of three notched sections of sapling that were assembled in the form of a number 4. To bait the trap, a piece of jerky was firmly bound to the projecting end of the horizontal stick of the 4, which pointed well into the shelter beyond the raised log. An animal had to reach its head and possibly its front paws into the shelter to reach the bait; in the process, its upper body was positioned beneath the fall log. Gnawing the baited trigger stick released the log, which was guided in its fall by the pairs of guide posts. The log crushed the upper body of the prey to the ground or to a base log placed beneath the fall log.

Fox pointed out to the boys that his imported iron tomahawk and knife facilitated the chopping and carving of the various parts of deadfall traps, but they did not effect the traditional procedures. The introduction of *pièges,* iron traps with jaws and springs, however, did alter a number of native trapping techniques; for one, the hunters who used them did not produce the actual capturing devices themselves.

Iron traps were in common usage in France throughout the 1600s. A number of these devices were transported to New France and carried into the interior. The traditional snares and deadfalls of The People usually killed the captured animals very quickly. In contrast, European iron traps most often grasped a foot or leg and held the tormented animal until the hunter arrived, unless the trapped part was broken or chewed free. The exceptions occured when these traps were set underwater; then, the captured prey usually drowned quickly.

Over time, The People slowly began to acquire increasing numbers of iron traps. However, a great many native hunters continued to construct pit traps and deadfalls of forest materials, and to set snares with nooses made from trade cord or wire. These inexpensive nooses could be easily constructed and repaired by each hunter; they also took up very little space in a shoulder bag, pack, or canoe, and weighed almost nothing. In contrast, the relatively expensive iron traps were heavier, bulkier, and often required a blacksmith to make repairs. In many instances, these traits discouraged their usage by native hunters, especially in remote areas.

Eagle and Hawk had learned much concerning trapping, but they still needed experience with various baits, scents, and ingenious sets which would not be noticed by the animals. With patience, this knowledge would grow in the years ahead, as it had for Fox. He and numerous other Frenchmen had learned many techniques of trapping from The People.

When the family had earlier examined the "sugar bush," Eagle had discovered a fist-sized burl growing at about his shoulder height on one of the maples deep in the grove. The burl was a gnarled round mass of wooden growth which had been produced when some injury to the tree had healed in the distant past. Using Fox's tomahawk, which required a two-handed swing for a boy, Eagle carefully chopped the burl free from the trunk. The chopped flat side of the growth would be hollowed out, using a *couteau croche* (crooked knife), to produce a drinking cup. The twisted grain of the gnarled mass would be virtually unbreakable, even if the cup were dropped onto a hard surface.

While Eagle was occupied in the maple grove, Hawk located an interesting natural growth as well. A thick woody vine had grown in a spiral pattern tightly around and around a sapling. Fox felled the sapling with its captor vine for his son, and cut off a section nearly as tall as Hawk. Since the younger son did not yet have a *couteau boucheron* (butcher or sheath knife) of his own, he used Otter's knife to carefully peel the fresh green bark from the two intertwined elements, to fashion a walking stick.

Sitting before the canvas shelter, Otter busied herself with an iron *alesne* (awl) and a length of sinew thread from an elk leg tendon. She resewed the central toe seam of one of Fox's moccasins, where a knot in the original sinew had become untied and had slipped a few stitches. Keeping footwear in repair was a common and recurring task of woodland life; but it was of no concern at all to the two crows that circled high above Otter as she worked.

One grey afternoon, the boys asked if they could do one of their favorite tasks, molding lead balls for the wheellock pistol. In preparation, Fox found a slender bar of *plomb* (lead) in the scarred old trunk, and brought it to the fire, along with his hunting bag. He drew the tomahawk from its sheath, which was sewn to the long shoulder strap of the bag. Placing the bar on a log, he chopped the soft metal into chunks about the size of a finger joint. The newly-cut surfaces glinted with a bright silver color, in contrast to the dull grey color of the other, older surfaces.

Now the boys could safely take over. Hawk jammed the pointed shaft of the black iron *louche* (ladle) into one end of a forearm-long section of green sapling. Into the cupped end of the ladle he dropped two of the cut chunks of lead, and placed it in the base of the flames. The wooden handle allowed him to remain at a comfortable distance from the fire while the metal heated. When the lead reached the melting point, it quickly dissolved into a thick silvery liquid. A bit of thin grey scum floated on the top, the remnants of the dull grey coating which had been on the outer surfaces of the metal when it was in chunk form.

In the meantime, Hawk opened the pliers-shaped *moule de balles* (ball mold) of iron, and heated its head in the coals. The heat from the head traveled past the central rivet and into the handles, but he removed the mold from the coals before the handles became too hot. Eagle then held the pliers mold in a closed position in his left hand. Positioning the spout of the ladle over the hole or vent in the top of the mold, he filled the hole until it overflowed slightly, and carefully laid the partially empty ladle aside. Opening the mold, he dumped the hot silvery ball onto a piece of old deer hide. The heat of the metal singed and puckered the hide slightly. Before the remaining lead in the ladle had a chance to cool, Hawk quickly filled the mold a second time, and dropped a second hot ball onto the hide. As they cooled, the silver color of the two spheres slowly turned a bit grey.

The first couple of balls were somewhat misshapen, due to uneven heat within the head of the mold. But after the first pours, each product was a complete sphere. However, each ball had a short cylindrical projection, which had been formed by the lead which remained in the hole of the mold. These sprues Fox trimmed off with a knife after the balls had completely cooled, saving the trimmed remnants to be later remelted to form more gun balls. The boys traded off in the molding production during the afternoon, and took much pride in the pile of balls that they finally loaded into the small moosehide ball pouch in the hunting bag.

While his sons admired their products, Fox described to them other types of ball molds. His iron mold formed only one ball at a time. Using other larger molds, made of iron or brass, up to fourteen small shot could be cast on each side of a mold in a single pouring operation, creating a total of twenty-eight balls at a time. In addition to ball molds made from iron or brass, others consisted of two halves carved from soft stone, such as soapstone. The halves were either tied together for the molding procedure or were mounted into two wooden handles that could be fastened together and released. Many molds were also carved from hard wood. To minimize the burning damage of the hot lead, these wooden varieties were dipped into water immediately before and after being filled with the molten metal.

The notches in Fox's stick finally indicated that a week had passed at the camp; the day of departure had arrived. In the quiet of early morning as the sun came up, a northbound wedge of geese honked over the little island of serenity and ancient ways. The family broke camp and loaded the canoe, reluctant to leave the life of the island and return to the modern world.

A leaden sky closed in, a brisk wind picked up, and light rain began to fall. It required all the efforts of Fox and Otter, against the strong headwind and whitecaps, to paddle out to Isle Drummond and the twentieth century.

———————————————

On the evening after departure from the island, at a motel just north of the Straits of Mackinac, I could not bear to break the spell of the enriching week by taking a shower and changing into modern clothing with the rest of the family. Instead, I spent the evening in solitude on the shore of Lake Huron, envisioning canoes rounding the point centuries before.

Chapter Two

The campsite was a good one, in a small clearing on the south bank of the Rivière Tahquamenon, about a mile upstream from where it emptied into Lac Supérieur. Clean, cool water flowed in the river beside the camp, and not far away a stand of dead trees, blown down by the wind some years before, offered a plentiful supply of firewood for an extended stay. The clearing was large enough to allow breezes to waft through the camp, cooling it during the heat of the day and helping to keep the mosquitoes at bay during the evenings. The early morning rays of the sun could filter through the tops of the surrounding forest to warm the clearing, while the angle of the bend in the river enabled Sunning Otter to enjoy the last rays of sunset from across the river at dusk. It was a comfortable place.

Fox held in his right hand a narrow bar of steel that had been bent into an elongated C shape, with his fingers fitted through the central opening of the C. In his left hand, he firmly grasped an irregular piece of broken grey flint about two finger joints long. Chick. Chick. As the *batte feu* (firesteel) struck a razor-sharp edge of the flint, several tiny orange-hot sparks of steel were sliced off. One of them flew onto the small square of linen charcloth that Fox held on top of the flint. The little spark smoldered on its black bed of charred fabric as he placed the cloth into a nest-shaped wad of dried grass. Holding it above his face, Fox blew steadily; the charcloth glowed orange, then the wad of dry tinder suddenly burst into flame. He lost no time plunging the little fireball into the teepee-shaped arrangement of firewood, and in seconds the flames had consumed the tiny twigs and were licking at the kindling wood. Shortly, the breakfast fire was ready, with a plentiful supply of firewood limbs stacked near at hand, the result of much labor by the boys.

The container holding the supply of charcloth and tinder fibers, a small black cow horn, was carefully closed with its wooden stopper, to ensure that the contents would stay dry. The stopper, an oval slice of wood, was gripped by a short loop of deerhide thong that protruded from a hole in the middle of the oval. Fox then returned the firesteel and flint to a small deerskin pouch, and dropped the pouch and the storage horn into the *sac à feu* (fire bag) which hung from his belt.

The tubular bag, made from a complete pelt of a striped skunk, had glossy black fur and a white stripe that extended the full length from the nose down to the tip of the tail. A lengthwise slit in the underside between the front legs provided an opening into the bag. Fox wore the *sac* with its head and neck tucked up behind his waist belt and folded over the belt. He had inserted the skull of the skunk back into its original position inside the head; this prevented the thin hide bag from sliding out below his belt. To reach inside the bag, Fox raised the skunk's head and neck and pulled the bag downward until its top was halted at the belt by the thickness of the skull. The slit opening was then exposed below his belt.

Fox had earlier created his fire-starting charcloth by placing a stack of cut squares of linen into a small round tin box, a *boite de fer blanc*, that had a tiny hole punched through

Upper: Eagle and Hawk learn of the magical powers of a firesteel and flint for starting a blaze.
Lower: A watched pot never boils, in any century.

Fox's *sac à feu* or fire bag, made from a complete skunk pelt, hangs from his wide moosehide belt.

Upper: Harvesting jack pine roots for stitching birchbark.
Lower: Hawk fashions a miniature birchbark canoe, beside three one-piece dishes of folded bark.

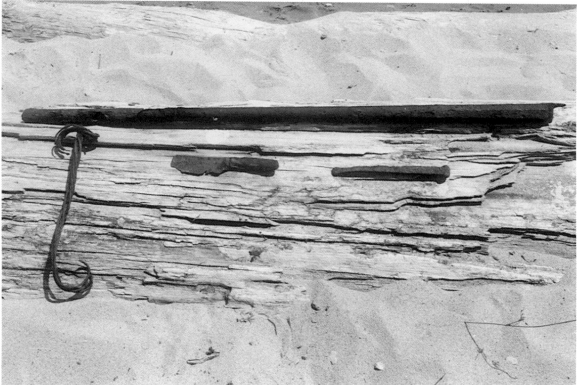

Upper: Each player earns dried beans by casting five bone dice.
Lower: Ancient items discovered by the boys: barrel of a trade gun, gaff hook, sheath knife, and hand-forged spike.

Upper: Ready for a swim in the Tahquamenon.
Lower: Three card players on a buffalo robe.

Surveying the forest from his high pine perch, Eagle watches for the approach of friends or foes.

Upper: Hawk looks forward to the day when he will have his own *mousqueton* for hunting.
Lower: No intruders will escape Eagle's notice.

its lid. When the box was heated on glowing coals, the fabric inside had carbonized instead of burning, since it was sheltered from oxygen in the closed container. After the smoke had stopped flowing from the hole, Fox had brushed the box from the fire and let it cool before opening the lid. He then transferred the rather delicate blackened fabric to the protection of his cowhorn container.

Some Frenchmen lit fires by igniting *allumettes* with their firesteel, rather than using charcloth. These items, made of either slightly twisted linen cordage or splints of wood, had been dipped at their end in sulfur.

Partially decayed "punky" wood, particularly from a soft maple, was also effective in maintaining a hot spark from a firesteel. When dried and pounded, this wood barely burned, much like the charcloth. Dried and crushed fungi from such trees as birch, sugar maple, and red maple also worked well.

Although the system of firesteel and flint had been readily adopted by many of The People, Fox still sometimes saw individuals igniting their fires with a wooden fire set. Two pieces of wood were used, a horizontal flat split section (the hearth) on the ground and an upright spindle or shaft. Various woods could be used for these two elements. The tip of the spindle was set into a shallow pit near the edge of the flat hearth, and was twirled with downward pressure. This was done either between the palms or by using a curved section of limb strung with cordage much like a bow.

Friction between the two pieces of wood caused them to burn slightly, producing a hot charred powder. This powder fell through a notch which had been cut halfway into the side of the shallow pit in the hearth. The black powder accumulated into a tiny pile, where it finally reached a peak temperature and formed a tiny ember. This ember was maintained on a bit of dried punky wood or crushed fungus, and was transferred to a wad of tinder, in much the same manner that a hot spark from flint and steel was handled.

Fox's firesteel system was considerably less laborious than the friction method, and his set of equipment was much smaller and thus more portable. If the flint and steel became wet, they could be wiped dry very quickly and made ready to use. In contrast, a wet friction set had to be used a bit to create friction and heat to dry the wood of the spindle and hearth before they were ready to create an ember. Over time, Fox was certain, the wooden friction set would be abandoned by The People.

Even the firesteel and flint method was occassionally replaced, by the use of a small magnifying lens. This tool was especially useful for lighting tobacco in a pipe. Red-tailed Hawk carried one of these thin lenses of glass in his fire bag, carefully protected inside a tiny deerhide pouch. On days of bright sunshine, he focused a thin beam of sunlight through the lens onto a square of charcloth. After a short time, the fabric began to smolder in a tiny spot, in the same manner as when a little spark fell onto it from a firesteel.

At the fire, Otter began cooking preparations. Her pot hanger, a long straight iron rod with a U-shaped crook bent into one end and a sharp point at the other, had been fashioned from a round iron rod salvaged from the rim of a large brass kettle. Pushing the pointed end of the rod deep into the ground beside the fire, she suspended the copper pot on the crook end over the flames. Deciding to bring the pot nearer to the heat for faster cooking, she then suspending it from the crook with an S-shaped iron hook.

The People thought that most of the copper and brass cooking containers that were carried into the interior regions were much too valuable as sources of exotic materials to be used for cooking. Instead, they cut up most of them to make bright, flashy ornaments, as well as scrapers, knives, and arrow and lance points. However, as a trader with a ready and renewable supply of trade goods, Fox had plenty of pots, pans, and kettles; so his family cooked with them.

The delicious smells of wild rice and jerky, spiced with ginger root, began to waft from beneath the blackened wooden lid of the pot, encouraging Otter to wield the stirring stick. As she stirred the steaming, savory meal, the bird head effigy carved at the end of the handle seemed to do a little dance in the air.

Hawk ambled off to fill the water bottle from the handy supply at the riverbank. He added a few wintergreen leaves to the long, wide neck of the *bouteille*, and placed it in the sun near the fire to make tea. The light green glass glistened in the sunlight, making the globular body and long neck of the bottle look quite elegant.

By the woodpile, Golden Eagle sorted through the ancient *cassette,* a wooden trunk with a rounded top. The solid construction of its dovetailed corners and wooden pegs, plus its strong, handforged iron hinges, handles, and bands, had helped it endure many years of service before it had come to Otter. Its deep scars and stains spoke of numerous adventures. A fist-sized square piece of sheet brass, cut from a kettle, had been nailed over the hole in its front where a key lock had long before been pried out.

Eagle lifted from the trunk drinking cups of box turtle shells and dishes of both snapping turtle shells and birch bark. From a lidded *makuk* (birchbark storage container) he produced a twisted serving ladle carved from a tree root, four mussel shell scoops or spoons with their edges carved smooth, and a little salt container of cowhorn. Everyone was ready for a feast, including Jacques, the *petit chien* with the *grand appétit.*

After the meal, Fox and Otter slid the canoe from under the canvas lean-to which had been set up at the riverbank, and the family set out to explore a little upriver. The glassy surface of the water reflected the puffy white clouds in the azure sky. As the canoe rounded the first broad bend, Hawk spied an otter sunning himself on a small log that jutted out from the reedy far shore. The otter watched the people while they watched him. When the canoe approached, he slid quietly into the water, dived, and surfaced in midstream behind the craft.

As the family proceeded upstream, Eagle rummaged in his fire bag on his belt and located his brass *boussole,* a sundial-compass. After removing its brass cap, he positioned the little round instrument on the center thwart, and called out the directions that the canoe turned around each bend. This item was handy for noting directions while traveling during the daytime, when no stars were visible as guides. However, The People had developed over thousands of years acute skills for determining directions by carefully observing their environment. To them, the compass was more of a novelty than a useful tool. However, it was of considerable value to a foreigner such as Fox when he first began orienting himself to their region, and for drawing maps en route.

When Eagle had tired of announcing the direction of travel, he raised upright the little fold-down brass sundial, and rotated the compass so that it was aligned with north. The shadow cast by the sundial fell onto the symbol X on the rim of the compass. Fox explained that in New France and France, this would mean that the time was ten o'clock. The boys thought it was both strange and laughable that many people in those far-away worlds arranged their entire lives around such a clock.

With his sharp eyes, Hawk discovered a large birch tree that had been toppled to the ground by the wind, not far back from the riverbank. It still had some of its roots connected to the earth, so that its sap flowed and its leaves were still green. Thus, Fox could remove a good supply of fresh bark yet not damage or destroy a standing tree. With the knife from his neck sheath, he scored around the trunk in several places, as well as making one long cut down most of its length. The thick bark peeled off in broad white sheets.

The best root for making *watap*, the long strands used for sewing birchbark containers and canoes, came from the black spruce, which grew in boggy, swampy areas. Since this area of the Tahquamenon was well-drained, no black spruce grew there. However, jack pines would provide good substitute roots. After a search, Eagle located a small stand of these scraggly pines, with their stubby, bent cones and greyish brown, scaly bark.

A couple steps from the base of one of the trunks, Fox dug in the sandy soil with his hands and a stick. A little below the surface, he located one of the slender roots, which he severed by pulling it upward. Tugging the brown root with both of his hands near the surface of the ground, he advanced away from the tree and pulled it free out to its end, a distance of three or four paces. Otter harvested several other roots from the neighboring pines in the grove, using the same technique.

Meanwhile, the boys had located a sapling with a strong crotch form at about their shoulder height. Facing each other, one on each side of the sapling, they pulled one of the freshly-dug jack pine roots back and forth through the crotch area of the young tree. Each firm pull stripped the thin bark from the root and removed its little branching rootlets. The exposed surface had a clean, shiny appearance; its color was very light tan, almost white.

The better part of the afternoon was spent harvesting and peeling a good supply of these long, slender roots, which were rolled into small coils and securely bound. En route back downstream to the campsite, the family sang in celebration of their very productive harvesting trip.

> *Entendez-vous sur l'ormeau,*
> *Chante le petit oiseau?*
> *Tra la la la la la la la la la la,*
> *Tra la la, tra la la.*
>
> Do you hear in the elm,
> The little bird singing?
> Tra la la .....

Having only snacked lightly during the day on dried grapes and walnuts, everyone was famished. At the evening meal, they feasted on bean soup plus squash, baked whole in the coals and eaten with maple sugar. As a treat, Otter fried *gallette* (corn meal cakes) with blueberries in the *poele à frire*, the copper frying pan. She turned the fist-sized cakes with an ivory-handled iron *fourchette* (fork) and a bent spatula carved from the juncture of a limb and its tree trunk.

Some of the cakes were laid aside for the next morning's breakfast. Placing them into the copper pot, Otter tied a long piece of trade cord to its handle. Throwing the end of the cord over a sturdy limb of one of the tall pines at the camp, she hoisted the container of treats out of reach of nighttime marauders, both animal and human.

After a long, active day, the family watched the fire for only a short while before retiring to the shelter and snuggling into the blankets and robes. For Otter and Fox, the distant calling of the whippoorwill in the distance brought back many childhood memories of falling asleep on summer nights.

Suddenly, Fox was awakened by slow, splashing footsteps in the river. Since the shelter had been erected at the very edge of the riverbank, about four feet above the water, the footsteps sounded as if they were close enough to soon be stepping right on him. He listened intently for a long time. Finally, he heard a few more splashing steps, now sounding as if from more of a distance. The next sounds he heard were the birdsongs of early morning.

Hawk and Fox were the first awake and out of the shelter. As they stretched and admired the start of a beautiful sunny day under a blue sky, a huge bull moose rose up from his resting place in the expanse of tall grass and reeds on the broad curve of the river directly across the river from their camp. As the black bull ambled off unconcernedly into the distant trees, Fox realized that the splashing steps in the river during the night had been his, probably while he had fed on underwater plants near the water's edge. This day, the lucky moose would avoid being transformed into jerky.

After a breakfast of leftover *gallette* plus walnuts, washed down with berry tea, everyone spent the morning fashioning items from the supply of birchbark and *watap* that had been harvested the previous day. Otter retrieved several coils of roots from the river, where they had been soaking to keep them as pliable as when they were freshly dug. With his fingers, Fox split the roots into halves or quarters, to make them more flexible for sewing. Cutting the bark to shape with a pair of loop-handled iron *ciseaux* (scissors) and piercing holes with an iron awl mounted in a deer antler handle, the boys fashioned simple toy canoes, as well as a sun visor for their mother. Otter and Fox made one-piece eating and serving dishes, and a ladle with a long peeled stick for a handle.

Afterward, everyone enjoyed making dental pictographs with thin layers of bark. To make these traditional tooth-bitten imprints in birchbark, Otter peeled off a thin layer of reddish tan inner bark for each person. These were then cut into a square or rectangular shape, and folded several times. A design was firmly bitten into the folded bark, using mainly the incisor teeth. Unfolding the layers revealed the repeated pattern that had been formed by the teeth marks. Eagle and Hawk enjoyed producing complicated designs, and tried to predict how the pattern would look before they unfolded the layers.

For the midday meal, Otter crushed dried corn with the flat stone mortar and pestle for corn soup, accompanied by jerky eaten plain. The boys enjoyed heating water for tea in a birchbark vessel hung directly over the flames. They never tired of seeing that the liquid contents kept the bark moist enough that the flames could not burn through the container.

Boys and parents whiled away a lazy afternoon on the buffalo robe spread out under the trees, playing games of chance. Eagle's favorite was a native dice game. Five deer ankle bones had each been carved with a different symbol on each of the three sides of the small bone; pulverized hematite stone mixed with fat had been rubbed into each of these cut-in designs. The lid of a birchbark storage box served as the tray on which the bones were shaken. The player earned dried bean markers by having three, four, or five matching symbols land facing upward on the tray. All winnings of beans were later thrown into the next day's bean soup.

Another of the traditional native games involved guessing under which of four over-turned mocassins a certain object was hidden. Hawk "accidentally" poked his father regularly with the pointer stick while indicating where he guessed the lead gun ball lay hidden. The family ended the afternoon by playing some gambling games with French playing cards, involving high stakes and high pressure.

That evening after the meal, the youngsters brewed wintergreen tea in a traditional pottery bowl of The People. Decorated on the exterior with impressions of a wooden paddle wrapped with twisted cord, the thick vessel had been fired to a mottled gray with areas of dark black. Tiny flecks of crushed granite that had been mixed into the wet clay as tempering material glinted in the firelight. After filling the round bowl with water, the boys balanced it atop three small stones, and raked glowing coals around it; when the water began to simmer, Eagle added wintergreen leaves. To cool the clay bowl and its tea, Hawk raked away the coals, leaving the bowl in position until it had cooled.

As the warm drink was sipped from turtle shell cups, darkness fell and the evening grew chilly. The adults donned *capotes* and the boys deerskin mantles, and everyone found a place on the buffalo robe before the fire, with backs against the venerable trunk. The story that evening focused on Fox's ancestor Claude David dit Lacourse, who in 1660 had paddled westward on Lac Supérieur past the mouth of the Rivière Tahquamenon, not far from the family's campsite.

Radisson and Groseilliers were the first two known French traders to venture from the St. Lawrence settlements into the upper Great Lakes region. In 1660, they came out from Lac Supérieur to Trois-Rivières, on the St. Lawrence River, with the Ottawa and Huron canoe brigades. When these brigades returned to their villages on Baie Chequamegon, near the western end of Supérieur, seven French traders from Trois-Rivières accompanied them. The ancestor Claude David was one of those seven, the gunsmith of the group.

Born some time between 1621 and 1627 in France, Claude had been in Canada since at least 1647. He was about age thirty-three to thirty-nine, the father of five sons ranging in age from one to ten. He had been settled with his wife in Trois-Rivières, across the street from Groseilliers's house, for over eleven years at the time this trading expedition began in 1660.

Claude and his six colleagues traded during the following fall, winter, and spring with the Ottawas and Hurons, and accumulated many furs, as did also a number of native traders and hunters. When the time drew near for the brigade to transport the furs out to Trois-Rivières, the Ottawas, having clashed with the Sioux to the west, decided not to make the trading trip to the French settlements on the St. Lawrence River; they expected retaliatory raids from the Sioux. So Claude and his friends spent a second year with the villagers on the bay.

After this second year, in the summer of 1662, Iroquois raiding parties menaced the canoe route to the St. Lawrence settlements. A large party of Ottawas, Ojibwas, and Nipissings defeated a major Iroquois war party in the Sault Ste. Marie area; but again, the Ottawa and Huron brigade did not journey out to the French trade fair. Thus, the seven Frenchmen were obliged to spend a third year in the interior.

Finally, in the summer of 1663, the brigade was able to proceed safely down from Lac Supérieur with the supply of furs. The group was made up of one hundred fifty Ottawas and Hurons in thirty-five canoes, in addition to Claude and the other six Frenchmen. En route, they passed by the mouth of the Tahquamenon, near the present campsite of Fox and his family.

The three-year trading venture in the interior did not end as a financial success for the seven French traders. The debts they had incurred in 1660 to outfit the expedition with equipment, provisions, and trade goods had been accruing interest for three years instead of the expected one year. The hard-earned furs which they brought out did not cover the total cost of the expedition. However, the traders did transport out a large copper ingot, as well as bringing reports of copper mining by The People in the Supérieur region.

Claude apparently made no further trading trips himself into the *pays d'en haut* (the upper country), although he did join with other traders, including Nicholas Perrot, as an investor. Others of the seven Frenchmen of the 1660-1663 expedition did return to the interior. Adrien Jolliet, older brother of the later famous explorer, returned to trade for four or five years, beginning in 1666, until his death. Antoine Trottier (brother of another of Fox's ancestors, Pierre Trottier) founded one of the most active fur-trading families in New France, which participated in the trade for many years. Claude's only daughter and last child was born a year after his return from Chaquamegon Bay. None of his three sons who lived to adulthood worked as voyageurs, but his daughter married a Detroit trader. In addition, Claude's nephew Jacques Denoyon worked for Tonti in the Illinois country trade; he also was the first recorded French trader to venture as far westward from Lake Superior as Rainy River and Lake of the Woods, in 1688.

Claude lived to about age sixty to sixty-six, in Trois-Rivieres and across the St. Laurence at Gentilly. He died at nearby Cap de la Madeleine, where he was buried on December 2,1687, survived by his wife and four of his six children.

Fox and his family retired for the night with their fur trade ancestors very much in mind.

The following day dawned bright and sunny. At an early hour, the canoe once again was launched, this time heading downstream about a mile to the mouth of the Rivière Tahquamenon, on Baie de Poisson Blanc (Whitefish Bay) near the eastern end of Lac Supérieur. On the way, Otter caught a glimpse of a doe near the edge of the forest, at the top of a high sandy bank. The canoe also disturbed a tall, dignified heron that had been fishing in the quiet shallows; he flapped away, as if in slow motion, to a spot further upstream. At the mouth of the river, a brood of tiny mallard ducklings was led in an obedient line across the watercourse and into a shadowed inlet by their quacking mother.

The big lake was unusually calm; only an occasional light breeze ruffled its blue surface. Fox could see clearly about twenty miles across the bay to Pointe des Iroquois, where Supérieur funnels down its last few miles into the Rivière Ste. Marie near Sault de Ste. Marie.

While Otter and Fox enjoyed the warmth of the sun and the sand, and reflected on the past history of the place, Eagle and Hawk were finding tangible relics of that history. In the shallows of the lake near the river mouth, they found a complete barrel from a trade fowler made by Richard Wilson, the main supplier of trade guns to the Hudson's Bay Company. [This particular gun barrel bore markings indicating that it had been made in the period of about1785, when Wilson's shop was located on Minories Street in London.] In addition, the boys found a bone-handled sheath knife, a hand-forged flared-bit spike, and a gaff hook that had been fashioned from a number of slender iron rods twisted together.

After a meal of smoked whitefish with dried strawberries and apples, the family began the return trip back to camp. By this time, a stiff westerly headwind had picked up. The waves were advancing downstream, against the direction of travel, making forward progress tough and slow. Fox resorted to the only known remedy: a voyageur song.

> *Vent frais, vent du matin,*
> *Vent qui soufl' aux sommets des grands pins,*
> *Joie du vent qui soufl',*
> *Allons dans le grand vent.*

> Fresh wind, wind of the morning,
> Wind that blows in the tops of the tall pines,
> How wonderful is the wind that blows,
> Let's go into the strong wind.

Fox knew well the magic that these old songs could conjure, by helping to pass difficult or tedious miles. The family had also learned years before that the songs helped quench fear in dangerous paddling situations; it was impossible to be scared to death while belting out an old *chanson*. With the singing assisting their paddles, they finally returned to the friendly camp.

The next morning, in preparation for fishing, the boys harvested two long but light saplings, and pulled off their slim branches. Eagle tied a length of tan-colored linen trade line to the tip of each pole. Meanwhile, Fox produced two barbed iron *hamecons* (fishhooks) and two *empiles*, thin strands of brass wire which were used to fasten each hook to its fishing line. These filaments were imported in bound skeins, with each strand pre-cut to the proper length. The wire, secured to the shaft of the hook with a special lashing, was prevented from sliding off by the broad flattened area that the blacksmith had created at the upper end of the shaft. Eagle lashed a pebble to each line for a sinker, while Hawk gathered insects for bait from beneath overturned rocks.

As Fox watched his sons standing in the shallows, casting their lines toward the depths of the river, he considered what changes his trade goods had wrought on the fishing practices of The People. The traditional methods of fish harvesting had been little altered by his trade items. Fishing was still done by hook and line, spear with one or more prongs, bow and arrow, club, dip net, gill net, and woven trap. Various of these articles were used while standing on shore, wading in the shallows or rapids, or afloat in a canoe. For easier harvesting, fish were sometimes attracted by a torch, or were corralled into restricted areas by means of weirs made of walls of stones or of sticks pushed into the bottom. Much fishing was done in winter via holes through the ice, using hook and line, spear, or net. Gill nets were set beneath the ice by passing them from hole to hole with long poles.

Fox's linen cords and lines of various weights were sometimes substituted for native cordage in the various nets, woven traps, and hook lines. In addition, finished *filets de peche* (fishnets) were also occasionally imported. *Harpons* and *darts* were iron harpoon and spear heads which had either a wide triangular tip at the end of a shaft or one or more broad barbs on one side of the shaft. These implements often replaced native versions of the same two styles, made of wood, bone, or antler. Heads for fish spears were also sometimes fashioned by native craftsmen from pieces of iron or thick sheets or plates of brass that had formerly been portions of trade items. These metals were salvaged from such sources as knife and sword blades, lugs and bodies of brass kettles, and gun hardware.

Blacksmith-made iron arrow points, *fers de flèches*, also sometimes replaced traditional ones made of stone, bone, antler, or native copper for fishing. In addition, The People often fashioned homemade versions of arrow points from iron and brass that they salvaged from trade items, producing both flat and conical styles. These conical points copied the native versions that were made of antler or native copper.

Fishnets and traps made from trade cord did not function, for the most part, any more efficiently than traditional versions made of native cordage. However, harpoon heads and fishing arrow points of iron and brass had cutting edges which were thinner, sharper, and more even than the edges of the native versions made of wood, bone, antler, or stone. In addition, the metal articles were much more durable. Finally, the considerable labor that was involved in producing native cordage and working antler, bone, stone, and native copper into fishing equipment was eliminated by the importation of Fox's trade items.

The iron fishhooks that he brought, in a wide variety of sizes, also functioned more efficiently than the traditional ones, due in part to the fine, sharp barb at the end of the hook. Native hooks were usually fashioned of bone or wood, in a one or two-piece construction. The two-piece versions often consisted of a tapered straight splint of bone mounted at an angle into a vertical wooden shaft. A barb that was carved or ground into the tip of a wooden or bone hook could be easily broken if it were made sharp and thin enough to be fully effective. Thus, the majority of native-made fishhooks did not have pronounced barbs; many had no barbs at all. In contrast, the barb that was cut by a blacksmith into even the smallest iron hook was both needle-sharp and very durable. This barb, tending to prevent a fish from slipping off the hook, greatly increased the likelihood that a hooked fish would be successfully landed. Iron hooks were also more durable than ones of bone or wood, and were less visible to the fish, due to their slender form and black color.

Equipped with efficient and durable barbed iron hooks of various sizes, The People often abandoned their other traditional style of fishing hook. The gorge hook consisted of a short straight shaft of wood, bone, or antler which tapered at each end to a sharp point. The fishing line was attached to the midpoint of the shaft, either tied directly to it, or fastened to a length of thin brass wire which connected the line to the shaft. The gorge hook was then inserted into a piece of bait. When a fish took the baited hook into its mouth, the fisherman yanked the line, causing the straight gorge to catch inside the fish so that it could be hauled to the surface.

Iron axes and *tranches* (ice chisels) were also quickly adopted by native fishermen, for chopping holes through the thick ice for winter fishing. These tools, replacing traditional stone and antler implements, were generally more efficient. However, the iron versions sometimes became brittle in extreme cold; they then tended to crack, at the eye or the bit of the axe and the body or the bit of the chisel.

Fox was jolted from his thoughts on fishing equipment by the return of the boys. Unfortunately, they had had no luck in landing any finned creatures for the cooking fire.

The remaining days passed quickly, filled with wood gathering, cooking, games, crafts, tree climbing, evening fires, and soaking up the sun and history. Eagle enjoyed clambering up the tall pines that stood at the edge of the clearing. He seemed oblivious to the dark splotches of pine pitch that accumulated on his mocassins, leggings, breechclout, and chemise. He was only interested in the long distance that he could see both up and down the river from that vantage point.

One afternoon, as Fox sat in the warm sun on the riverbank, he carved and ground a spoon from a moose antler tine. The white and blue pottery jug of *eau-de-vie* (brandy) sat within easy reach, in the shade of a bush. As the afternoon progressed and the liquid in the flask reduced, the hard antler seemed to become easier and easier to work. With each nip from the jug, the smile on its wooden effigy head stopper also appeared to become broader and broader.

The mild effect that brandy and wine had on Fox was many times stronger on The People, who had not developed a tolerance for alcohol over many centuries like Europeans had. He had often noted that many natives lost all sense of judgement when under its influence;

some even reached the point of maiming and killing their own loved ones without provocation. Certain French traders used to their own advantage this loss of judgement when natives were under the influence of alcohol. Trading sessions often began with a gift of a drink of brandy. After that, many native customers would exchange every possession they had, sometimes even their own family members, to acquire more of that magical brew which had never before been available in their world. Fox clearly saw that drunkenness was one of the greatest problems that had come to The People with the arrival of the French and their trade.

From the cooking area, Otter watched her two sons at the river. Wearing only a breechclout, Hawk waded in the warm shallows, gathering opened mussel shells from the sandy bottom. His parents would later produce from them scrapers, knives, and spoons. Eagle, squatting on the sandy bank, cut green twigs into short lengths, which he then lashed together with long strands of grass to make a tiny raft for playing in the river.

Another day, the main project of the boys consisted of making little cases of brain-tanned deer hide for their sundial-compasses. With scissors, an awl, and some strands of sinew thread, each one fashioned a pouch of his own design.

On the last day of the stay at the camp, Fox arose early with Jacques. Man and dog made their way in the quiet of early dawn over the soft bed of moss which covered the forest floor. Passing thousands of tiny delicate white flowers, they reached the large fallen tree which had been the family's source of firewood during their entire stay. Fox reviewed its years of slow growth, from a tiny twig to a young sapling to a mature tree. He then considered the fierce wind which must have swept through a few years before, breaking the large tree off at about his head height and partially uprooting several others nearby, which now leaned at an acute angle to the north.

In the manner of The People, he thanked the spirit of the broken tree for providing the family with branches for fires that cooked their meals, warmed them each evening, and gave a cheerful light for times of stories, songs, and quiet. Then, Silver Fox turned and reluctantly stepped back into the twentieth century.

Chapter Three

The strong breeze off Lac Huron made the candle flame flicker a little, even inside its protective *lanterne*. Sunning Otter was glad that Silver Fox had brought her the tin lantern, along with an ample supply of *chandelles* (tallow candles), when he had returned with the new stock of trade goods the previous fall. He had also acquired a good supply of fluffy white cotton fibers, which she would later twist into candle wicks and dip in melted fat to make more candles.

The lantern's light in these windy conditions was much steadier than the light from her traditional native torches of pine knots or rolled birchbark. In addition, the lantern did not give off fire-threatening sparks like the torches did. The yellow light that spilled from the little open door of tin shed a dim but steady glow on the path which led from the camp in the forest clearing out to the lakeshore. Focused shafts of light beaming from the many pierced slits in the rounded sides and conical roof of the lantern played upon the leaves and branches beside the path.

As the two figures with the lantern emerged from the edge of the dark forest onto the beach, the bright light of the nearly full moon lit the scene. A continuous row of sand ridges, piled up along the shoreline by many years of pounding storm waves and heaving winter ice, wore a thin cover of low bushes and tufts of coarse grass. From these hillocks, a wide flat area of bare sand and scattered driftwood extended to the water's edge to meet the incoming waves. Frothy whitecaps reflected on the dark surface of the water far out into the Bay of Thunder, Anse du Tonnerre.

Since the breezy shore area was bathed in moonlight, Otter blew out the lantern to save her precious candle. Clouds hid some of the stars overhead, but to the west, very low near the forested horizon, gleamed three bright stars [Jupiter, Venus, and Mars], nestled together in a triangular pattern. Even the oldest members of The People could not recall ever having seen those bright stars there before.

A short distance to the west down the shoreline, the Rivière du Diable, Devil's River, flowed into the bay. At the mouth of the river stood two large stones of unusual shape, revered by The People as images of two members of the Spirit World. Thus, this place was called *Shing-go-ba-wa-sin-eke* (stone images of the spirits) *go-ba-wat* (leave more than one offering). At these stones were left offerings of food, *kin-nik-i-nik* (tobacco), and personal items, as tokens of thanks as well as for future good fortune in such areas as hunting, fishing, and traveling.

Canoe travelers left these offerings to appease the spirit creatures that lived in the lake, the giant serpents and Mi-shi-pi-shu, the horned panther with a long spiked tail. They prayed that the creatures would not lash their tails and whip up dangerous waves while the canoes were en route. The People felt that these prayers were much more likely to result in a safe journey than the prayers that were offered by the French to the mother of a man who had died while tied to a tree in another world.

Upper: Jacques and his main master beside Lac Huron, with Pointe des Rochers in the distance.
Lower: The mortar and pestle of granite easily crush dried corn kernels.

Fox tests the effectiveness of a hatchet with a granite bit in cutting green wood.

Upper: A stone adze efficiently removes charred wood in the burn-and-scrape procedure.
Lower: The traditional native crooked knife: a beaver incisor tooth mounted into a wooden handle covered with rawhide.

An iron version of a crooked knife easily cuts green or dried wood. In the same manner as its native predecessor, the tool is pulled toward the user.

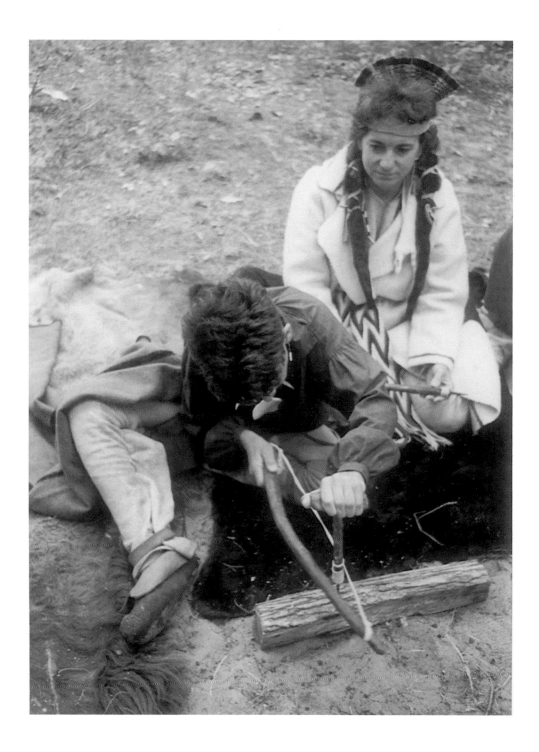

Using a bow drill, Hawk tests an iron-bitted spindle, while Otter holds a stone-bitted version. A similar set, containing a bow, hearth, spindle, and spindle cap, was used by The People to start fires by the friction method.

The broad cover flap of the holster has been folded behind and tied in place with its deerhide thong. An iron spanning wrench hangs from its leather loop, beside the wheellock pistol.

Upper: Fox showing how the wrench is used to prepare the wheellock gun for firing.
Lower: A *mousqueton* or carbine fitted with a flintlock ignition system.

The People sometimes painted pictures of the underwater creatures and other members of the Spirit World on the tall faces of cliffs, particularly at locations where the rock ledge towered over the edge of a waterway. The red paint was made from hematite stone ground to a powder and mixed with water, grease, oil, or native glue. The pigment was often applied by scaling the cliffs or while reaching upward from a canoe afloat. Travelers left gifts to the spirits at the cliffs, or shot an arrow into a crack or opening in the rock face as an offering when they passed by, in hopes of safety and good fortune.

Otter and her people had heard stories of Fox's people, in a faraway land called France, laboriously cutting stones into pieces and piling them one atop the other to build huge long-houses for leaving offerings to their spirits. They had even heard that some men spent their entire lives piling up stones in this manner. The People wondered why the French chose not to use tall cliff faces, which naturally stood high and impressive, direct channels to the spirits. Many of the ways of the French were difficult to understand.

Otter and Fox contemplated the long history of the two spirit stones at the mouth of the river, and marveled at the unusual stars in the west. As they quietly spoke, a low, shadowy figure emerged from the dark forest edge and moved toward them: Jacques had left the two boys at the camp, nestled in their blankets and robes under the canoe shelter, to join his masters on the beach.

Following the chilly night, the day dawned bright and clear. After a breakfast of smoked whitefish, fried cornmeal cakes, and strawberries, washed down with blackberry tea, the family relaxed in the warmth of the sun at the lakeshore. The day was so clear they could see entirely across the Bay of Thunder to the northern point of the bay, as well as the offshore islands well out in the Lake of the Hurons.

Jacques alternated sessions of frantic gull-chasing with naps on the warm sand. Red-tailed Hawk was anxious to see how his newly-captured pet, a large painted turtle, would take to the waves of the big bay after a lifetime in a small inland lake. As was the custom with The People, Hawk had bored a small hole with an awl through the outer edge of the turtle's shell, where it would not harm him. To this hole he attached a long line, so the turtle could swim and roam freely, yet be kept as a pet. The boys enjoyed watching in the clear water the turtle's effortless swimming style; they were amazed to see how far he could swim under water before bobbing his head above the surface for another breath.

Having only munched on walnuts, dried apples, and some leftover cornmeal cakes at midday, the family was ready for a feast by evening. After Fox kindled a fire with flint and steel, he poured water from the gourd bottle into the copper pot, covered it with its carved wooden lid, and hung it from the pot hanger over the fire. All the while, he heard the soft thunk-thunk of the stone mortar and pestle, as Otter crushed dried corn.

Sitting on the buffalo robe spread out near the cooking area, she first placed in front of her on the robe a deer hide, then upon it a small boulder of grey granite with a flat top. From the birchbark *makuk* beside her, Otter took a small handful of dried corn kernels, which she pounded and ground on the mortar with an oblong pestle of light brown granite. As more and more kernels were added to the center of the mortar and were crushed, the white and yellow corn meal worked its way to the outer edges of the mortar, where it fell onto the deer hide. After finishing the corn, Otter also crushed two tiny black balls called *poivres* (pepper corns), as spice for the soup. When Fox had first brought these peppers, she had not liked the strong flavor; but now she enjoyed the interesting zest it added to meals.

Into the steaming pot, Otter poured the corn meal, ground pepper, and jerky. With a *jambette* (clasp knife) from the bag at her belt, she also cut in a few shavings of ginger root. As she pared the root with the folding knife, with its pine wood handle and thin iron blade in the shape of a hawk's bill, she smiled at the memory of the first time she had ever used such a knife. At first, it had seemed awkward to maintain a steady pressure with her thumb or palm on the small button at the back end of the blade, to keep it in its fully opened position. But after only a few painful pinches between blade and handle, she had made it a habit to keep the pressure steady all the while the knife was in use.

After the evening meal, the family drew close around the fire on the fur robes, and passed the time with stories of long ago, before The People had contact with the French. Otter, the last to speak, told the tale of the Moose and the Woodpecker. This was a long, entertaining story that warned against boasting. As the evening waned, the dancing yellow flames turned to sparkling orange coals and finally to darkness, with only the heated sand of the fireplace radiating its warmth.

The weather at dawn was chilly and overcast, with the sky the color of a bar of lead. Otter raised the hood of her *capote* for added warmth. This was to be the long-anticipated day the family had planned, when they would begin comparing the traditional woodworking tools and techniques of The People with those of the French, Silver Fox's people. The boys were eager to do the experiments, since they had not grown up using the traditional tools of stone, bone, antler, shell, teeth, and native copper. All their lives, iron tools had been available to them through their father.

Eagle brought from the shelter the tool storage box, which had been made from a sapling-banded wooden cask or *barrique*. When the cask was cut down in height, one stave on each side of the cask had been left a finger's length higher than the other staves, like a tall ear. A hole had been carved through each of these rounded projecting ears. The flat wooden lid had two broad notches carved into its edge on opposite sides; these indentations fit around the two ears on the rim. When the box was to be carried, a peeled stick was run through the holes in the ears, just above the lid; then a thick cord handle was looped around each projecting end of the stick.

From the storage box, Eagle produced a traditional stone axe. The rectangular celt or bit, made of greyish tan granite, had been pecked to shape with a hard cobblestone and ground to a smooth finish with finer grained stones. The poll of the celt had been firmly set into a cavity carved in a dry oak limb. Everyone was ready for the first step, felling a pine tree that was about as thick as a man's hand with outstretched fingers.

As Eagle repeatedly struck the tree with the stone axe, the bit first dented, then bruised, and finally broke the layer of bark and the outermost layer of wood fibers, little by little. It was clear that it would take a great deal of labor to fell even this moderately small tree with such a tool. The cutting edge of a pecked stone axe could only be moderately sharp; if a thin, sharp edge were attempted, the edge would only crumble away when it reached a certain thinness. Also, the entire bit of the axe had to be relatively thick and wedge-shaped to avoid breakage during use. This thickness created a rather angled taper of the bit, reducing its cutting efficiency. An extremely sharp cutting edge and a moderately thin blade with a gradual taper could be easily produced by flaking an axe out of flint. However, The People did not generally make axes of this material, since it tended to break too easily under such heavy usage as that of an axe.

In contrast to the pecked and polished stone axe, the axe bit of native copper had been hammered into shape so that it had a moderately thin and very gradually tapered bit; its cutting edge had been ground extremely sharp and fine with a grinding stone. When Eagle chopped the tree with this tool, it cut easily into the wood; but it dulled very quickly, and would actually bend out of shape with heavy usage.

Thus, The People did not have in their traditional tool kit an axe which alone could effectively chop down a large tree or cut it into appropriate lengths without expending considerable time and effort. These procedures were most often carried out by the burn-and-scrape technique.

To try this method, Hawk mixed a thick paste of clay and water in a small brass kettle. He then broke away the bark in a wide band above the base of the tree with the stone axe, and at the upper edge of this area of exposed wood applied a band of pasty clay. Placing firewood around the base of the tree, he lit it with a burning brand from the cooking fire, and let the flames do their work. After the exposed portion of the tree below the band of clay had been heavily charred, he pushed away to the side the burning fire with a limb. Now the usefulness of the stone axe became clear, as it effectively cut and scraped away the soft charred wood. Repeated cycles of burning and scraping away the charred material eventually felled the tree, and also cut off a section about as long as a man's arm.

Compared to the traditional native tools, Fox's iron *hache* (axe) was able to fell trees of any size in a much shorter time and with much less effort, since the axe was able to cut the wood directly, without any burning procedure. Its bit was thinner, and the cutting edge much sharper, than those found on stone axes.

However, his axes sometimes became quite brittle in extremely cold temperatures. They then tended to break at the bit or at the eye, where the iron looped around the handle. Native axes, made of stone or native copper, did not have a hollow eye. The solid head either fit into a cavity in a thick straight handle or was lashed to a sapling handle that was bent around the head. When an iron axe broke at its eye, The People sometimes chiseled off the damaged eye portion, and used the remainder as a splitting wedge or mounted it like a native celt into a cavity in a handle.

The family's next experiment involved hollowing out the arm's length trunk section, as was done when making a bowl, a cooking vessel, or a dugout canoe. One side of the log was split off, producing the flat surface which was to be hollowed out. For this splitting task, an iron wedge or *coin de fer* was sharper, thinner, and more durable than native wedges of stone, bone, antler, or hard wood. Eagle discovered that the full array of native axes, adzes, scrapers, and knives proved to be of little use in hollowing out the log; again, the technique of burning and scraping was traditionally used to remove larger amounts of wood with these tools.

Eagle applied a narrow border of clay paste around the perimeter of the flat side of the split log, to prevent these areas from being charred. He then built a small fire on the flat area left exposed, and again let the fire do the heaviest part of the labor. His efforts mostly entailed fanning the fire with a piece of birchbark to hasten its progress. He also applied water or fresh clay paste as needed, especially in areas where the flames began to undermine the exposed side of the previously coated edge areas.

After the exposed wood had been charred to a sufficient depth, each family member took turns testing the effectiveness of the various native tools in removing the burned wood. Fox tried several adzes: one had been pounded and ground to a fine edge from native copper, another had been pecked and polished to shape in green granite, and a third was flaked from greenish grey slate. These adzes included examples of both straight and concave cutting edges. The heads were either set into a carved hole in a straight handle or firmly lashed with rawhide thongs to an L-shaped junction of a limb and its adjacent trunk.

Hawk used a series of hand-held scrapers, made from a narrow deer leg bone, a mussel shell, a two-point deer antler, a long flat flake of light grey flint, and a palm-sized curved piece of conch shell that had been carried from the Atlantic coast to the Great Lakes region by inter-tribal trade. Eagle pared away considerable charred material with a snub-nosed scraper chipped from dark grey flint that was lashed with a rawhide thong to the end of a wooden handle.

Otter tried two versions of a crooked knife or chisel which utilized the incisor tooth of a beaver. The first version was simply one side of a beaver's lower jaw, with its long, slender orange chisel tooth still in its socket at the end of the jaw. The other tool had a similar long curved tooth projecting from the end of a hand-sized section of sapling. The base of the tooth was held firmly in position in a deep groove in the handle by a glued strip of wood and a wrapping of rawhide which covered the entire handle, firmly sewn with elk sinew thread. The rawhide, wet when installed, had shrunk tightly to the handle when it had dried.

Otter gripped each of these tools in her upturned palm, with the beaver tooth in a horizontal position and curving toward her. She cut by pulling the implement toward her, utilizing the natural chisel edge at the tip of the tooth. She also sometimes held the tool in a vertical position when carving, with the tooth pointed downward. Fox noted that he used the opposite method when wielding his sheath knife and clasp knife of iron: with his palm facing downward, he pushed the tool away from himself.

Each of the native tools that the family tried seemed to be equally effective in removing the soft charred wood, regardless of the hardness or durability of the tool. The hafted larger tools would make quicker work of large projects such as hollowing out a dugout canoe. The hafted small flint scraper, with its rounded snub nose and thick, steeply inclined scraping edge, was especially useful for the final scraping process down to the browned wood beneath the layer of char. Due to its small size and rounded end, it could reach easily into rounded interior corner areas. Since iron woodworking tools were not yet available in plentiful supply in many areas, The People sometimes fashioned adzes and scrapers from salvaged iron and brass, which they utilized like the native tools in burn-and-scrape procedures.

The final step in the procedure involved a thorough sanding of the scraped surface with handfuls of dry sand and a hand-sized piece of deer hide. The boys were surprised to discover that the final surface resulting from the burn-and-scrape technique was a clean, browned, gently undulating surface, with no lingering traces of blackened wood.

After becoming familiar with the native tools, it was time for the boys to try the iron versions of axe, *herminette* (adze), and *couteau croche*, the crooked knife. The latter tool had a rather heavy knife blade that had been bent into a quarter-round curve at its tip. Like its beaver tooth predecessor, it was held with the palm upward and pulled toward the user. The curved tip portion of the blade was useful for hollowing out cavities, while the main straight span of the blade was used for general cutting procedures. Unlike a beaver tooth crooked knife or chisel, the cutting edge on the iron version was on the edge, running along the full length of the blade, rather than at the end of the tip like a chisel.

Fox had used his crooked knife to finish the carving of a shallow oval platter, which he had roughed out from a split section of basswood with a small adze. The iron crooked knife, adze, and axe made quick work of shaping wood and hollowing out cavities, compared to the native burning procedure. Using these tools, it was considerably easier to control the evenness and regularity of the carved surfaces as well as the dimensions of the product, since the wood was cut under close observation and control, rather than being burned away.

Since everyone was famished from a day of woodworking activities, they especially enjoyed the evening meal of smoked whitefish and boiled wild rice with grapes. After relaxing around the cozy fire, they all turned in early, to dream of more good days ahead.

After a quick breakfast, the family returned to their woodworking experiments. This time, they focused on woodcarving tasks in which only a little wood needed to be removed, such as in making tool handles or a bow drill. For this project, the family worked with a series of flaked flint tools: a hafted knife which had the notched base of its blade lashed into the grooved end of a sapling handle, a hand-held knife consisting of a long sharp flake, a hand-held scraper, a spokeshave (a scraper with a concave or indented cutting edge), a graver with a very slender point for boring and scoring, and a serrated saw blade as long as a man's finger. In addition, they also used a knife of native copper mounted in a deer antler handle, and a sandstone abrading stone.

These tools cut, scraped, sawed, and sanded away small amounts of wood, especially green wood, without requiring the charring process. However, the procedure was quite slow and laborious, since the sharp cutting edges of nearly all of the flaked stone tools tended to be uneven and undulating, and the body of the tools tended to be thick. This thickness, designed for strength, made the taper of the blade to its cutting edge considerably angled, rather than a slight, gradual taper. Such an angled taper reduced the cutting efficiency of the tool. The exception was the flint flake knife, which had a thin and razor-sharp cutting edge and a rather thin body. Its drawbacks included the irregular curve of the blade and the tendency of the cutting edge to break off in small chips during usage. The edge of the copper knife was even, thin, and straight, but it dulled quickly. To remove a substantial area of wood with any of these tools, it was necessary to cut a deep groove or a series of holes around the area to be removed, and then split out the isolated section.

From these experiments, Eagle and Hawk learned that such woodworking projects were rather slow and laborious when using the traditional tool kit. To reduce the amount of shaping work, The People would usually choose a piece of a tree as close to the desired shape as possible, and split away as much waste wood as they could with a knife or wedge before beginning the cutting procedures. This reduced the total amount of wood that had to be removed by carving.

The boys observed that the iron blades of the sheath knife, clasp knife, crooked knife, and chisel cut much more easily and evenly than the native tools, since the iron versions were much thinner in the body and had straight, even cutting edges which were very sharp. Also, they were much less likely to break under heavy usage. The edged tools made by The People of hammered and ground native copper had slender bodies and straight, even cutting edges similar to the iron versions; however, the edge dulled quickly, and the tools would even bend out of shape under heavy use. Thus, their usefulness in woodworking was primarily in the burn-and-scrape procedure.

Otter brought out the bow drill for the final tool tests. A slender tapered drill bit of flaked tan flint had been lashed with a rawhide thong into the hollowed and split end of a forearm-long section of narrow sapling. This spindle was entwined once through a deerskin thong that had been tied to each end of a bow-shaped section of limb. The spindle was spun with its attached drill bit in one direction when Otter drew the bow toward her and in the opposite direction when she pushed the bow away from her. The more downward pressure she applied on the upper end of the spindle with the wooden end cap, the faster the stone bit drilled into the wood. Then she tried another spindle, into which had been mounted a straight iron awl with a diamond-shaped cross section. This iron bit was able to drill more effectively, since it had straight, even cutting edges on all four sides, compared to the undulating, flaked cutting edges on only two sides of the flint drill. In addition, the iron bit could produce narrower and deeper holes, since it could be much longer and slenderer than its stone counterpart without danger of it breaking during use.

Frenchmen in the interior regions sometimes drilled holes with a brace and bit, a curved brace of wood which had a series of interchangable iron bits. They also utilized a *vrille* (gimlet) and a *tarière* (auger), which were small and large versions of another drilling implement. The iron bit of those tools was mounted perpendicular to a straight handle, which was turned by hand to slowly twist the drill bit.

After all of these experiments, Eagle and Hawk could visualize how Fox's iron tools had spurred woodworking for The People, allowing larger and more intricate projects to be done with much less time and labor. However, Otter noted that it had taken a long time before the Old Ones had grown accustomed to the light color and tool-marked appearance of bowls, cooking vessels, and dugout canoes that were produced by direct carving. They had been long accustomed to the warm browned hues and smoothly undulating surfaces of items produced by the traditional burn-and-scrape method. Iron tools also greatly facilitated the felling of trees, both for harvesting a supply of wood to serve various needs and for clearing forested land for gardening areas.

Fox described to the boys a number of larger, bulkier woodworking tools of iron that were sometimes brought into the interior by other Frenchmen, to build major posts and mission centers. These included a *hache à doler* (hewing axe), a *bisaiguë* (mortise axe) for chopping narrow grooves into upright corner posts, *scies* (saws) of various sizes, from the small scroll saw to the huge plank saw, and a *masse* (sledge hammer) for driving splitting wedges. They also used a *couteau à deux manches,* a two-handled knife (drawknife), a *verlope* (smoothing plane), and a *marteau et clous,* hammer and nails. The iron hardware for these buildings included hinges or *pentures* , pintles and strap hinges or *gonds et fiches,* a door bolt or *verrou*, and a door lock or *serrure.*

His mention of the bolt and lock prompted Otter to explain that, before the arrival of Les Francais, the world of The People had not included locking devices that prevented access to shelters, storage buildings, and storage containers. Their traditional ways of living valued a great deal of communal sharing. However, many articles of personal equipment, particularly items for hunting and warfare, were imbued with the spirit of the owner, and would not function properly if used by others. Consequently, those items were not often shared. In contrast, Otter felt that the French lived in a world in which individual ownership and hoarding of possessions was much more dominant. She believed that the world view of the French, as well as their supply of exotic articles that had never before been found in the native world, had begun to erode the communal ideals of some of The People.

The family passed the remaining days at the campsite exploring the coastline, relaxing beside the lake, cooking feasts, playing with French cards and native games, and singing voyageur songs around the evening fire. In addition, the boys spent much time discussing with Fox the changes that had come to their forest life with the introduction of his items for hunting and warfare. Truly, the boys thought, the traditional ways were being altered. They understood the anguish that these changes brought to the Old Ones, but they also found exciting the new items that had been imported by their white father.

Eagle and Hawk had known since early childhood that the traditional weapons that were used by The People included the knife, club, lance for thrusting and throwing, and the bow and arrow. Native knives which had blades of stone or native copper were usually mounted in a handle of wood, bone, or antler. Some knives were fashioned with both the blade and the handle all in a single piece, using a complete half of a mussel shell or carving a bone such as a deer leg bone. Fox provided iron *couteaux boucheron* (butcher knives) hafted in wood, as well as *jambettes* (folding knives) with wooden or bone handles. The People also sometimes made sheath knife blades from iron or heavy brass that they salvaged from various trade items.

Fox's sons admired the *couteau boucheron* that Fox wore in a sheath suspended by a strap around his neck. The base of the iron blade was set into a slit in a handle of deer leg bone, held in position by two iron pins running through handle and blade. The entire grip area was spirally wrapped with a wide thong of deer hide, from the blade out to the projecting ball socket at the end of the bone. This enlargement served much the same purpose as a pommel at the end of a sword hilt, providing a more secure grip for the hand, especially when the handle was slippery.

The clubs of Otter's people were usually carved from a single piece of wood, in one of two basic styles: either a long handle with an enlarged ball at the outer end, or a form similar to that of an extended hind leg of a rabbit, with its broadened "thigh" portion at the far end angling upward slightly. One or more spikes or blades of stone, bone, antler, or native copper sometimes projected from the front of the ball head or the outer edge of the leg-shaped club. With the introduction of metal trade items, The People sometimes substituted one or more iron knife blades, lance heads, or arrow points for native varieties on their clubs, or fashioned spikes from salvaged iron or heavy brass. Some of them replaced their wooden club with a *petite hache,* a small axe or tomahawk.

Their traditional lance points, fashioned from stone, bone, antler, or native copper, usually had a triangular point at the end of a short or long shaft. Other varieties, with one or more barbs on only one side of the shaft, were made of bone or antler. Iron versions of both of these forms, called *darts* and *harpons,* were supplied via the trade. In addition, unhafted straight sword blades, *épées à emmancher,* were often included among the trade goods, to be mounted on lances. Native craftsmen also fashioned lance points from iron and heavy brass salvaged from trade items, producing both flat and conical styles. These conical points copied the native variety that was formed by hollowing out the tip section of an antler tine.

The boys clearly saw that the most complex weapon of The People was the bow and arrow. Small points for arrows were crafted of stone, bone, antler, and native copper. The majority of these were in triangular form, although some had a short stem at the base of the triangle. Arrow points of antler and native copper were made in both flat and conical shapes.

Fox's iron arrow points, called *fers de flèches,* were usually of the stemmed triangular form. The People often made homemade versions from salvaged iron and brass, creating both flat and conical styles. The majority of the flat points were triangular in shape. Flintknappers also chipped points from pieces of glass which they salvaged from bottles and drinking vessels.

Many hunters realized that blades for knives and clubs, as well as points for lances and arrows, which were made of European metals functioned more efficiently than native varieties. The bodies of the iron and brass versions were slenderer, and their cutting edges were sharper, thinner, and more even than traditional ones made from stone, bone, and antler. In addition, the articles made of European metal were more durable. Native copper knives and flat points had slender bodies and sharp, even cutting edges; however, they dulled easily and bent under heavy usage. Finally, the great deal of labor that was involved in working forest materials into hunting equipment was eliminated by the importation of Fox's trade goods.

Those goods, however, did not appreciably alter the techniques of hunting and warfare that had been practiced by The People for centuries. Fox often observed hunters using such methods as tracking and stalking, hiding in a blind, attracting game to an offshore canoe with a torch, harvesting animals as they crossed a waterway, casting woven nets over birds on land or on water, setting underwater nets for such prey as beavers, and chopping open lodges of beavers and muskrats. More durable and efficient French equipment did little to change those time-honored traditions. In fact, The French had adopted many of the native techniques themselves. However, the bonebreaker created for native people entirely new vistas in the areas of hunting and warfare.

The bonebreaker had made an immensely powerful impression on The People, as well as on all of the other native groups. This magical tool created a sharp crack of sound like thunder, and at the same time gave off a puff of thick white smoke. When pointed at human or animal prey, it could wound or kill them at a considerable distance. Arrows and lances tended to deflect off of bones in the prey and remain embedded in fleshy areas. In contrast, the little stone that was thrown from a bonebreaker tended to break and shatter most bones in its path; thus, the weapon earned its name from The People. This shattering of bones created wounds in humans that were much less likely to heal well; injuries inflicted with this implement were thus even more serious in many cases than those caused by knife, lance, or arrow.

Fox's long holster hung at an angle beside his left hip, handy at a moment's notice for reaching across with his right hand. Fashioned from thick moose hide, the holster was suspended from a broad moosehide strap that passed over his left shoulder. His moosehide hunting bag hung on his right side; its broad strap angled upward across his body, and was attached atop his left shoulder to the holster strap.

Fox untied the thong which held the broad flap of hide securely over the open end of the holster, and drew out his wheellock *pistolet* (pistol). In length, it spanned from his fingertips to his armpit, with a hand grip that angled only slightly downward from the alignment of the barrel. The butt cap and trigger guard were of gleaming cast brass, while the sideplate and single ramrod ferrule were of iron. The rear half of the long iron barrel was octagonal in form, with the forward half rounded. The octagonal areas of the barrel bore deeply chiseled ornamentation, as well as an inlaid silver stick man effigy on the top surface near the breech.

The wide rounded lockplate was dominated by a large central wheel cover of iron, which bore three bold chiseled *fleurs-de-lis*. From the center of the wheel cover projected a horizontal four-sided shaft of iron, about the size of a man's finger joint. At the upper forward edge of the lockplate stood an ornate brass cock, with a man's face engraved upon its side. Clamped between the jaws of the cock was a thin rectangular slab of tan colored pyrite.

To begin loading the weapon, Fox removed the gunpowder flask or *pulvérin* from his waist belt, where it was suspended by a long iron hook. The flask, made of greenish tan cowhorn, was closed at each end with a triangular piece of thick sheet iron. From its wider end projected an ornate cast brass spout and a slender iron rod that was attached to a flat spring of steel. Pointing the spout downward while covering its end with his index finger, Fox depressed the iron spring handle with his thumb. This opened a sliding door inside the base of the spout, allowing the spout to fill with powder. Releasing the handle closed the door and left a measured amount of powder in the spout, the proper amount for one shot.

Fox poured the measure of powder down the vertical barrel of the gun, and followed it with a lead ball which he had drawn from the shot pouch within his hunting bag. Removing the wooden ramrod from its position below the barrel, he rammed the ball firmly down to the breech area of the barrel, firmly seating it atop the load of powder, and returned the ramrod to its ferrule.

The gun was actually loaded at this point; however, several steps were required to prepare it to be fired. Above the wheel and its cover on the lockplate was a small rectangular pan to hold priming powder. Next to the pan was a tiny hole which extended through the breech of the barrel. When the priming powder was set off, its flame would pass through the tiny touch hole to ignite the powder charge within the barrel. This explosion would suddenly create gases that would forcefully push the ball out of the barrel. Such was the basic operation of all cannons and firearms since they had first been invented, more than three centuries before Fox's time.

In his younger years, Fox had heard stories about the history of firearms. For about one hundred fifty years, shoulder and hand guns had been set off by applying a smouldering match or wick to the pan of priming powder. At first, this was done manually, and later by pulling a trigger which caused a mechanism to place the tip of the matchcord into the pan.

In the late 1400s and early 1500s, the wheellock mechanism was developed in western Europe. This was the first firelock system, in which a spark was mechanically produced to set off the priming charge. The wheellock mechanism or *platine à rouet* of Fox's pistol was based upon sparks generated by the friction of steel and a stone called *pyrite* (pyrite).

To prepare his gun for firing, Fox drew from a loop on his holster a spanning wrench. When the blacksmith had forged the spanner from a slender bar of iron, he had broadened one end and punched through it two sizes of square holes; at the other end he had fashioned a screwdriver. The latter end was used to make adjustments and to remove the lockplate for cleaning, greasing, and simple repairs, such as replacement of parts. The smaller hole in the wrench fit the head of the bolt which tightened the top jaw of the cock onto the pyrite slab.

Fox fitted the larger hole of the wrench onto the spindle that projected from the middle of the wheel, and rotated it three quarters of a turn, to tighten its interior spring. He then slid forward the little iron lid, decorated with a grotesque cast face, which covered the priming pan. Using a finger-long thin pointed rod of iron which hung by a thong from his shoulder belt, he cleared the touch hole in the barrel of any obstructions and residue of spent powder. He also brushed the adjacent priming pan clean of residue.

A small wooden flask of fine-grained priming powder was suspended by two thongs from his shoulder belt. Pulling its wooden stopper free with his teeth, Fox filled the pan with powder, restored the stopper, and slid the pan cover closed. He then rotated the cock downward over the pan cover so that the pyrite slab rested firmly upon the cover. The pistol was now ready to fire.

In addition to his powder flasks of cowhorn and wood, Fox also carried a small wooden cartridge or charger, which was suspended by two thongs from his shoulder belt. The tubular cartridge, bearing a wooden cap, held a single shot worth of powder plus enough to fill the priming pan. This was used when a fast second shot was needed, without having time to draw from the two powder flasks. Each thong passed through a projecting ear on the side of the wooden cap, and was tied to another ear near the rim of the charger. To empty the cartridge, Fox simply slid the cap upward along the two thongs and poured out the powder. Soldiers typically carried a dozen or more of these chargers, hung in a long row along a wide shoulder belt that angled diagonally across their chest. In some instances, these refillable containers were now being replaced by paper-wrapped cartridges or *cartouches*, which were carried in a cartridge box suspended beside the hip from a shoulder belt.

Aiming his gun at a distant birch, Fox pulled the trigger, which caused the pan cover to suddenly slide open. The cock then pushed its pyrite through the priming powder in the pan, down to the steel wheel which lay at the open bottom of the pan. Simultaneously, the wheel spun back the three-quarter turn to which it had been wound. This caused the pyrite to scrape against the serrated edge of the wheel at the bottom of the pan full of priming powder, creating sparks; the sparks ignited the powder in the pan, which set off the gun.

The rather complex wheellock mechanism was somewhat expensive to produce, as Fox well knew from the price that he had paid for his *pistolet* many years before. In addition, the open bottom of the pan and the adjacent wheel easily fouled with spent powder, and the grinding action of the serrated wheel wore down the pyrite slab rather quickly. Finally, the mechanism was prone to breakage and drifting out of adjustment, and was difficult to repair. For these reasons, many soldiers were still armed with simpler and cheaper matchlock or *platine à mèche* weapons. However, for hunting and traveling, the wheellock offered a number of important advantages over the matchlock.

Of primary importance was the elimination of the smoldering match cord or *mèche*, which needed to be lit with flint and steel before using the gun. The smoldering cord created a little smoke that could be seen during the day and smelled at all times, and it made a glow which was visible at night. It also required much tending as it burned down, especially when brisk winds hastened its burning. Fox appreciated a weapon that did not rely on such a match.

He was glad that an improved ignition mechanism had been developed during the late 1500s and the first decade or two of the 1600s. From about 1625 on, France dominated the European production of these new *platine à silex* (flintlock) guns, which gradually replaced wheellocks and matchlocks throughout most of western Europe and in New France. However, gunsmiths in Paris and in other areas of France still continued to produce fine quality wheellock civilian weapons at least through the 1630s. In addition, good servicable wheellocks in the interior wilderness were not quickly discarded; they were used in New France through about the sixth decade of the 1600s. Fox now owned a carbine and a pistol that were fired by the new style of firelock, yet he still found his trusty wheellock pistol to be a valuable tool.

Eagle brought Fox's flintlock *pistolet* from the shelter, dreaming of the day when he, too, would own such a weapon. He drew it from its belt holster of moose hide, and carefully handed it to Fox. The gun, about as long as Fox's forearm, bore ornate raised designs on all of its iron hardware. The rear half of the barrel was of octagonal form, while the forward half was round. The grip curved moderately downward from the alignment of the barrel. A slender tapered projection extended forward from each side of the butt cap, running along the full length of the grip.

The flintlock mechanism of the pistol created ignition sparks by the action of stone against steel, as in the wheellock system; however, pyrite was now replaced by *silex* (flint). Instead of using a spring-loaded wheel that easily fouled with spent priming powder, the new system caused a sharpened slab of flint that was held between the jaws of the cock to strike a vertical frizzen of steel. As the frizzen was struck, it rotated backward, pulling the attached cover from the pan. A shower of sparks, caused by the scraping of the flint against the steel frizzen, fell into the pan of priming power and ignited it. The resulting flame passed through the touch hole in the side of the barrel and set off the main charge, firing the gun. This flintlock mechanism was less expensive to build and repair than the wheellock, and was much simpler to use.

In addition to his two pistols, Fox was also armed with a *mousqueton* (carbine). This shoulder gun, which reached from the ground only up to his sternum, had a barrel that was considerably shorter than those of standard hunting and military guns or *fusils*. He found this shorter, lighter weapon convenient when traveling through dense forests or by canoe. The fine quality gun had been fitted with gleaming brass furniture, and its stock was ornately carved with scrollwork designs. Fox carried it in a sheath made of dark grey blanket material, which was secured at its open end by two deerhide thongs. He had sewn a piece of thick moose hide about as long as his hand around the narrow end of the sheath, to prevent wear to the fabric and to further protect the muzzle of the barrel.

In his hunting bag, Fox carried pouches of various sizes of lead balls. He loaded his guns with either a single large ball or a number of smaller shot, depending on the intended usage. The small shot were held within the breech end of the barrel by wadding material, such as tree bark or dried moss. In addition, he also carried a *tire-bourre* (charge-puller). This tool, made of a very slender iron rod bent into a coiled spiral, was installed when needed onto the tip of the ramrod. When he wished to unload his weapons, he inserted the charge-puller or gunworm on its ramrod down the barrel, forced its sharp point into the soft lead ball, and drew the ball out of the barrel. When the gun was loaded with small shot, the gunworm drew out the wadding material, which released the lead balls. The worm was also used to scour the residue of burned powder that built up on the interior of the barrel, by attaching a piece of fabric to the worm and inserting it down the muzzle on the end of the ramrod.

Soldiers of Fox's time were also often outfitted with an additional item of equipment, the plug bayonet. The wooden handle of this dagger was shaped so that its end fit into the muzzle of a *fusil*, instantly converting the gun to a thrusting lance.

French traders in the interior such as Fox were usually well armed, with shoulder firearms as well as large and small pistols. Nearly all of these weapons were smoothbores, without any rifling or spiral grooves inside the barrel to increase the accuracy of the ball's flight. Each of the various sizes of firearms were traded and given to The People by the French, in ever-increasing numbers. Consequently, a number of native hunters had become very adept at the use of these new weapons, which were also very useful for terrorizing enemies who did not yet have ready access to these frightening items.

Fox was well aware that, as The People gradually increased the use of firearms and decreased the use of their traditional weapons, they began to require a greater supply of gun-related items. His canoe loads of trade goods for the interior now usually included casks of *poudre* (gun powder), bags of *plomb et balles* (lead and balls), and casks of *pierres à fusil* (gunflints) and *tire-bourres* (gun worms). He also often carried a stock of *cornes à poudre* (powder horns).

Fox pointed out to his sons that French firearms offered a number of advantages over some of the native weapons of hunting and warfare. With a gun, the prey could be wounded or killed at a much greater distance than with lance or bow. Thus, a hunter had a greater chance of successfully making a kill, since he did not need to approach as close to the prey and possibly frighten it away before making the shot. In addition, with a charge of several small lead shot, a hunter could down a number of birds with a single shot, rather than one bird per arrow or thrown lance.

Otter noted, however, that guns had certain disadvantages compared to the weapons of The People. Wet gunpowder, as well as a worn or improperly adjusted gunflint, sometimes caused misfires to occur. When a gun did fire properly, the first shot alerted all game animals and enemies for a considerable distance, in contrast to silent arrows and lances. If a gun were accidentally charged with too much powder, or if its muzzle became clogged with dirt while traveling, the barrel would sometimes explode rather than allowing the ball to exit, injuring the shooter. Even when a weapon fired properly, the time that was required for the shooter to reload for a second shot while remaining in a stationary position would allow an archer to shoot ten or fifteen arrows while quickly changing positions.

In spite of their disadvantages, firearms were increasingly replacing the lance and bow. However, both of those traditional weapons were still retained by a great many hunters, at least as supplemental weapons to the firearms, and for those times when supplies of powder and lead were depleted. With these changes of weapons, native armor made from wicker-work or slats of wood, as well as shields of wood and hide, were gradually disappearing from the northern woodlands. New kinds of war wounds, inflicted by the bonebreaker, were becaming more prevalent. Fox and each of his family members realized that guns would drastically change certain aspects of the traditional ways of The People.

The morning of departure from the camp dawned warm, but rain threatened. In short order, without much talk, Otter and Fox neatly stacked beside the canoe the folded roof and floor tarps of the shelter, its poles, and the bedding. Eagle and Hawk stored all food, cooking and eating utensils, and equipment in the wooden trunk, linen bags, birchbark boxes, and the cask container. Then Eagle called Jacques, Hawk gathered up his painted turtle on its line, and the family was ready to depart.

It was time for a last quiet look around the site, to fix it in their minds. They were leaving that quiet place and the seventeenth century, but from it they would keep in memory the experiences, knowledge, and contentment that had been gained there, as they stepped into the future.

Chapter Four

Each of the various parts of his canoe had once been living plants, growing near the Rivière de la Grande Fourche in the region to the west of Lac Supérieur. The outer skin of the canoe had covered and protected stately birch trees, while the canoe's wooden framing elements, ribs, and sheathing had reached upward for sunlight as long, straight trunks of northern white cedars. The split root lashings, as roots of black spruce trees growing in the boggy ground of a swamp, had provided solid anchorage as well as conduits for minerals and moisture.

As Silver Fox guided the canoe upstream, looking for a likely campsite on the banks of the St. Croix, he admired all the long-forgotten artisans of The People, both men and women, who had applied their minds and hands over the centuries to fashion these materials into a highly developed canoe. The craft was fast-paddling on all kinds of waterways, and light enough to be easily portaged around obstructions and from one waterway to another; yet it also had plenty of carrying capacity, even when paddled in shallow water. The fur trade could not have flourished in New France if this vehicle had not been used by both the native groups and the French as the main form of transport in the interior regions.

On this particular excursion, the canoe was loaded with all of the belongings the family would need for an extended trip. Canvas tarps and birch poles for the shelter, bedding, a good supply of dried foods, cooking and eating utensils, spare clothing, and various tools and raw materials nearly filled the little craft; yet it still floated quite high in the water. Perched atop the large wooden trunk just forward of the center thwart, Jacques, the ever-faithful hound, watched the shoreline intently.

When they reached a location about twenty *lieues* (fifty miles) south of the western tip of Lac Supérieur, the canoe rounded a broad curve which headed the family northeastward. Red-tailed Hawk pointed out an appealing campsite, a lush green point on the northern shore where a small river flowed into the St. Croix from the north. Above the low bank, a thick growth of bracken ferns and knee-high grasses, interspersed with a few white forest flowers, covered a broad, flat clearing on the point.

A short exploration by Fox back of the clearing revealed a forest of well-spaced silver maples and a few scattered bur oaks shading the fern-covered forest floor. A shallow ravine, now dry, extended across the rear of the point; long before, it had apparently been the course of the small river at its mouth.

Industrious beavers had at some time attempted to fell some fifteen to twenty large maples across this ravine, when it had carried water. Only some of the large trunks had actually toppled over the ravine; a number had fallen in other directions, and several had only leaned against neighboring upright trees. These standing dry wooden skeletons would provide an ample supply of firewood for the family's stay. This site would be excellent for a week-long sojourn.

Upper: Jacques acts as lookout from his position in the midsection, amid the baggage.
Lower: After the floor tarp is laid down, the roof tarp is drawn over the canoe.

Upper: The rear edge of the upper tarp is staked down, while its front is tied to forked poles.
Lower: Hawk kindles a fire with his magnifying lens.

Otter's elegant headdress, a ruffed grouse tail and an ermine pelt attached to a moosehide head band.

Upper: A folded bedroll atop the ribs of the canoe provides padding for knees and feet. A setting pole lies near at hand along the right wall.
Lower: The canoe offers an instant shelter en route for two paddlers and their canine companion.

Upper: A setting pole is handy for traveling on this shallow, sand-bottomed river.
Lower: Fox inspects the bark cover for any damage.

Canoe repair kit: piece of patching bark, sewing root, rolled birchbark strip holding pieces of gum sealant, sealant in split sapling holder, and a melting torch of folded birchbark in a split handle.

Upper: Removing a heated cooking stone from the fire with a long-handled spoon and a stick.
Lower: Three hot stones make the stew boil in the wooden bowl.

Upper: Brushing ashes from a heated stone before transferring it into the rawhide cooking pot. After cooling, the stone would be rinsed in the wooden bowl before being returned to the fire to reheat.
Lower: Tea and soup simmer in two pottery bowls atop a bed of coals.

Cornmeal mush flavored with dried blueberries cooks in a birchbark pot directly over the flames.

In the knee-deep shallows near the shore, Hawk and Sunning Otter stepped out of the canoe into the river to unload, as Jacques leaped happily over the gunwales, landing with a splash. He paddled to shore, shook himself, and began his earnest exploration of the site, with eyes, ears, and nose.

Otter held the floating canoe parallel to the shoreline, to avoid grinding or breaking the bark skin on the river bottom or on any submerged rocks or limbs, while Hawk and Fox hauled the family's possessions up onto the bank. Because of this offshore loading and unloading, which protected the canoe from damage, each family member usually wore only a *brayet* (breechclout) and a thigh-length *chemise* (shirt) when travelling by canoe, as did most voyageurs of the time. That way, there were no wet moccasins or leggings to bring water and sand into the canoe after loading in the cargo, or after jumping into the water to pull the canoe up a rapids or off a rock. Once the canoe and baggage were safely ashore, the family slipped on those welcome dry garments over bare legs and feet.

Erecting the shelter was the first task in preparation for the extended stay. After checking the area for any projecting sticks or stones, Fox and Hawk placed the canoe upside down in position as the rear of the shelter. In this overturned position, the canoe made contact with the ground at the tips of its high upswept prows and along much of the midsection length of one gunwale cap.

The high upswept ends of the canoe cut and deflected tall waves when traveling in boisterous open water and rapids, diverting the waves from sloshing over the gunwales and into the craft. The high ends also served another purpose when in camp. They provided enough head room underneath the overturned canoe to make an instant shelter that was large enough for two end-to-end paddlers, a dog, and a small amount of cargo. However, this traveling party included three people and a dog, plus a full cargo for an extended stay. So the canvas shelter would be erected over the canoe, to provide more comfortable room for working, sleeping, and storage.

Otter staked down one edge of the light tan canvas *prélart* (tarp) along the lower side of the overturned canoe. Using a fist-sized rock as a hammer, she drove stakes made of peeled sapling forks through a series of canvas loops that were sewn at intervals to the edge of the fabric. Then Hawk and Fox extended the tarp over the canoe, completely covering it and the area to be sheltered. At the front of the lean-to, Otter tied the tarp to the chest-high tops of five slender upright birch poles with forked tops, by means of a row of narrow canvas straps sewn to the tarp. Each pole was held upright by a guyline made of braided trade cord which angled from the top of the pole down to a forked sapling stake driven into the ground.

At the front of the shelter, on the inner side of the row of upright poles, the canvas extended vertically down from roof level to the ground. During most days, this front wall was rolled up and secured by means of straps sewn to the roof, to be unrolled and let down as needed for protection against rain, cold, or humming hordes of biting insects.

A second, smaller canvas tarp was laid down as a floor, with its rear edge tucked under the canoe. On rainy days, this tarp, with its attached canvas tie straps, could be removed and erected nearby as a cooking shelter.

As soon as the family had stowed the gear inside the shelter and arranged the bedding of blankets and robes, Jacques curled up in one corner for a welcome nap.

With the camp set up, the family gave the area a closer inspection. It was clear that they were not the first travelers to have appreciated this excellent site. The edge of the bank of the main river in two places was deeply worn into a narrow passageway, with the grass above each area flattened down; here, beavers or otters regularly slid into and out of the water. A forearm-long section of poplar sapling floated beside the bank, recently severed and peeled by sharp incisor teeth. The freshness of the exposed wood indicated that not long before, a beaver had enjoyed a meal here. At the rear edge of the clearing, a family of deer had very recently spent a day sleeping, hidden in the tall grass and ferns. Three oval areas, in which all of the vegetation was completely flattened, revealed where they had lain.

Soon after Hawk and Fox had gathered a generous stack of dry maple branches for the wood pile, Otter had a fire crackling and a pan of *rubbaboo* cooking. In the copper frying pan, she first simmered in water a good amount of pemmican; this consisted of a mixture of dried meat that had been pounded fine with a mortar and pestle, dried blueberries, and rendered (melted) animal fat. The solid, hearty concoction made excellent traveling food: it was a complete meal in itself, it could be eaten unheated, and it would keep indefinitely if stored away from moisture. To this heated and thinned mixture she added a handful of corn meal, which absorbed much of the fat as it cooked and lightened the heavy mixture, and finally some maple sugar.

Just as the meal was ready, the threatening sky finally made good on its threats, driving the family under the shelter to eat. As the heavy rain poured down, the tarp gave off a hollow drumming sound, which Jacques endured but definitely did not like. Accompanied by the pouring rain, Fox explained to his family the device called a *parapluie* that was used by certain important men and women in the French world. Otter chuckled at the mental image of a dignified person carrying a little cloth-covered roof above her head on a stick.

The rain sometimes slowed during the remainder of the afternoon and evening, but it never did stop. So everyone stayed beneath the shelter, with its front wall rolled up. After the family had enjoyed the meal, Jacques happily licked the pan clean, thoroughly greasing his long drooping ears in the process.

The afternoon passed quickly, as Fox taught his family card games that his ancestors had played for generations. Since Otter and Hawk were both quick learners, they were soon as adept as Fox at counting the *diamants*, *coeurs*, *trèfles*, and *piques* on the cards.

Otter was particularly interested in the items of clothing that were worn by the *Rois*, *Reines*, and *Valets* pictured on the cards. Most of these elaborate articles had never been worn by the few members of Fox's people that she had seen. She especially admired the headgear that was worn by the *Reines*, which was apparently made of gleaming brass like the kettles which Fox brought each year. Yet she still preferred her own headdress, which consisted of a band of brain-tanned moose hide that was adorned with an elegant splayed tail of a ruffed grouse, two shiny black dew claws of a deer, a pair of tinkling cones made of kettle brass, and a long, soft ermine, pure white with a black tip to its tail, which hung down her back to just below her waist. At the midpoint of the ermine was tied a ball-shaped *grelot* (brass hawk bell), which occasionally jangled when it was disturbed.

As evening closed in, Hawk produced from the old trunk a snapping turtle shell platter filled with walnuts, maple sugar, and dried strawberries, as well as three cups made from box turtle shells. He had earlier steeped red raspberry tea in the long-necked bottle of green glass. After this light meal, everyone snuggled into bed for the night.

Otter's *couverture* (blanket), medium blue in color, contrasted with the deep red ones of Hawk and Fox. Each of the woolen blankets had been folded in half in the long direction, and one end and the side seam had been sewn closed with thread; these bedrolls were much warmer than open blankets. Since the nights were not very chilly in this season, the buffalo and black bear robes were placed under the bedrolls, on the floor tarp. In colder weather, a soft insulating layer of boughs or ferns was laid down, and some of the robes covered the sleepers. When Fox slept on such a layer of padding, he was reminded of his years in the St. Lawrence settlements, when he had slept each night on a thick *paillasse,* a linen mattress stuffed full of straw. The drumming of the steady rain on the canvas roof soon lulled everyone to sleep.

Rat-tat-tat-tat. As Fox lifted the canvas wall to locate the woodpecker that was busily searching for a breakfast of grubs, the brilliant light of the new day made him blink. In the deep blue sky above floated a few stationary fluffs of white clouds. The warmth of the sun on his back was welcome after the previous day of grey skies and rain. But Fox was not the first that day to bask in the warm sun in the clearing: a large dark grey snake lay tightly coiled beneath a group of five bluish-purple irises. With a little gentle urging, he uncoiled to the length of a man's arm and slithered off beneath the ferns.

Hawk filled the copper kettle half-full at the river, threw in one handful each of jerky, wild rice, and whole kernel dried corn, and hung it on the iron rod hanger above the little fire. While Hawk prepared breakfast, Otter and Fox unstaked the rear of the shelter, removed the canoe, and restaked the tarp. After placing the canoe in the river to soak, they tied to trees on shore the two mooring lines of braided cord which were attached to the end thwarts.

When dry, the bark skin of the canoe was relatively hard and brittle. Soaking the canoe for a time before each loading and usage made the bark quite flexible. This increased the likelihood that, if the canoe were to strike an underwater object, especially one with rounded edges, the bark would flex and bend, rather than being broken or pierced. In some instances, a collision with a rounded rock or log could displace the ribs and sheathing strips inside the bark skin, and even move the adjacent cargo, without causing a break in the canoe's covering.

The mirror-like blue surface of the river accentuated the rich hues of the birchbark skin. Most of the covering had been made using various shades of tan bark, which had been gathered in the early summer. However, the canoe builder had artfully chosen to alternate every other narrow side panel in dark brown or reddish-brown bark, which he had gathered in early spring. Likewise, he had used the same contrasting dark-colored bark to fashion the gunwale reinforcement strip, which appeared as a long narrow strip of bark just below the outwales along their full length.

It only took a few moments after the meal to gather the paddles, a setting pole, blankets, and a little food before all was ready for a day of exploring upriver. Even before the mooring lines had been untied, Jacques leaped from the bank into the canoe; he quickly claimed the stern paddler's location, hoping to become the first canine *gouvernail* in history. Otter placed her blanket bedroll over the ribs in the bow paddler's position, as padding for her knees and ankles, then stepped in from the knee-deep shallows; Fox did the same at the stern. Since they wore no leggings while in the canoe, kneeling on the edges of the ribs would have been rather uncomfortable for a long day of paddling, if no padding were used. When the family traveled with the full complement of gear loaded into the canoe, the folded shelter tarps made handy paddling seats or knee and ankle padding.

To indicate which of the apparently identical ends of the craft was the bow, Fox had carved shallow shoulders into the sternward edge of two of the main thwarts. In addition, he had incised a round circle representing the sun on the face of the headboard at the bow end (so that Sunning Otter could always paddle facing toward the sun). Knowing which end of the canoe was the bow was important, since the builder had positioned the exposed overlapping edge of each of the bark panels so that it faced toward the stern (the only exceptions were the edges of the two panels that formed the stern end itself). Overlapped in this direction, the seams would cause a little less drag as the craft advanced through the water, and would be less likely to catch on vegetation, rocks, or sandbars.

Before departure, Hawk, who sat just forward of the center thwart as a passenger with Jacques, scattered a silent offering of shredded tobacco onto the placid surface of the water. This he did to appease the spirits that lived in the river, in hopes of a safe journey. The People knew that, in addition to the spirit creatures that inhabited all areas of the world, all things also had a spirit. Showing proper respect and offering gifts to those myriad spirits tended to appease them, making them a bit more likely to cooperate and less likely to cause harm.

Tobacco, one of the most important gifts, could be either a native or a French variety. The People made tobacco from such items as dried leaves of the bearberry and scrapings of inner bark of the red-osier dogwood. French *tabac,* often imported from Brazil by way of Portugal, was traded in both flat leaf and twisted rope forms. Native people often created a mixture that included both a forest version and trade tobacco. Some French traders occasionally imported *tabac en poudre*, powdered tobacco, which they sniffed up their nose.

An offering of tobacco to the spirits could be laid or sprinkled upon the ground or the surface of waterways, or it could be burned in a fire or a pipe, producing tobacco smoke as the offering. The head portion of a sacred pipe used for such offerings was carved from soft stone, bone, antler, or hard wood. Some wooden versions were fitted with a liner of kettle brass inside the bowl, to inhibit the burning of the pipe itself. The tubular pipe stem that fit onto the head was fashioned from wood, cane, or occasionally a slender bone.

As Otter and Fox settled into the rhythm of laboring upriver against the moderately strong current of the Rivière St. Croix, Fox reflected on its name: The River of the Holy Cross. Had the name been applied to the river because of the sensations it evoked in ascending it? It could also have been named by some earlier traveler who had first encountered it on the church holiday of Holy Cross Day, September 14.

The Rivière St. Croix and the Rivière Bois Brule, with their connecting portage, formed one of the two principal canoe routes between the western end of Lac Supérieur and the upper reaches of the Rivière Mississippi. Daniel Greysolon, Sieur du Luht, had been the first recorded Frenchman to travel this route, during the summer of 1680; however, other French traders may have plied its waters during the two decades preceding his voyage.

As they traveled upstream, Fox reflected on the features of his canoe which helped or hindered its progress. The canoe had been built with a narrow, slightly rounded bottom and well-rounded lower walls. Thus, the portion of the canoe that was actually in the water was very long and narrow when the canoe was lightly loaded like this and floating high in the water. This made paddling easier than when all of the family's gear was loaded aboard and the canoe sank lower. The taper of each end was rather long and gradual, which also facilitated the forward movement. The form of a canoe was the most important element in determining how it would handle.

However, several aspects of the birchbark skin tended to hinder the smooth flow of the craft through the water. First, the exterior surface of the canoe was less than perfectly even: shallow undulations were scattered over most areas of the bark. In its natural condition after it was removed from the tree, the bark had numerous uneven areas. In addition, the two different surface levels at each place where bark panels overlapped each other also created an uneven surface, even though the obstruction was reduced slightly by facing the exposed overlapping edges sternward (or upward on the side panels).

The inner side of birchbark, which formed the canoe's outer surface, was not perfectly smooth. Ridges and grooves occured in intricate oval patterns wherever limbs had once grown from the trunk of the tree. Also, many rounded knobby growths, up to half the size of a man's fingernail or larger, projected from the surface of the bark in scattered areas.

Other impediments to the smooth flow of the canoe were the pitched areas that sealed seams, holes, and repairs in many locations on the canoe's surface. In some of these areas, the pitch, applied thickly enough to provide an effective seal, sometimes projected well out from the surface of the bark, especially after many repeated applications.

Even the thickness of the bow end of the canoe, which cut through the water, hindered forward movement somewhat. Rather than a thin, sharp edge, the end of Fox's craft was as thick as the width of his thumb. This edge was created by the combined thicknesses of the stempiece, the bark panel of each side of the prow, the stitching of split roots that lashed these three elements together, and the pitch that sealed the cutwater edge.

Fox, Otter, and Hawk lived in an imperfect world at that time. Thus, Fox could only dream that some day some other canoe covering would be found which would be more effective and durable than bark or hide.

The People also made dugout canoes, and with the iron tools that had been imported by Fox they could now carve the hulls of those canoes thinner and lighter, with a smooth, even exterior surface and a sharp cutwater edge at the ends. The People understood the value of both dugouts and bark canoes; in Otter's region, they made and used both types, for different purposes.

Some distance upstream, the family encountered a large midstream island half-filling the channel. Its long, sandy shores looked inviting, so Hawk, Fox, and Jacques waded ashore to explore. Otter took a paddling position forward of the usual place of the *gouvernail* (stern paddler), and departed for a short solo trip.

As she paddled, the solitude and the beautiful sun-drenched weather heightened the brightness and clarity of everything around her. She appreciated the special paddle that Fox had carved for her with his crooked knife. The bold decorative grooves and ridges that encircled its shaft had a dramatic look that was accentuated by the reddish-tan color of the spruce wood, and the knobbed handle fit her palm just right. As Otter admired her husband's knife-work, she was again reminded of the special link that often formed between the maker of a handcrafted item and the person who used that item.

An irridescent blue-green and black dragonfly landed gracefully on one gunwale cap, between two of the carved wooden pegs, and folded its thin, transparent wings above its back. After a time, it flew off, as another identical one landed on the center thwart to hitch a ride. As Otter watched her new passenger, she also observed the graceful lines of the flared shoulders near each end of that thwart. The shoulders had been carved into the light tan cedar to hold the tumpline cords from slipping when they were tied on to portage the canoe. She also noted that the split root lashings looked firm and strong where they bound the ends of each of the five thwarts into their mortise holes in the inwales, and along the top of each wall where they lashed the gunwale elements and the bark wall together beneath the gunwale cap.

The angle of the sun's rays exaggerated the contrast in color between the ribs, split out of light reddish-brown heartwood of cedar, and the sheathing strips, running lengthwise beneath the ribs, which had been split from the off-white sapwood of the same cedar. Interesting patterns of parallel wavy ridges covered many surfaces of both the ribs and the sheathing strips. These ridges had been caused by the separation of the wood along its grain lines when the builder had split these pieces to size.

A group of crows, cawing noisily overhead as they flew down the course of the river, reminded Otter of her raucous family back on the island. She made a few broad sweeping strokes with the paddle to turn the canoe around, and floated easily back downstream.

While the family sat on the sandy shore, munching jerky and dried apples, Fox automatically noted the outline of the canoe pulled up on the shore, with its high upswept ends and nearly vertical gunwale tips. The most obvious difference between canoes built by different native groups was in the profile of the prows and gunwale tips. Observing the outlines of canoes at a distance was an ingrained survival technique, particularly important to Fox each year as he made the trip out to the French settlements on the Fleuve St. Laurent. During the eastern portion of the trip, on the Outaouais and the St. Laurent, it was especially crucial to be ever watchful for raiding parties of Iroquois, in their low, flat elm bark canoes.

After the meal, Hawk paddled away on his own, with his canine friend Jacques peering out over the gunwale in the bow. A short distance upstream, he nosed the canoe into a long, quiet lagoon. Long before, a narrow island of sand had formed on the inside of the broad curve in the river. Some time later, a sand bar had accumulated at the upstream end of the island; the bar finally grew into a solid spit of dry land connecting the island to the shore. This closed off the flow of the river on the shoreward side of the island, turning it into this placid lagoon.

Quietly plying his paddle in the still water, Hawk looked and listened carefully. As the canoe passed through a bed of tall reeds and water grasses, the reeds scraped against the bark hull, with its myriad little grooves and growth bumps, and made a quiet announcement of his presence. The many little empty spaces between the bark skin and the sheathing strips inside acted as sound resonating chambers, like many tiny drums. Hawk was reminded that dugout canoes, carved from a single solid trunk of a tree, did not have such hollow resonating areas within their walls.

Hawk mulled over the strange object that lay on the floor of the canoe, attached by a cord to the center thwart: dark tan in color, irregularly round, about the thickness of a man's outstretched hand, with many long slender holes running through it. When Fox had first brought the unusual item, Hawk had been amazed at the amount of water it could soak up from the bottom of the canoe when waves were splashing over the gunwales or when heavy rain was pouring into the craft. He had become accustomed to its use, but he was still unsure whether to believe the fantastic story that Fox still told about where the *éponge* had come from: a bad-tasting lake many times bigger than *Gitchi-Gumi* (Lake Superior)! Even after all these years together, it was still sometimes impossible to tell whether Fox's stories were really true, or were just made up for fun, like the ones about his people in France riding moose and drinking milk from buffaloes.

The whole family was once again afloat. Fox, now down to just his breechclout and broad-brimmed felt hat in the afternoon heat, stood in the stern, using his long setting pole to propel them back to camp. The St. Croix seemed ideal for poling, with its solid sandy bottom, moderately shallow depth, and many shallows and sandbars, especially at the upriver and downriver ends of islands and on the inside of curves. As he pushed downstream, Fox offset the tendency of the canoe to turn away from the side on which he was poling by leaning toward the pole side; the craft glided along a straight course with little effort.

These traveling conditions offered few perils. The few scattered boulders were, for the most part, tall enough to cause telltale ripples on the water's surface. However, as Fox poled leisurely, his mind drifted back to many dangerous situations that the family had encountered during their years of canoe travel. He knew that if their bark canoe ever broke open against a boulder in deep powerful rapids, most of their gear and cargo would sink to the bottom. In addition, the broken canoe, full of water, would not be buoyant enough to keep the family members afloat, in their heavy, watersoaked clothing of leather and fabric.

Back beside the campsite, Fox and Hawk switched back to paddles to explore up the small tributary river. After working their way up for a distance, scraping on several of the many barely-submerged rocks, the canoe finally hung up on an unseen submerged boulder in midstream. After they had jumped into the river to free the canoe, a hasty family conference determined that further exploration of this small river was pointless without a dugout canoe.

Returning to the camp, Fox and Hawk hauled the slightly heavier canoe out of the shallows onto shore, and turned it upside down to drain. When dry, the five-paces-long craft weighed some sixty *livres* (pounds); after a thorough usage, it had gained about five pounds by water absorption into the bark. However, after a long day of water intake caused by climbing in and out, waves splashing in, or rainfall, the canoe would gain more weight in interior water than the five pounds worth that was absorbed by the exterior bark. Unlike water that lay on the rather even floor of a dugout, water in a birchbark canoe collected in each of the spaces between the ribs, up to a finger thickness in depth, along the full length of the craft. This water was impossible to bail out from between the ribs, and was a chore to sponge out. Some of it percolated through the narrow gaps between the sheathing strips, to fill the spaces between the sheathing and the bark cover. Even after sponging between the ribs, this trapped water remained until the canoe was eventually turned upside down on shore to drain. That was the reason that the builder had left the upper portion of the stitched cutwater edge at each end of Fox's canoe free of any pitch sealant, so that trapped water could drain out freely.

During the day's usage, a certain amount of water inside the canoe had been also absorbed by the sheathing strips and ribs. However, that absorption had not been extensive, since the most absorptive end grain of the wood was exposed only at the tapered ends of the sheathing, and not at all on the ribs.

With the canoe's bottom exposed on shore, Fox made a thorough inspection for any damage that might have been caused by the hangup on the submerged boulder. Luckily, there were no breaks in the bark, just a few long scrapes. Often, it was not possible to pinpoint by eye the exact location of small leaks while examining the exterior. It was also difficult to locate a small leak from inside the canoe while afloat, since its interior was covered by cedar sheathing strips. In those cases, Fox placed the craft in its upright position atop one or two logs on the ground, and poured water inside it. Rolling and tipping the canoe so that the water ran to all locations, it was very easy for him to observe on the exterior where the water exited through holes or cracks in the bark or pitch sealant. Those areas were then marked, dried, and repaired.

The canoe repair kit, stored in a birchbark *makuk* at the bow, contained several pieces of birchbark, a number of coils of peeled and split roots of black spruce, a supply of finger-sized pieces of gum sealant, and a small torch of rolled or folded birchbark for melting the gum. The sealant was a solid mixture of pitch, animal fat, and pulverized charred wood. Pitch hardened after it was extracted from a slash in a pine or spruce tree and was melted; it became brittle, and was easily broken. The addition of a certain amount of animal fat tempered the pitch, so that the sealant would be more likely to bend rather than break when the bark wall of the canoe flexed or was struck by an object. If too much fat were added to the mixture, it would tend to melt in the heat of the summer sun. A small amount of black powdered charcoal was added simply for decorative purposes, so that the gum-sealed seams of the craft would stand out in contrast to the tan and brown hues of the bark.

Around the fire that evening, the family discussed the various modes of transportation that were used in the worlds of the French and The People. Otter and Hawk again marveled at the story of people in France riding on tame moose and teaching those animals to pull large toboggans loaded with trade goods along wide paths. Fox called that creature a *cheval* or horse; he noted that very few horses had been brought in the giant canoes from France to New France since the first ones had arrived in 1665. He explained the use of wheels, but indicated that few horse-drawn carts or wagons were used in the St. Lawrence settlements, due to the scarcity of both horses and roads.

Although a few Frenchmen had brought *patins* (ice skates) into the interior, they did not find them very useful for long-distance travel on frozen waterways. The iron runners that they attached to the bottom of their footwear only worked well in those places where the wind had swept the ice clear of snow.

In the interior regions, the French had adopted virtually all of the native methods of transportation. Canoes of various sizes and materials were found to be much more useful than heavy wooden plank boats on most of the water routes. The canoes far exceeded such boats in speed of travel, ease of portaging, and simplicity of repairs. South of the birch-bark region, the French often used the canoes that native builders fashioned from the bark of other trees, such as elm and hickory, as well as wooden dugouts. In time, Fox thought, some Frenchmen would probably bring boat builders into the interior, to construct plank boats and a few sailing ships. However, those vessels could never replace the canoe as the most practical craft for most interior water travel.

On land, the French had just as quickly adopted native methods for winter travel. Snowshoes, constructed of a webbing of rawhide thongs laced within a slender frame of bent wood, enabled the wearer to walk atop deep snow. Fox called these items *raquettes,* since they reminded him of rackets that he had once seen being used to play a game. A lightweight toboggan with an upturned front was fashioned from two or three long thin strips of wood lashed side-by-side, or from a long section of elm bark; with this vehicle, a considerable amount of cargo could be slid on top of the snow, pulled by a person or one or more dogs.

The French also adopted another native land transport item, which was used for carrying loads upon their backs. The tumpline, which Fox called a *collier à porter* (carrying strap), consisted of a broad leather or woven band to which was fastened two long leather straps. The straps were tied to the parcel to be carried, and the band was placed across the forehead of the portager. Leaning forward, he carried the item nestled in the small of his back, with its weight supported mainly by the band across his forehead. A second parcel or item was often placed atop the first one, balanced between the shoulder blades or held in place by one or both hands of the carrier.

As Fox and his family drifted off to sleep that night, each of them was very aware of the great debt that the French owed to The People for sharing their various modes of land and water transportation. Native travelers had shared even more than their ingenious inventions. They had also guided numerous Frenchmen like Fox into the interior by canoe, teaching them the vast network of waterways and showing them how to travel upon those liquid paths.

The next morning during the meal, another subject arose concerning the different ways of the French world and the native world. On occasion, Otter had discussed with her sons the various cooking methods that had been used by The People before Fox had come to live with them. Otter's extended family now had a good supply of copper pots and brass kettles for cooking, renewed annually by Fox. However, many others in the region felt that those items were still too scarce and valuable to be used as cooking vessels; they were much more useful as sources of ready-to-use raw materials for making jewelry and other decorative items, as well as for making scrapers, awls, and arrow and spear points. Since Hawk had seen his mother cooking with metal pots and pans all his life, he was interested in learning about the traditional cooking methods. He wanted to compare those methods to the procedures that were used when cooking with the metal containers that Fox supplied.

Otter explained that native cooking without containers was still carried out as it always had been done. Many food items were grilled, roasted, or dried, on a spit, a rack, or heated stones. Foods were also baked directly in the hot coals or ashes, either on the surface or in an earth-covered pit. Baking pits were sometimes lined with stones, which retained the heat more efficiently than a simple pit. Some of the baked items included unpeeled squash, unhusked corn, and foods that were wrapped in green leaves or corn husks.

After contact with the French, the major changes in cooking methods which took place were in the procedures that involved containers. Traditionally, native cooking containers were made of wood, bark, rawhide, gourd, and clay. For cooking, those vessels were either hung over the fire, placed directly on the coals, or placed on the ground and the contents heated with hot stones from the fire.

To prepare to demonstrate hot stone cooking, Otter searched in the old dry stream bed behind the point. There, she located a number of small, rounded, fine-grained cobbles of granite and basalt, which would retain heat well. She also showed Hawk which stones to avoid, since they might explode when heated in the fire. Those were ones that had fine cracks, as well as pieces of sandstone, shale, or slate. Otter also picked a generous handful of bracken ferns as she returned to the cooking area.

From the wooden chest, she produced an oblong cooking trough carved from a split section of a basswood log, a seamless folded birchbark container, a long-handled cooking spoon, a stirring stick, three flat pieces of birchbark, and a stirring spoon.

She also brought out a rawhide pot, which she had fashioned by pressing a piece of water-soaked deer rawhide into the cavity of a pottery bowl. The edges of the hide had extended over the rim of the pot and down to the ground. After the hide had dried and hardened, the pottery bowl was removed, leaving a rawhide pot which had an interior cooking cavity as well as a second vertical wall around the exterior. This outer wall would remain dry and firm, even after the interior cavity wall became pliable when it was filled with liquid.

Otter placed nine or ten of the gathered stones into the bed of hot coals beneath a moderate fire to heat, and filled the containers of basswood, birchbark, and rawhide nearly full with water at the riverbank. Into the basswood trough of water she placed dried beans and jerky, to soak a little. Jerky could be eaten without any further cooking, since the thinly-sliced meat had actually been cooked during the drying process; however, Otter preferred to soften it by further cooking. She poured into the bark container of water some crushed dried corn, dried slices of squash, and a few parings of dried ginger root which she sliced off with her clasp knife. These items would also soak before being cooked.

After a short time, the stones in the fire were heated sufficiently. Positioning one of the flat pieces of bark on the ground beside the fire, Otter took one of the stones out of the fire with the long-handled spoon and the stirring stick, and placed it onto the bark. After wiping off any sand and ashes that adhered to the stone, using a wad of ferns, she transferred the hot cobble with the same two tools into the cooking trough. The liquid around the stone immediately began to sizzle and steam.

In quick succession, two more stones were removed from the fire, wiped clean, and deposited into the beans and jerky stew. Immediately, the entire liquid contents of the trough reached a simmering temperature. A flat piece of birchbark was placed on top of the trough as a lid, held in place by a hefty piece of firewood.

Each cobble remained hot enough to maintain the high simmering temperature for quite a long period [two to three minutes]. For keeping food warm after it had been cooked, they would radiate enough heat about three times longer than when used for cooking. The stones heated the food most effectively when the level of the liquid completely covered the stones; then, all of the heat radiated into the liquid, rather than some of the heat from the top of the cobbles radiating into the air.

After the stones had given off their most effective heat, all three were removed and placed into the rawhide pot of water to rinse. Otter stirred the stew with the stirring spoon, afterward placing the spoon on the third piece of bark, to keep it out of the dirt. Another three hot cobbles from the fire were transferred into the stew, after being first wiped clean of ashes. Then the three cooled stones were removed by bare hand from the rinse bowl, where most of the adhering food pieces and grease had been rinsed off, and were placed back into the fire. (Later, as an experiment, some of the stones were trasferred directly from the cooking pot back into the fire, without a rinse; when they next emerged from the fire, they were nearly impossible to wipe clean of ashes and burned particles.)

Now there were three sets of cobbles in position: one hot set of three was cooking the stew, another set was hot and ready to replace the first ones as soon as they cooled, and a third set was reheating. The speed of cooking, and thus the total cooking time, depended on how often Otter chose to replace the stones in the cooking trough with ones of maximum heat that were fresh from the fire.

After some time, the vegetable ingredients that had been soaking in the bark container were added to the partially-cooked beans and meat in the trough, since the former items needed less cooking time. For maximum effectiveness of cooking, Otter explained, the ingredients had been pre-soaked back to nearly a fresh state before beginning the hot stone procedure.

While being heated in the fire, a couple of the stones cracked open, but did not explode. None appeared to have cracked at the moment they were dropped into the liquid; however, that sudden cooling may have actually caused the cracking, which only became apparent after they had been placed back into the fire.

The family circled hungrily around the cooking trough after the stew had cooked sufficiently. One pink granite cobble was left in the stew to keep it warm during the meal. During the process of cooking, some of the liquid in the trough had soaked into the dried foods, some had escaped as steam from under the edge of the bark lid, and some had soaked into the trough, especially into its end grain areas. The light-colored corn and squash and the broth had acquired a light grey cast, indicating that a few unnoticed ashes had ridden into the stew aboard the hot stones. If Otter had not wiped most of the ashes from the hot stones before adding them to the pot, the grey color would have been considerably darker. However, if the flavor were altered at all because of the ashes, it was covered by the pungent flavor of the ginger root. Fox rated the meal as outstanding, based on the number of times he needed to use the sleeve of his *chemise* as a handkerchief for his nose during the meal. As Jacques gobbled down his share, he never once hinted that he noticed the light grey color.

Otter explained to Hawk that the same hot stone cooking method could be used just as effectively in the rawhide bowl or the bark container, if a grid of criss-crossed twigs were first bent into those vessels. The twigs would keep the hot stones from making direct contact with the bottom and walls, thus preventing any holes from being burned in the containers. Hot stone cooking was also effective in a gourd bowl, but it would be somewhat risky in a clay pot, since eventually some stones were bound to be accidentally dropped into the pot, cracking or breaking it.

After the filling meal, each member of the family drew near the fire as the last rays of the day fell onto the far shore across the river. Sitting on the fur robes, they wrapped themselves in blankets or put on *capotes* against the cooling night air. As darkness closed in, the pewter mug of *eau-de-vie* (brandy) was passed from hand to hand, warming the family's insides while the fire warmed their outsides.

As the bird calls of daytime ceased, a host of fireflies emerged, flitting like tiny blue-green ghosts as high as the tallest treetops that surrounded the little clearing. About the time the cheery fire had burned down to dim orange coals, Fox had finished his tale of Les Feux Follets, the magical spirit lights that appeared in swamps at night to lead travelers astray. An owl called intermittently from deep in the woods, signaling the end of a good day.

Starting the new day with hot raspberry tea sounded appealing, considering the chilly, overcast weather. At Otter's direction, Hawk wielded a stick to position three small stones in a little triangle in the middle of the bed of glowing coals. He then nestled the semi-pointed bottom of an elongated clay pot onto this stone tripod, so that the pot made direct contact with the hot coals. In a few areas of the pot's smooth black and grey exterior, bits of pulverized granite gleamed in the early-morning sunlight . The family did not have to wait long for the cool river water in the pot to reach a steaming simmer [five to six minutes].

In the meantime, Otter fashioned a lid for the pot. Cutting two round pieces of birch-bark, she positioned one atop the other so that the direction of the grain of one crossed the grain direction of the other, with the white outer surface of the bark facing outward on both pieces. Positioned in this manner, the inward curling tendency of one piece was offset by that of the other piece when the lid was heated. With the antler-handled iron awl, she pierced a row of holes around the perimeter of the bark sandwich, and quickly stitched it together with a length of peeled and split root of black spruce.

After dropping three finger-length red raspberry twigs into the steaming water, Hawk lidded the pot and laid out a basswood platter of jerky. Otter showed him, on another clay pot, the damage which could result by building a flaming fire around a vessel so that direct flames created too much heat: a number of fine cracks had formed between the rim of the pot and the level of the liquid in the pot at the time of the damage. Even when clay vessels were used which had loop handles at the rim for suspension, they were usually hung over a bed of coals, rather than over open flames, to avoid cracking.

When the tea had steeped long enough, Hawk scraped the radiating coals away from the pot with a maple limb, and dipped the tea from the pot with his cup of box turtle shell. Removing the heat from the pot rather than the pot from the heat minimized the risk of breakage. If an entire meal had been cooked in the pot, infusions of new hot coals would have been scraped into position around the pot at intervals, as the previous ones burned down.

After the light meal of jerky and tea, Fox began preparing a treat of wild rice with blueberries. He had earlier fashioned a cooking vessel from a single piece of folded birch-bark. After filling the seamless pot half-full at the riverbank, he hung it by its long handle of basswood inner bark over the fire, and added a double handful of rice and a generous amount of dried berries.

During the extended simmering process, the flames were allowed to reach the bottom and lower walls of the bark pot. Those areas were eventually singed to a dark black color on the exterior; they also warped out of shape a little. However, any areas of bark which were kept moistened by the liquid contents of the vessel would not burn through. Fox had to carefully limit the degree to which the flames reached the two folded exterior flaps at each end of the pot, since those areas had no contact with the liquid inside the vessel, and thus could burn through.

After the wild rice had cooked to a soft consistency, he stirred in a generous scoop of maple sugar, took the pot from the fire, and passed out mussel shell spoons to Otter and Hawk for the feast. Sitting on the robes, enjoying the sweet treat, the family reviewed the various traditional container-cooking methods of The People.

Hot stone cooking, whether in containers of wood, rawhide, bark, or gourd, produced the highest temperatures, since the liquid actually boiled around the stones as soon as they were first placed into the pot. The high temperatures, in turn, made possible the shortest cooking times. Drawbacks to this method were the considerable labor and tending that were required, the ashes that made their way into the food, and the lack of significant heat retention by the various types of containers. Each of the containers could be reused many times, and could be cleaned of food remains moderately well after each usage.

Cooking in a birchbark container directly over the fire produced medium simmering temperatures and thus moderate cooking times. One major drawback was the very close attention that was required to keep the flames high enough to provide effective heat yet not burn the upper walls or exterior end flaps of the container; others included the one-time usage of the singed and warped bark pot, and the pot's virtual lack of heat retention.

Cooking in a clay pot likewise produced medium simmering temperatures for moderate cooking times. However, unlike the bark pot procedure, the temperatures were kept quite steady by a bed of hot coals, without the fluctuations that were caused by flareups and burn-downs of direct flame cooking. Even more significant, the amount of labor and tending that was necessary was minimal; tending only required the occasional addition of new hot coals around the pot. Other advantages of clay pot cooking included the easy cleaning of the pot's interior due to its smooth, even surface, and the great many times it could be reused if care were taken not to break the pot or cause cracks by direct flames. Particularly useful was its heat retention feature, both for efficiency in the initial cooking process and for keeping foods warm after they had been cooked. Thus, clay pot cooking was the most effective and efficient, overall, of the three native methods. It was especially useful for long, slow simmering, as well as for keeping a pot of food ready and available over much of the day, which was a common custom of The People.

In addition to discussing the various cooking methods, Otter also pointed out a number of traits of the containers themselves. Those made of wood, bark, or clay did not tend to impart any obvious flavors to the food, either during cooking or when food was left to stand in the containers. However, liquids tended to pick up some flavor when they were left for an extended period in a rawhide or gourd container.

As to durability, the most fragile cooking vessels were those of birchbark; they tended to develop cracks along the fold lines in the bark, for which there was no practical repair solution. Clay and wooden vessels followed in increasing degrees of hardiness. Cracks which developed in the upper wall areas of clay pots were sometimes repaired by drilling a hole on each side of the crack and binding the crack together through those holes with cordage. Cracks which formed in wooden vessels, primarily in the end grain areas where they absorbed the most liquid, were often repaired using the same method. Containers made of rawhide were extremely durable, nearly indestructible if not burned, especially if they were allowed to dry well between usages.

In discussing the ease of transport of each of the container types, the factors of size and weight were considered, in addition to durability. Wooden vessels were the heaviest and most bulky; they were sometimes left overturned at camp and village sites by The People when they moved, to be reused when the owners returned to the site in another season. Seamless cooking containers of folded birchbark were not often transported, due to their generally one-use lifespan when used in direct-flame cooking. Even if they were not ruined by the first cooking usage, as in hot stone cooking, they were generally impractical to transport empty, due to their fragility, even though they were extremely light. Transporting flat panels of bark was much more practical; they could be quickly folded into new cooking pots at a new site. Many pottery vessels were moderately transportable, if care were taken against breakage, since many of them were not overly large or heavy. Rawhide pots, very light and not too bulky, were easily transported.

Now that Hawk had been exposed to each of the methods that The People had used to cook food in their traditional containers, he understood why the pots and kettles of copper and brass which Fox supplied were some of the most hightly prized of his various trade goods. Cast iron kettles were only occasionally transported into the interior by French traders; the excessive weight of the larger versions of such vessels was often impractical for canoe and foot travel, for both the traders and The People. When Fox traveled, he carried, in addition to a copper pot and skillet and a brass kettle, a small *marmite de fer* (cast iron kettle) which stood on three short legs. In diameter, it only equalled the length of his hand; this size was useful mainly for brewing hot beverages.

Chaudières (kettles) had walls which usually angled outward as they rose. Those vessels were usually fashioned from brass; they were not often covered with a thin coating of tin on the interior surfaces. *Marmites* (pots) were usually constructed of copper; they nearly always bore a coat of tin on the interior surface of the bottom and walls, since copper reacted much more quickly to food acids than brass, producing poisonous corrosion. The walls of pots usually rose straight upward, or narrowed near the rim, often with a shoulder area around the perimeter. Many were fitted with a lid, which often fit over the rim down to the shoulder, or within the rim. Fox's copper pot had originally been equipped with a copper lid, which had fit over the rim and down upon the shoulder that ran around the perimeter of the pot. That lid, lost during a voyage years before, had been replaced by a round one carved from wood.

Cooking was often done with the copper and brass vessels suspended or supported directly over the fire, which was the location of greatest heat efficiency. There was no concern about damage to the containers due to high flames, extreme temperatures, or long duration of cooking. Since the heat was applied efficiently, cooking times were greatly reduced, compared to cooking with traditional native vessels. Labor was also much reduced, since the only tending that was necessary involved keeping the fire built up and occasionally stirring the contents of the pot. Due to the efficient conduction and retention of heat by the copper and brass, the contents remained very hot while cooking. This heat retention by the metal also kept the food warm for a long time after the cooking was completed. The interior of such vessels was very easily cleaned of food remains, even when the surface was covered with shallow hammer marks, which were sometimes produced in the manufacturing process.

These containers were extremely durable, both the body of copper or brass and the iron bail or handle; they held up under heavy usage for years. Holes or cracks in the bodies were often repaired using riveted patches, with both the patches and the rolled rivets being cut from pieces of the body of an irreparable vessel. Copper and brass containers were very easily transported, since even the larger ones were quite light in weight, in addition to being extremely durable and easily carried.

The only minor drawback to the usage of such vessels involved the slight flavor which the interior surface, even though tin-plated in many cases, imparted to foods if they were left standing in the containers while cool or only slightly warm. This did not occur if the foods were kept quite warm. The elimination of the familiar light grey cast of foods that had been formerly cooked with hot stones was seen by some of the Old Ones as another sign of the changing times. After a lifetime of eating grey stew, they missed that hue at meals which were now cooked in metal containers.

After the family had completed their several days of experiments with the traditional native cooking methods, they filled the following string of warm, sunny days with further explorations of the river, as well as fashioning birchbark containers, braiding trade line into cordage, feasting, telling stories of the ancestors around evening fires, and singing their ancient *chansons*.

Noone enjoyed those old French songs more than Otter. At first, she had delighted in hearing the new melodies with their variety of moods, and then in learning to pronounce the new sounds and words of Fox's people. It heightened her enjoyment even more when he later translated the words for her.

> *Ah, si mon moine voulait danser!*
> *Ah, si mon moine voulait danser!*
> *Un capuchon je lui donnerais,*
> *Un capuchon je lui donnerais.*
>
> *Danse, mon moin', danse!*
> *Tu n'entends pas la danse,*
> *Tu n'entends pas mon moulin, lon, la,*
> *Tu n'entends pas mon moulin marcher.*

Otter laughed each time they sang that song. She was tickled by the mental image of a dignified blackrobe being bribed into dancing by gifts of a frock, a belt, a hooded cape, a rosary, and a prayer book.

One day, Hawk spent the entire afternoon making a priming powder flask from a small glass bottle. Over the pale green glass, he stitched a protective covering of brain-tanned deer hide, using a long deerhide thong. He then carved a little stopper of wood, drilled a hole through its broad end with an iron awl, and attached it by a thong to the neck of the flask. He proudly stowed the powder container in his fire bag, looking forward to the day when he would have a weapon of his own to load.

On the last evening before departure from this sojourn on the St. Croix, the sun dipped beneath the treeline and the air began to chill. An eerie, whispy mist rose from the surface of the warm river beside the camp. In the waning light, the family began making plans for future voyages into the past.

Chapter Five

Before coming to live with The People, Silver Fox had never seen the process of tanning a hide to make leather. In his French world, that work had been done by professional tanners, in their own buildings. But here in the camp of Sunning Otter's people, most of the women and girls tanned the hides and furs that were needed by their own families. Their products were utilized for footwear, clothing, bedding, floor and wall coverings, and myriad other items.

Fox decided to learn each step of the extensive procedure himself, so he could determine how the importation of his European trade goods had affected their tanning process. He also wanted to understand why The People so avidly sought the blankets and fabrics that he brought each year in his cargo of goods. Sunning Otter thought it was rather strange that a man, especially as wealthy and prominent a man as Fox, would want to do this woman's task of hide tanning, especially in camp, where there were women available to do the job; however, she complied with his wishes.

Soaking

Using freshly-cut saplings and large stones, Fox weighted down underwater a large, heavy hide of a buck that had been killed by a single lead ball through the base of the neck. During the following days, as the hide soaked, he gathered all of the implements that would be needed for the wet-scrape method of tanning. (In the alternative dry-scrape method, the hair was scraped from the hide without a pre-soaking step to first loosen the hair.)

After a few days of soaking underwater, the skin had expanded enough to cause the hair to loosen; it could now be tugged out of the skin rather easily, which was the indicator that the hide was ready for processing. It gave off a pungent, rather sweet smell, since the adhering fat and flesh had begun to deteriorate during the days of soaking.

Fleshing

Fox draped the hide over a fleshing and beaming platform, which had been made from a length of rounded outer section of a peeled tree trunk. The platform was about as long as a man's height. Two limbs, about the thickness of a man's wrist, served as legs to support one end of the section of log at waist height. The tip of this raised end had been carved round and smooth, and its thickness had been tapered. The log platform was positioned in the shade, so that the hide would tend to stay moist, and its layer of fat would remain solid in the cooler air.

The interior side of the hide faced upward on the platform, ready for the fleshing procedure. In this step, the thick layer of fat that the buck had stored up was to be removed, plus the thin membrane between the fat layer and the skin, as well as any flesh adhering

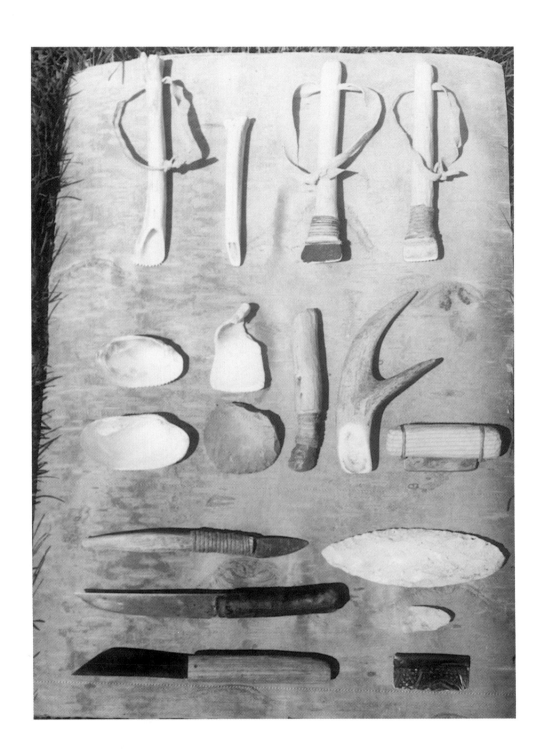

Fleshing tools.

Chisels, upper group L to R: deer leg bone, with serrated edge and plain edge; hafted iron bit, plain edge; and hafted brass bit, serrated edge.

Scrapers, middle group L to R: mussel shells, with serrated edge and plain edge; conch shell; hand-held flint; hafted flint; deer antler; and hafted brass.

Knives, lower group: native copper; iron sheath knife and clasp knife; flint bipointed oval; flint flake; and kettle brass with rolled upper edge.

Fleshing the interior side of a deer hide on the platform, while Jacques waits for a morsel.

De-hairing beamers (lower): iron bit hafted in a wooden handle, and a grooved deer leg bone.
Nap-raising scrapers (upper): native copper bit (L) and brass bit, mounted in elk antler handles.

Removing the hair with a beamer. A rawhide apron keeps the front of Fox's clothing dry.

While the hide slowly dries in the stretching frame, vigorous work with the breaking tool turns it from rawhide into soft leather.

Upper: At intervals, scrapers are used on both sides of the hide, to reduce thick areas and to raise a velvety nap on the surface.
Lower: Fox sewing the hide into a bag form, in preparation for smoking.

Hawk creates a smudge with punky wood to smoke the hide, the final step in tanning.

to the skin. Three techniques could be used for this fleshing process: slicing, scraping, and chiseling.

Trying the slicing technique first, Fox chose a large, graceful knife blade of flaked white flint; it had been shaped into a long oval form which gradually narrowed to a point at each end. The knife had the slightly undulating cutting edge which was typical of flaked stone tools. Holding the unhafted blade directly in his hand, Fox sliced with his right hand while pulling the flap of loosening fat and membrane back and down with his left hand. As he worked gradually down the hide on the angled fleshing platform, the flap of loosened material grew larger and larger, coming off the entire hide in one broad piece. Jacques stayed close by, in case any loose morsels might be sliced off and fall his way.

Next, Fox tried another hand-held blade, a long, slender flake of grey and white flint; its cutting edge was quite straight and was razor-sharp. This flake knife was followed by a hand-held blade that had been made from a rectangular piece of brass from the rim of a trade kettle. The rolled rim area of the kettle provided a secure handhold along the entire back edge of the thin blade. After a period of fleshing, the fat from the deer hide made these hand-held blades somewhat slippery and a little difficult to hold.

The hafted knives did not present this problem. Fox first used a tan flint blade which had been mounted into the end of a pine handle, then a knife with a thin blade of native copper. Hammered out of a pure copper nugget that had been mined by The People in the Lake Superior region, the blade had been ground and polished smooth and flat; it was lashed into a handle of deer antler with a rawhide thong. The last two knives which Fox used were ones that he had brought as trade goods: a *couteau boucheron* (butcher knife) with its wooden handle covered with sinew-sewn deer rawhide, and a *jambette* (clasp knife) with a folding handle of pine.

The fat and the adjacent membrane layer of the hide were cut relatively easily by each of the slicing blades; however, those with sharper and straighter cutting edges required less effort. With the slicing method, Fox had to be a little careful not to cut the skin itself in the process of removing the fat and membrane. A second drawback of this techique was its tendency to leave attached some of the membrane layer that was closest to the skin. However, this was not a problem when using the flaked flint blades, since their undulating cutting edge caught and pulled up the thin membrane layer as the blade cut. In Fox's experiment with a knife of bone (with its handle and cutting blade ground from a single length of deer leg bone), he learned that its blade could not hold a sharp enough edge to effectively slice the membrane from the skin.

Next, he tried various scrapers to remove the fat layer and membrane, beginning with a series of unhafted, hand-held ones. The round scraper of flaked grey flint, about the size of a man's palm, had two broad flat sides and a steeply beveled edge around most of the perimeter; its cutting edge had the usual undulations of flaked stone tools. Fox first sliced through the fat and the layer of membrane down to the skin. He then vigorously pushed the scraper at a downward angle against the exposed skin, separating the flap of fat and membrane, which he peeled down and away with his other hand. The scrapers of mussel shell were tried next, one with an even cutting edge and another with a serrated edge. The conch shell scraper was the last hand-held one; the shell had been transported all the way from the Southern Sea [the Gulf of Mexico], through an extensive network of inter-tribal trade which had been in operation long before the French had first ventured from Europe to New France.

The hafted scrapers were a little easier to grasp than the hand-held ones, after fat from the hide had coated both tools and hands. The flaked flint end-scraper, about the size and shape of the end joint of a man's thumb, was bound with a rawhide thong into the end of a pine limb handle. Its steeply beveled cutting edge was on the narrow, rounded end of the flint bit. The final scraper that Fox used had been fashioned from a strip of heavy kettle brass; its rear edge had been set into a deep slit in a wooden grip. The cutting edge of all of the scrapers had one beveled side and one flat side; they were used with the flat side against the hide. The corners of each scraper had been rounded, so there would be no danger of piercing or cutting the skin.

Generally, the scraping technique removed the fat and the membrane layer more efficiently than the slicing method. In addition, the scrapers left no membrane on the skin, nor could they accidentally cut the skin. Fox found that the thinner the cutting edge and the more gradual the incline of the beveled side of the edge, the greater the efficiency of the scraper. However, a key factor was the irregularity of the cutting edge: greater irregularity produced greater efficiency. Thus, the thin and slightly beveled brass scraper, with its very even cutting edge, was not as effective as the hand-held flint scraper with its undulating, irregular flaked edge, in spite of the much steeper bevel of the edge of the stone tool. The most effective scraper of all was the mussel shell scraper that had a serrated edge: not only was its edge thin and only slightly beveled, but its serrated edge was very irregular. The even-edged scrapers produced a surface on the fleshed skin which was nearly as smooth and even as the surface that was produced by the slicing knives; those scrapers with an irregular or serrated edge produced a slightly rougher surface. This roughened surface was not a negative trait, however, since the entire hide would be later scraped to raise a velvety nap on its surface.

Now it was time to experiment with the third fleshing technique, chiseling. Fox began with an even-edged chisel of deer leg bone. With a downward chopping motion, he chiseled the flap of fat and membrane away from the skin. Pulling the ever-growing flap away with the opposite hand facilitated its separation from the skin, the same as when using the knives and scrapers; but the chisel did the job well even without this pulling assistance.

Next, Fox chose another deer leg bone chisel, this one with a serrated cutting edge. It had a deerhide strap which ran through a hole near the upper end of the chisel and was tied to form a fist-sized loop. Fox placed his hand up through the loop strap before grasping the chisel, so that the strap looped from the upper end of the chisel down across his palm and around the back of his wrist. As he used the chisel in a downward chopping motion, the strap kept the chisel from sliding upward out of his hand, without having to grasp it tightly. Fox then used a chisel made of deer antler: two spikes of the antler branch served as the handle, while the beveled chisel edge was on the basal end of the antler branch. While Fox was busy working with this chisel, Jacques, unnoticed, ate the delicious deerhide wrist strap of the chisel of bone.

The two remaining chisels each had a metal bit mounted into the end of a straight wooden handle, lashed in place with a cord of elk sinew. The iron bit, made from a section of broken knife blade, had an even cutting edge, while the brass bit, fashioned from a piece of heavy kettle metal, had a serrated cutting edge. These two chisels were also fitted with a deer-hide wrist strap. The cutting edge of every chisel, as on the scrapers, had one flat side and one beveled side; during usage, the beveled side faced upward, with the flat side against the hide. The corners of each tool had been rounded, to avoid cutting or tearing the skin.

Fox found that chopping with chisels was the fastest and most efficient of the three fleshing techniques. It required the least physical effort to cleanly remove all of the fat and membrane from the skin in a single step, without any danger of cutting or damaging the skin. Actually, the chisels and scrapers worked in the same manner; however, the long, straight handles of the chisels provided leverage for a stronger downward motion, thus requiring less effort than most of the shorter scrapers. In comparing the various chisels, those with sharper and thinner cutting edges tended to be more effective; but again, a major factor was whether the edge was irregular or even. In Fox's estimation, the serrated chisel of deer leg bone with a leather wrist strap was by far the most effective tool for fleshing a hide, in a comparison of all of the various knives, scrapers, and chisels.

During the fleshing procedure, the thick layer of hair on the opposite side of the skin had acted as a spongy cushion, keeping the skin away from direct contact with the wooden fleshing platform. This allowed the knives, scrapers, and chisels to be pushed quite vigor-ously, and thus effectively, against the skin, while greatly reducing the possibility that the tools would cut or tear the skin.

The hide, draped over the fleshing platform, hung down over both sides nearly to the ground. Fox noted that the fleshing procedure could be done on the areas of the hide which hung loosely down over the sides, as well as on the area which lay on the platform, without having to move the hide. However, he could do a better job, and with less effort, by repositioning the hide at intervals, so that the area being fleshed was always lying on the platform, immobile. The weight of the wet hide kept it in position on the platform, even during the vigorous fleshing procedure.

After Fox had completed the fleshing process, the exposed white skin had a slimy but not greasy surface; it felt cool to the touch. Nearly all of the pungent, sweet smell of decom-posing meat was now gone from the skin, since the layer of fat, membrane, and flesh had been removed. Fox was glad to hear that, within a few hours, the smell would also fade from his hands. Otter explained that a hide was sometimes fleshed before the several days of underwater soaking, to avoid the decomposition and its smell.

The testing of all the knives, scrapers, and chisels had taken Fox a considerably longer time than would normally be needed to simply flesh a deer hide. On a later occasion, he used his favorite tool, the serrated chisel made of deer leg bone, to flesh a deer hide in about an hour.

Fox had learned that the introduction of his European items had not altered the fleshing procedure of traditional tanning. First of all, the techniques had not changed at all. As for the tools, he had learned that the thinness, angle of bevel, and serration of the cutting edge which was required to efficiently flesh a hide could be easily achieved on tools of stone, bone, shell, and native copper. Thus, the substitution of iron or brass for these traditional materials in the blades of some of the knives, scrapers, and chisels did not really increase their efficiency; it only offered some more alternatives.

Durability of the tools was not much of a factor, since the traditional tools showed no evidence of dulling or breakage after being used for fleshing. It would take a great many usages to begin to dull their edges. Thus, Fox could foresee a long period of continued usage of his two favorite fleshing tools, the serrated chisel of bone and the serrated mussel shell scraper.

Beaming

It was now time to begin the beaming process, in which the hair would be removed from the exterior side of the skin. Fox turned the hide over on the platform to expose the hair side, positioning the tail end of the hide at the raised end of the platform. He then took up the traditional beamer of The People, which was made from the complete lower leg bone of a deer. On one narrow side of this bone, two natural parallel ridges ran along its entire length. A flaked flint scraper had been used to deeply scrape out the narrow space between these two raised ridges, making them high and sharp. These two sharp-edged ridges became the scraping edges of the beamer.

Fox pulled the end of the tail area of the hide over the raised end of the beaming platform, and leaned forward over that end; his stomach pressed the hide tightly against the platform and held it in place. A rawhide apron kept his *chemise* from becoming wet from the hide, but nothing prevented the water from dripping onto his ankles and moccasins. Gripping the beamer in both hands, with the scraping edges placed downward against the hide, he firmly pushed it down the hide on the angled platform. With each long stroke of the beamer toward the head end, against the direction of the natural lay of the hair, a swath of hair, loosened by the days of soaking underwater, was pushed off the skin. It came loose very easily in the central area of the hide, but was much more tenacious in the perimeter areas (the deer's shoulders, upper legs, and belly). At intervals, the hide was repositioned on the beaming platform, so that he could work on all areas of the hide.

At the same time that the hair was removed, the thin layer of greyish tan scarf skin was also scraped off with the beamer. This thin layer grew on the outer surface of the skin at the base of the hair. Removing this outer layer of skin, with its hair follicles, gave a native-tanned hide its characteristic fuzzy surface, compared to the smooth surface of the grain leather that was produced by the French, who left the layer of scarf skin in place.

An improved version of the beamer had been developed by The People after the introduction of iron knives. A forearm-long section of tree limb, about as thick as a man's wrist, was cut for the handle. The blade portion of an old broken knife was driven into the middle area of the limb, in the long direction, so that only about a third of the blade's width was left protruding out from the wood. This exposed back edge of the knife blade became the scraping edge of the beamer, with its corners ground off to avoid cutting the hide.

This tool scraped out the most persistent areas of hair from the skin more effectively than the bone beamer. During the process, however, Fox had to take care not to slide the iron blade in its long direction, or it would cut the skin. Another advantage of the iron-bladed beamer was its durability: the beaming procedure would not dull the back edge of the blade very much over many repeated usages, and when it eventually dulled it could be easily retouched. In contrast, the scraping ridges of the bone beamer would eventually wear down into a deeply concave surface, caused by the rounded shape of the tree trunk beaming platform beneath the hide. In time, the worn beamer would grow too thin in its middle area, and break under the vigorous usage.

Most of the hide was de-haired rather quickly; however, by the time all of the tenacious areas of hair had been removed, about three hours had elapsed. When Fox rinsed and wrung out the fleshed and beamed hide, he marveled at how light and thin it now was.

Braining

Ages before, The People had learned to work cooked brains into a hide during the tanning process: the oil content of the brains did not turn rancid, and it helped to keep the hide soft and supple later during usage, even after repeated wetting and drying. Due to this application of brains in the tanning method of The People, it was often called brain-tanning. The process involved the use of brains for something besides thinking.

In preparation for the braining procedure, Fox covered about one and a half deer brains with water in the bottom of a moderately large brass kettle. Sometimes, pieces of raw liver of the animal were also cooked with the brains, but Fox chose not to include that ingredient this time. After simmering the mixture until the brains had turned a greyish tan color, he mashed them with a long-handled wooden spoon into a creamy sauce with many lumps.

After the mixture had cooled, Fox added the hide to the kettle, and kneaded the brains into the hide. The mixture felt very oily and slippery, but not unpleasant. Then he spread the hide out on a grassy area, and worked the brains thoroughly into each side of the hide, until the mixture had been almost completely absorbed. For this procedure, he used a smooth, fine-grained basalt cobble with a flat side, which was a little smaller than his palm. During this last step, Jacques licked the emptied kettle clean, marveling at the good fortune that had brought this gourmet delight his way. Fox rolled the hide up tightly, and placed it aside to let the brains penetrate for the night, out of Jacques's reach.

Breaking

The next morning after breakfast, Fox turned to the next stage of processing the deer skin. The steps of fleshing and de-hairing the hide on an angled platform had been the very same as those that were used by the French. However, the actual tanning of the hide, which involved the stretching and breaking down of the fibers of the skin to turn rawhide into permanently soft tanned leather, was done in very different ways by the two cultures. The French soaked the skin for long periods in vats of chemical solutions, while The People suspended and stretched the hide on a pole frame and rubbed it for hours with a wooden tool.

Fox wrung the moisture out of the rolled hide, and unrolled it on the grass. The day before, when he had applied the freshly-cooked brains, their smell was not at all unpleasant. But after the night-long wait, the new odor reminded him of those times years before when Eagle had been a baby and the padding of dried moss in his cradleboard was long overdue for changing. Fox was glad he had not eaten much for breakfast.

At this point, he sewed closed the two neat round holes that had been made in the hide by the lead ball when it had passed into and out of the deer. He made many small stitches, using a short needle with a round cross section and tan-colored trade thread of unbleached linen.

In preparation for stretching the hide, Fox cut short slits with his sheath knife tip around the entire perimeter of the skin. Through these holes, he passed a long trade cord, in one hole and out the next.

In the shade, he had previously constructed a stretching frame, using four long peeled poles. Two of the poles were set deep into the ground, about as far apart as Fox's height; the remaining two were lashed horizontally to those upright poles with trade cord, one at knee level and the other above his head.

The hide was now suspended with a couple lengths of cord in the center of the pole frame. Then it was stretched taut in the frame by spiraling a cord around the frame poles and through the in-and-out cord lacing which ran around the perimeter of the hide. The in-and-out lacing distributed the tension of the spiralled stretching cords rather evenly over all areas of the perimeter of the hide; this kept the edges of the hide quite even, instead of being stretched out into deeply scalloped edges.

If Fox had wanted to make this deer skin into rawhide, which had many uses in woodland life, he would have omitted the braining step and would now let the stretched hide dry into finished rawhide on the pole frame. However, he intended to finish the tanning process, by stretching and breaking the fibers of the skin.

For this purpose, he had carved a breaking pole from a thick pine limb. About the length of his leg, its head was carved into the shape of a snake's head, with a blunt point, while the butt end widened into a rounded grip like that of a canoe paddle.

Gripping the pole with one hand on the end grip and the other above the wide head, like a paddle, Fox rubbed the skin in the frame vigorously in long, sweeping strokes. Pushing hard and working on both sides of the hide, he rubbed every area except very near the edges; in those areas, strong pressure of the tool directly on the cord which held the skin taut could cause the cord to break. As he worked, the hide stretched considerably; at intervals, he tightened the spiralling cordage to restore the tautness to the skin in the frame.

As the hours passed, the cold, clammy white skin began to dry, turning a creamy white color and feeling only cool to the touch. The only sounds were the swish of the breaking pole against the surface of the hide and the soft creak of the lashings of the pole frame. The pungent odor of the hide gradually faded to the vague smell of an old fish-cleaning area (mixed with Fox's own odor, as he worked up a good sweat).

After the hide had dried partially, Fox halted the pole-rubbing process occasionally to use scrapers on both sides of the hide. A series of hand-held and hafted flint scrapers were moderately effective in roughening the surface to raise a velvety nap on the skin. This nap was a trait of native-tanned leather that was not present on leather produced by the French. Other scrapers, mounted in elk antler handles that were shaped like a bent elbow, were more effective and required less effort. Their thin, sharp-edged scraper bits, made of native copper, an old iron blade, and a piece of heavy kettle brass, all worked equally well to roughen the surface of the skin.

After about three hours of strenuous pole-rubbing, with intervals of scraping, the skin had dried completely. Fox removed the soft, tanned hide from its cords in the pole frame.

Smoking

One final step remained in the processing of the deer hide, that of smoking it. This process tended to deter insects from snacking on the hide, and it helped to keep it supple even after repeated wetting and drying during usage. In addition, the coloration which was aquired during the smoking tended to conceal somewhat any future soiling of the hide, as well as any remaining deep blood stains that had not been removed during the tanning process. Occasionally, garments and other items were made from unsmoked white tanned hides, but the majority of hides that were utilized by The People were smoked.

Fox sewed the hide into the shape of a long bag with one open end, by threading trade cord through the perimeter holes that had been cut for the stretching procedure. Then Hawk inserted a tripod of saplings up into the bag, so that it would stand upright. After the midday fire had burned down to a good bed of hot coals, Hawk stood the bag on its tripod over the coals. He then added to the coals shredded rotten pine wood that he had just gathered, still moist, from an old stump in the ravine beside the camp.

A thick smudge of smoke rose, filling the hide bag and escaping through its loosely sewn top and side seams. Hawk alternated between adding more punky pine wood and blowing on the coals; in this manner, he nurtured a steady, smouldering fire that produced a good supply of smoke yet never burst into flames that would shrivel the hide at the base of the bag. After about an hour, the smoke had stained the inside of the hide bag a brownish tan color. Then the bag was turned inside out, and the opposite side was smoked in the same manner. When the cord was removed and the bag was opened, the pungent smell of smoke wafted from the hide; it had permeated the skin, where it would remain for many years.

Different smudge materials and lengths of smoking time would have produced different colors, Otter noted. Rotten poplar, cedar, or hemlock wood, dried willow or sumac twigs, chips of green wood, crushed cedar bark or soft inner pine bark, and dried corn cobs were some variations that would produce a range of colors from light cream to dark brown, with hues of tan and orange in between.

Now, Fox had completed each step of the extensive procedure of tanning a deer hide by the traditional methods of The People. Otter pointed out that the very same process was used to tan the larger hides of elk, caribou, and moose. Virtually the identical steps were required to tan furs and robes, except that the water soaking and hair removal steps were omitted. The smaller skins were often worked to break down the fibers by rubbing them back and forth over an upright stake or through the hole in the pelvic bone of a large animal, rather that stretching the hide out in a frame and working it with a breaking pole.

Fox had learned that the native techniques of tanning hides and furs had not changed with the introduction of his French goods. The same procedures of soaking, fleshing, beaming, braining, stretching, breaking, and smoking were still followed, as they had been done by countless previous generations. The French method of chemical tanning was not adopted by The People.

Some of the traditional tanning implements had been altered, such as the incorporation of brass and iron blades into some of the knives, scrapers, chisels, and beamers. However, for the most part, those altered tools did not perform their tasks better than the traditional versions; they only offered more varieties to the tanners.

Some tasks that were peripheral to the actual tanning process did involve significant use of French trade goods: the axe and knife that were used to construct the wooden fleshing and beaming platform, stretching frame, and breaking pole; the brass kettle which was used to cook the brains; and the trade thread and cord that were substituted for native cordage to sew the ball holes closed, stretch the hide, and sew it into a bag form for smoking. Those European items had considerable impact on many of the daily activities of The People, much greater than the minor alterations that were involved in hide tanning.

Otter explained that the real change which involved tanning had been caused by the introduction of woolen blankets and linen and woolen fabrics. The People avidly adopted these fabrics whenever possible for most of their garments, in place of leather and furs. With minimal tailoring, they made with these fabrics moccasin liners, foot wrappings, leggings, garters, breechclouts, skirts and dresses, belts, robes and capes, sleeves, scarves, turbans, hoods, and mittens. The two cloth garments which required major tailoring skills, the shirt and the coat, were imported in large numbers as finished garments by the traders.

Compared to leather garments, those of cloth were generally lighter, more flexible, and cooler in warm weather. They were also easily washable, they dried quite quickly, and woolen ones were even warm when they were wet. In addition, the dogs had no interest in eating them, as they did with leather clothing.

Otter knew from considerable experience that one negative aspect of cloth garments, compared to those of leather, was the much poorer durability of cloth under heavy usage. Also, no fabric could block cold winter winds like a thick, heavy bear or buffalo robe. Finally, clothes made of fabric did not emit the deep, satisfying smoked odor like those that were made of smoked hides, nor could they be eaten in the starving times.

After Fox and other traders had brought cloth to The People, the number of hides and furs that needed to be tanned was considerably reduced. However, many tanned hides were still used for footwear, some durable garments for daily work, a number of traditional garments for ceremonial occasions, and numerous other articles that were used in woodland life. Also, many heavy fur robes were still used for winter sleeping. Since the task of tanning was performed by Otter and the other women and girls, they particularly welcomed the introduction of trade fabrics and the consequent reduction of the tanning workload.

In the course of learning the traditional brain-tanning procedures of The People, Silver Fox had gained a deep appreciation for the extensive labor that was involved. He had also learned to appreciate something else: holding the hide that he had tanned, Fox made a silent offering of tobacco in thanks to the spirit of the buck that had worn this skin for a number of years, protected and warmed by it from the day of birth to the day of death. Now this skin would warm and protect another of Earth's creatures.

Chapter Six

The twisted mass of gnarled roots of the old maple arched out from the riverbank over the surface of the water. Crouching down on the root platform, Red-tailed Hawk was able to fill the copper pot and gourd bottle with river water without slipping down the embankment and wetting his moccasins. Even on a sun-drenched morning such as this one, the water flowing beneath Hawk's feet had a dark brown cast, which would appear almost black toward dusk. *Ou-ta-kou-a-mi-non* The People called this river, "Blood-colored Water." It did not have the bright red color of fresh blood, but the brown of dried blood or blood in water. They believed that the river acquired its dark hue from the great cedar and hemlock swamps that it drained, many miles further inland from *Gitchi-Gumi* (Lake Superior).

Hawk followed the narrow path back up the steep incline to the top of the high sand bank. Most of the sloping banks along this stretch of the river were lined with maples, pines, and scattered birches. But here the slope was open, covered with tall grasses, a few delicate white flowers, and a profusion of blueberry bushes, with their berries still hard and green at this time of year.

On the previous day, the family had set up camp atop the bluff, beneath a stand of jack pines. They had erected their canvas shelter over the overturned canoe, with its low rear side facing the direction from which the prevailing westerly winds blew. The shelter was nestled amid a thick growth of bracken ferns, on a spongy bed of green and red mosses. The fireplace had been positioned near the edge of the embankment, where it afforded a clear view both up and down the river.

During Hawk's absence, Sunning Otter had not been sunning herself. Drawing from the pile of dry twigs and limbs that had been gathered from several downed pines and maples found near the camp, she laid up a small fire; then she lit it with the fire kit that she always carried in a moosehide pouch on her belt. A couple of quick strokes of the firesteel against a small piece of flint produced several orange sparks, which fell onto a small square of linen charcloth that she held wrapped around the flint. She inserted the charcloth with its sparks into a wad of dried grass tinder, held it high, and blew on it; the sparks caused the fabric and tinder to burst into flame, which she then used to start her fire.

Jacques seldom strayed very far from Otter, wherever she went in the camp area. But when she had begun snapping limbs for firewood, he had moved clear, and he was careful not to venture too near the fire.

Into Hawk's copper pot of water went a handful of bite-sized pieces of jerky, plus the same amount of dried corn kernels, a few thin shavings of ginger root, and a generous dollop of fat. Hawk slung the pot on the iron hanger over the fire, rolled two dark green acorn squash into the ashes, out of reach of the licking tongues of flame, and let the fire take over the work.

Otter finds the flint and steel method of fire-starting much quicker and less laborious than the wood friction method.

Upper: Dining inside the shelter, out of the rain.
Lower: Hawk sweeps the floor tarp with fronds of bracken ferns. The pierced tin lantern hangs from the central forked pole.

Pounding an elk leg tendon with a stone pestle against a log anvil, the first step in creating sinew threads. A strip of buffalo back tendon lies beside Hawk's left leg.

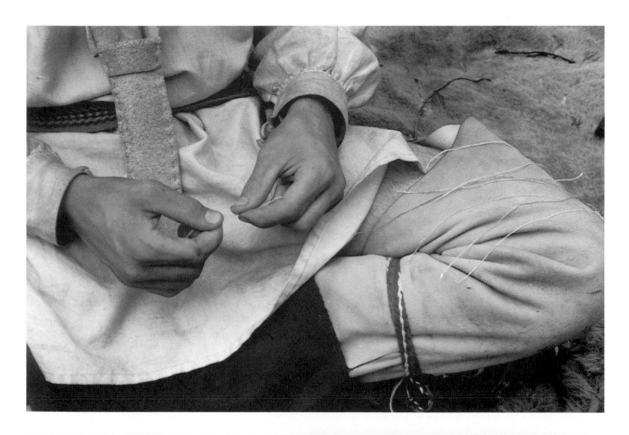

Upper: Hawk twists connected strands of sinew to form a thread. Six completed threads lie drying across his upper legging.
Lower: Otter stitches a moosehide knife sheath with a deer ulna bone awl and sinew thread.

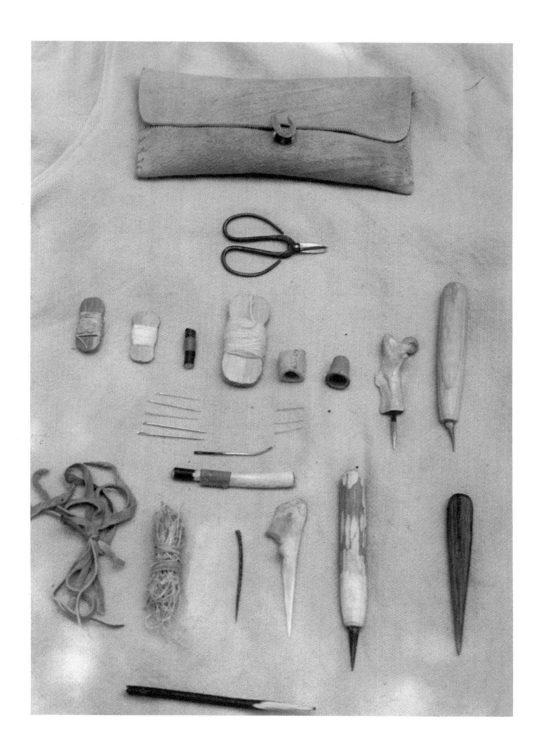

Otter's sewing kit, arrayed beneath its moosehide pouch (top to bottom, L to R): scissors; natural and bleached linen threads; cotton thread and wool yarn; thimbles of moosehide and wood; awls with iron and brass bits; bone needle case and a variety of needles and pins; deerhide thongs; sinew threads; awls of thornapple thorn, deer bone, and native copper; thread pusher; and a charred marking stick at the bottom.

A petite harvest of wintergreen berries, in a little basket of folded birchbark tied at each end with sinew cord.

Otter is carried in style from the riverbank out to the canoe, so that she can enjoy the rare luxury of wearing moccasins and leggings while afloat.

Upper: Hauling the canoe out of the river after an exploratory trip upstream.
Lower: Storage case made of rolled birchbark with cedar ends.

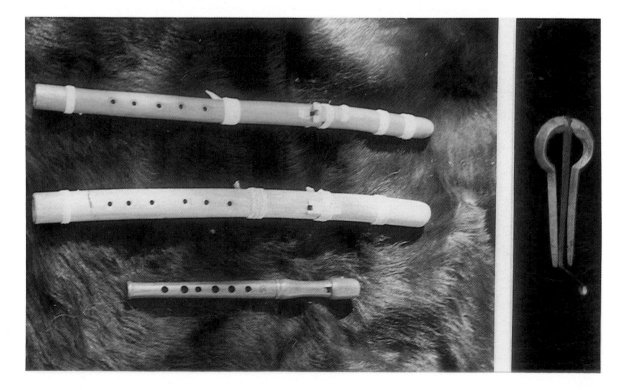

Upper: Flute songs of The People float out over the Tahquamenon.
Lower: Two native flutes, a shorter French flageolet, and a brass jew's harp.

Braiding new guylines for the lean-to shelter from three strands of trade cord.

Upper: Father and son load the canoe while it floats offshore, to avoid damaging the craft.
Lower: Paddling downriver to Lac Supérieur.

Soon the compelling aroma of cooking stew reached Silver Fox's nostrils, as he continued his exploration of the woods near the camp. Earlier, he had encountered a set of tracks where a deer had recently walked slowly across an open area of sand which was still moist from the previous night's rain. Now he was down at the bottom of the deep ravine which ran beside the camp, drinking deeply with cupped hands from the cold little creek which tumbled over rocks and long-dead tree trunks to flow into the main river. As he clambered up the steep incline out of the deep ravine, he wondered how many generations of The People had come and gone while the little creek had slowly gouged its way so far below the level of the forest floor, forming the narrow ravine.

After the family had finished its feast, and Jacques had licked from the dishes every edible morsel, it was time for the main activity of the day, leather working. Otter intended to finish the moosehide neck sheath that she was making to hold her son's butcher knife. Hawk wanted to replace the case of deer hide that protected his fire-starting lens from scratches, and Fox planned to fashion a *sac à feu* (fire bag) for Hawk. While working on the leather projects, the family intended to compare the traditional implements and techniques of The People with those that they had been using since Fox had come to live with them, bringing his parcels of trade goods.

Unrolling a thick brain-tanned moose hide on the ground, with its interior side facing upward, Fox determined the dimensions of the piece he would need to fashion the long rectangular bag, which was to be nearly as long as his arm. Then, using the charred tip of a sharpened willow stick, he marked tiny black dots at intervals along the lines which he intended to cut. Sometimes a sharp edge or tip of a knife, scraper, or awl was used to scratch the guide lines onto a hide; but these scratches were often more difficult to see than the fine dots of black char, on the velvety napped surfaces of brain-tanned hide.

To cut out the desired piece along the marked dotted lines, Fox placed the area of the hide that was to be cut onto a peeled log. His left hand and the surface of the log held the leather in place, while his right hand did the cutting. First he used a hafted knife of tan flint. Its irregular, undulating flaked cutting edge did not cut through the thick hide readily, but after considerable time it did slice and abrade its way through. The oval mussel shell knife, with its thinner and nearly straight cutting edge, cut slightly more easily; but again it required major effort to slowly abrade through the moose hide, while causing consider-able wear to the cutting edge of the shell. The knife which consisted of a single long flake of grey flint had a very sharp cutting edge, which was quite thin and moderately straight. With it, Fox was able to slice through the thick hide with a series of strokes, one on top of the other. The knife with a blade of native copper sliced through the hide the most efficiently, since it had a sharp, thin, and completely straight cutting edge. However, the edge dulled after a number of slices cut into the wood of the tree trunk which backed up the hide.

Fox then stood with one foot on a corner of the hide, and stretched the area to be cut between his foot and his left hand. In this manner, he could cut the hide without a backup log. In this situation, the long flint flake cut the suspended hide much more efficiently than did the knife of native copper. However, the sliced edge of the leather that was produced by this stretched hide technique was much more undulating than that which had been made when the hide was cut against a wooden backing. Thus, the best native method for making a straight, even cut in a hide was to use a single-flake flint knife while the hide was held against a backup log.

Compared to these traditional knives, iron trade knives (whether butcher or clasp knife style) had cutting edges which were thin, very sharp, absolutely straight and even, and did not dull readily. They cut the hide in a clean, straight edge when it was backed by a wooden surface, and produced a moderately even edge when the hide was stretched between foot and hand while being cut.

The greatest improvement in hide-cutting that Fox had introduced to The People had come with his iron *ciseaux* (scissors). Cutting leather with this miraculous tool did not require the use of either a backup log or stretching the hide between hand and foot to hold it in position while being cut. The lower blade of the scissors pushed the leather upward at the same time that the upper blade pushed it downward, so the hide simply remained in place as it was being cut. The cumbersome hide could now be left lying in one position, while the leather worker changed locations as the cutting progressed, instead of repeatedly changing the position of the hide over a backup log or between hand and foot. In addition, this wonderous tool produced straight, even edges, and it could cut even the thickest buffalo or moose hide without major effort.

Having cut out the piece of moose hide needed to make the bag, Fox now proceeded with the sewing steps. The two main thread or cordage materials that were used by The People to strongly sew leather were narrow thongs of tanned hide and sinew threads. Some other threads and cords were made from the inner bark of basswood and cedar trees, as well as fibers from the stalk of the false nettle.

Fox decided to sew Hawk's bag with leather thongs; the technique produced a somewhat coarse seam, but it was very strong. Taking a piece of brain-tanned deer hide which was left over from a previous project, he cut with the scissors around and around the perimeter of the leather piece many times, down to its center; this produced a long, narrow strip which was a little narrower than his little finger. When he stepped on one end of the thong and stretched the other end out fully, it increased considerably in length and narrowed to about half of its former width; these new dimensions then remained permanently.

To sew the seams on Hawk's bag, Fox first pierced a row of holes along the bottom and the one side that was to be sewn. He used a long, slender awl that had been fashioned from the ulna bone of a deer, the narrower of the two bones in the lower leg. The natural indentations and projections of the bone's broader end provided a secure hand grip on the awl. Its gradually tapered end had been ground to shape with a small chunk of coarse-grained sandstone.

Fox threaded the long deerskin thong through the row of pierced holes in a spiral stitch, pushing the end of the thong through each hole with a tapered implement of oak. Its pointed tip was dull, so that the tip pushed the thong through the holes rather than piercing the thong itself, as an awl would do. Sometimes he also used a thorn from a thornapple tree to nudge the thong tip through the holes.

After sewing the bottom and side of the bag, Fox suspended seven pairs of deer dew claws from the bottom seam. The shiny black cones, taken in pairs from the rear of a deer's leg above the hoof, were about the size of a finger joint. He hung each one by a slender thong running through a hole that he had drilled through the narrow tip of the cone and into its hollow interior.

Hawk proudly tucked the upper end of his new *sac à feu* behind the woven sash that he wore around his waist. When he walked, the movement caused the suspended dew claw tinklers to rattle against each other, producing a soft clacking sound.

The leather working projects which were planned by Otter and Hawk required fine seams that would also be strong. They needed threads of sinew, rather than the coarser leather thongs that Fox had used.

The People made the best sinew threads from the tendon than ran up the rear leg of an elk or along the backbone of a buffalo. The dried buffalo back tendon produced the longest and the greatest number of sinew threads, since the strip of tendon was about a full arm's length long and two or three fingers in width. In comparison, the dried elk leg tendon, about as thick as a person's little finger, was usable for making threads for only about a forearm's length. Beyond that point, one of its ends separated into two finger-long branches; there, the sinew fibers that made up the tendon were too intertwined to be easily separated into threads.

Hawk spread the buffalo robe out on the ground, and settled down on it to produce a supply of sewing threads. He positioned a small peeled log in front of himself, to be used as an anvil. Holding a dried elk tendon on the log anvil, he began pounding it with one end of an oblong pestle made from a fine-grained brown granite stone. As he pounded, the dark brown tendon slowly flattened out and turned a whitish tan color, as the sinew fibers of the tendon began to loosen and separate into strands. Hawk used a log for an anvil beneath the tendon, instead of a stone anvil, so that the pounding of the stone pestle would simply loosen the fibers from each other, rather than breaking them.

After considerable pounding on all areas of the tendon except at its double-branched end, Hawk wet the flattened tendon with water from the gourd bottle, and pulled from the tendon a narrow strand of fibers about as thick as a fingernail or two. He then pulled this strand apart into very thin groups of fibers, twisted each group between thumb and forefinger into individual sewing threads, and laid them aside on the robe to dry. Each thread, light tan in color, was about the length of a forearm; the thickness depended on the number of connected fibers which he had pulled from the strand and twisted together.

Jacques was also issued a dried elk leg tendon; but he used his much more sensibly than for making sewing threads. Hunkering down beneath the green fronds of the bracken ferns behind Hawk, he proceeded to eat the entire tendon, with great relish.

Otter brought her sewing kit from the shelter, and joined Hawk on the buffalo robe. Her kit was contained in a rectangular pouch made of thick brain-tanned moose hide, with its two end seams closed with deerskin thongs. The wide cover flap was held closed by a thong which looped over a toggle button; about the size and shape of a finger joint, the button had been carved from a section of willow sapling. A series of long, shallow gouges angling across several areas of the velvety surface of the pouch showed the effort that the tanner had expended in removing the hair from the moose hide with a beamer. The golden tan color and pungent smoky smell of the leather spoke of the smudge fire over which the hide had been suspended after being tanned.

Emptying the contents of the pouch out onto the robe, Otter chose out one of her awls plus a knife made from a single long flake of gray flint, and a few of Hawk's newly-made sinew threads. Taking up Hawk's moosehide sheath, which was nearly completed, she pierced several holes with the metal awl which The People had used for countless generations before Les Français had come. The four-sided awl bit, hammered and ground from a nugget of native copper, was mounted into the end of a pine limb handle. This copper awl was very rare; nearly all of the awls that had been used by her people before the arrival of European goods had been made of bone.

Choosing a sinew thread of medium thickness, Otter moistened it by passing it through her mouth a few times, wetting all areas of the thread except the tip of one end. After Hawk had made the thread, it had returned to its stiff rawhide state when it had dried. Otter moistened it to make it soft and flexible again for sewing, and tied its flexible end to the sinew thread projecting from the seam which she had previously sewn. The other end of the thread, which she had not moistened, remained hard and rather inflexible; this end she guided through the awl-punched holes in a series of in-and-out stitches. When she had used most of the forearm-long thread, Otter moistened and tied on a new strand, and proceeded to finish her project. This well-made sheath, hanging from its strong neck strap, would hold her son's butcher knife at his chest, ready at a moment's notice for any need.

While Otter was completing her project, Hawk fashioned a small pouch to safely store his magnifying lens, which he used for starting fires on sunny days. Having chosen a piece of brain-tanned deer hide, which was much thinner and therefore more flexible than the heavier moose hide, he cut it to size with the iron scissors. As he punched a row of holes along one side with the special awl that Fox had made for Otter, he noted how well the tool fit his hand. The handle had been made from the upper leg bone of a beaver; the projecting little ball of the ball joint served as a handy grip for his fingers. The four-sided iron bit projected out from the opposite hollow end of the bone, which had been cut off and filled with molten lead to hold the shaft of the awl firmly in place. To punch the remaining holes, Hawk tried an awl whose bit had been cut from the heavy sheet brass of a kettle lug. It had been ground to a round cross section and inserted into the end of a short length of maple limb.

To prepare for the sewing procedure, Hawk located Otter's needle case; it had been fashioned from a long, hollow section of wild turkey leg bone, permanently closed at one end with a plug of cedar. He removed from the other end its stopper, carved from a piece of willow sapling, and emptied the contents out onto the buffalo robe. Silvery iron *aiguilles* (needles) of various thicknesses and eye sizes mingled with *épingles*, straight pins of gleaming yellow brass, on the deep brown hair of the buffalo. He chose out a medium-sized needle, and replaced the other items in their bone case for safekeeping. If any of them were to fall off the robe, they would probably be lost in the pine needles and sand.

Before Fox had brought packages of iron needles, The People had not used needles for leather working. The moderately stiff, unmoistened tip of a sinew thread served relatively well as its own guide through awl-punched holes, and sewing thongs were pushed through the holes with a thorn or a tapered oak tool shaped like an awl. This pushing technique was also used when sewing with threads which were made of the inner bark of basswood or cedar or of nettle stalk fibers. The People did have various sizes of moderately thick needles, made of wood, bone, and copper. They were used for such tasks as sewing mats of bulrushes, making netting for snowshoes and fish nets, and weaving bags. However, eyed needles made of wood, bone, or copper could not be sufficiently thin and narrow, and at the same time durable enough, for producing the fine seams of leather work.

Now it was time for Hawk to choose his sewing thread. When Fox had first brought French needles, they had been used for sewing with the various traditional vegetable threads and sinew threads of The People. This year, however, his packs of trade goods had contained something new: *fil à coudre* (sewing thread) to be used with the needles. Hawk chose a heavy unbleached linen thread, in its natural color of light tan. The thread had been wound around the deeply indented concave sides of a thin, flat card of wood. The loose end of the thread was held in place in a slit at the end of the flat card. Another card or flat spool held windings of a light, thin thread of linen that had been bleached to a pure white color. Most of the threads that Fox brought were of flax (linen) fibers, but a few were of cotton. Some were also in colors of brown or grey.

Although Hawk had intended to sew his little leather pouch with a French needle and thread, he had still pierced the rows of holes with an awl before beginning the sewing. The thin, tapered needle, with its round cross section, tended to become caught up in the leather at its threaded end unless the holes were larger than the widest diameter of the needle. Also, needles did not pierce sturdy hides as readily as an awl did. Thus, Hawk had found that punching the holes first with an awl and then closing the seam with a needle and thread was the most efficient method for sewing leather.

Occasionally, Hawk's needle still became caught up in an awl hole, wherever the hole had been made too narrow. In these instances, he used a thimble made from a narrow strip of thick moose hide sewn into a loop, which encircled his index finger; this item forced the needle to pass through the awl hole in the hide — rather than through his own hide. He also sometimes used as a thimble the butt end of a wooden awl handle. The family did not have any manufactured *dés à coudre* (thimbles), since Fox and the other French traders of his day almost never included those little cup-shaped items of sheet brass in their packs of trade goods. After Hawk had completed his little deerskin case, he stowed his fire-starting lens inside, closed it with a loop of deerhide thong, and dropped it into his new fire bag that hung from his sash.

The hours of leather working had whetted everyone's appetite, so Fox fanned the fire back to life and soon had tea water simmering in the little cast iron pot. While dried raspberry twigs steeped in the water, Otter doled out a smoked whitefish into three dishes, with the secondary parts going to Jacques (indiscriminating as he was). For dessert, Fox fried a skilletful of the family's favorite treat, which he called *galette:* cornmeal cakes with dried blueberries mixed in, smothered in melted maple sugar and fat.

Over the meal, the family considered the effects that Fox's trade goods had had on the leather working activities of The People. Iron knives had readily replaced knives of native materials, and scissors were avidly sought as a great improvement over all knives, even iron trade knives. The introduction of iron *alesnes* (awls), however, had had much less of an impact.

The shape of the tip of an awl was the critical element in its effectiveness: the thinner the sharp tip and the narrower and more gradual its taper, the more easily it pierced leather. Those elements of thickness and degree of taper were more critical than whether the cross section of the tip was round, triangular, or square, or even the type of material which was used to make the awl. The choice of bone, native copper, iron, or brass for the bit of an awl did not effect the ease with which it pierced leather: each of those materials worked well when properly shaped.

None of the various awls dulled much, even after considerable usage. Breakage was not usually an issue, unless a light, thin bone awl was chosen to work on a thick, heavy hide. Otherwise, damage would only result if the awls were used against a hard surface, such as a wooden backing for the leather. Then the tip of the metal awls could bend, and the bone awls could break.

Therefore, the new materials of iron and brass which Fox had introduced had supplemented, but not replaced, bone for awls. However they did quickly replace the awl of native copper: when copper and brass trade vessels became available as a source of raw materials, The People quickly abandoned the laborious mining, transporting, and working of native copper.

The introduction of iron needles greatly facilitated the sewing of leather. The People's native technology had not been able to produce an eyed needle which was thin and narrow enough to fit through a tiny hole in leather yet still be durable enough for rather heavy usage. The trade needles of iron had each of these traits. Using those needles, native leather workers could now pull their native vegetable fiber threads through awl holes much more efficiently than they had formerly pushed the thread through the holes with a wooden or thorn tool. Even sewing with sinew thread had become more efficient, since it was easier to guide a rigid iron needle threaded with sinew through the awl holes than to guide through the semi-rigid tip of a sinew thread by itself.

The various threads and cords which Fox transported into the interior were a welcome addition to the native versions that were used in leather working. The traditional varieties, made of tanned hide, sinew, inner bark of basswood and cedar, and nettle stalk fibers, required a great deal of labor to produce. This labor could be entirely eliminated by using trade thread and cord. In addition, the unlimited length of the European versions was a very attractive feature, compared to the maximum arm's length of each sinew thread (although the native vegetable fiber threads and cords could be made in unlimited lengths).

In some cases, however, sinew thread was preferred over trade thread. The sinew thread, which was moistened to make it soft and pliable during sewing, again became stiff and hard after it had dried. This produced firmer, stiffer seams than those which were sewn by vegetable fiber threads, whether the thread was native or European in origin. These firmer seams were desirable in some instances. Also, there was sometimes simply a desire to retain the traditional methods of The People: "If an arm-long sinew thread was good enough for my grandparents, then......."

Overall, European knives, scissors, awls, needles, and threads for leather working were welcomed by The People. By trading for those ready-made items, they were able to apply to other activities the considerable amount of time that had been formerly used to produce knives, awls, thongs, and threads from native materials. The negative side of this was the reduction of opportunities for satisfaction that the production of those traditional items offered. However, the new European goods encouraged The People to make more elaborate and complicated leather articles, while requiring less time and effort; they even enabled the less skillful leather workers to produce neater products that brought more satisfaction.

After the filling meal and all of the heavy thinking about leather working, the family sat quietly, staring into the fire, unwilling to end a very good day. Finally, they entered the shelter and crawled into their blanket bedrolls. During the night, rain fell off and on, but all the creatures under the canvas roof stayed dry and warm.

The new day began heavily overcast and slightly chilly, as it would remain all day. Fox, Otter, and Hawk wore their woolen *capotes* and sashes, while Jacques wore his usual fur coat. Hawk built a new fire to brew cherry twig tea, while Fox spread out on the buffalo robe platters of dried cherries, walnuts, and maple sugar, plus a few leftover *galette* cakes. From somewhere upstream, a steady rat-tat-tat indicated that a busy woodpecker was searching for a morning snack of insects.

After the meal, Fox left to bring in more dry limbs for firewood, while Hawk took care of a few household chores. Drawing his knife from the new sheath that hung from his neck, he cut a couple handfuls of bracken ferns which grew behind the shelter, and bound their stems firmly together with a few wraps of cordage. Then he rolled up the front wall of the shelter and secured it with its canvas ties, folded the blanket bedrolls, and swept the canvas floor of the shelter with his whisk broom of fern fronds.

Otter pulled the buffalo robe near enough to the fire so that she could absorb the warmth of its flames, yet not so close that sparks might fly onto the hide and burn its hair. Gathering her sewing kit and a length of trade cloth beside her, she prepared to make a pair of moccasin liners for Fox, to keep his feet warm.

She spread out the tightly-woven blue woolen cloth onto the robe, and positioned upon it the flat birchbark pattern for Fox's size of moccasins. His liners would be the same size and design as his moccasins, in the typical one-piece style of The People. She could have marked the cutting lines with the pointed tip of the charred willow stick; but she simply cut the cloth with her scissors around the pattern, since precision was not really required for making liners. Choosing a medium-sized needle from the tubular bone case, she threaded it with a rather heavy linen thread of a natural tan color. After inserting a couple of brass straight pins to hold the edges of the cloth together, Otter proceeded to sew the single seam up the centerline of the toe area and the seam up the back of the heel.

Had she been working with leather instead of cloth, she would have held the edges of the leather together during sewing with a couple of widely-spaced awl holes bound with single ties of thong or thread. Inserting a few straight pins through the cloth was certainly quicker. However, the greatest advantage of sewing cloth was being able to sew in a one-step rather than a two-step procedure.

Leather working required first the piercing of a row of holes which were larger than the diameter of the iron needle, and then the sewing with needle and thread. Sewing cloth with a theaded needle accomplished both steps simultaneously: the needle pierced the holes and the attached thread immediately sewed through each hole. During the sewing process, the holes in the cloth expanded as needed to allow the threaded end of the needle to pass through without being caught up in the hole, unlike holes in leather, which expanded very little.

After completing the pair of moccasin liners, Otter decided to make a decorated breech-clout for Fox, using the same fabric. She first rolled out the long strip of blue cloth; it was about as wide as she was tall, and had woven finished edges along the two sides. At its end, she tore straight across the width of the strip, removing a swath of cloth as wide as the length of her forearm. Without having to do any cutting or sewing, Otter had made the basic breechclout, which already had a woven finished edge at each of its ends. She then proceeded to decorate those ends with an embroidered design.

From her sewing kit, she produced a flat wooden spool on which was wound sheep's wool yarn, pure white in color. In previous times, The People had used buffalo wool yarn. They now unraveled trade blankets to procure sheep's wool yarn, while Otter used a supply of yarn that Fox brought for her with his other goods. From her bone needle case, Otter chose an iron needle with an eye that was large enough to accomodate the fluffy yarn. Then she applied a zig-zag pattern of ornamental white stitches onto the blue fabric, along the finished edge at each end of the breechclout. This zig-zag design was one of the basic decorative elements that The People had used further back than anyone could remember.

As she admired the new moccasin liners and breechclout that she had made for Fox, Otter reflected on the fabrics and cloth items that Fox and his people had introduced to her world. Every year, The People avidly sought more woolen *couvertures* (blankets), as well as linen, woolen, and canvas cloth. With those fabrics, they could produce nearly every item of clothing except moccasins that they had traditionally made from leather. Those cloth garments were generally lighter, more flexible, and cooler in warm weather than the leather versions. They were also washable, they dried quickly, and the woolen ones were even warm when wet, all traits that were lacking in leather garments.

However, cloth was considerably less durable under heavy usage than tanned hides. That is why Otter and her family chose for daily wear leggings made of deer hide and shoulder and belt bags of moose hide; her daily dress was also of deer hide. In addition, they used moose and elk hides to make durable moccasins as well as heavy belts. Otter was pleased with the balanced combination of native-tanned leathers and traded European fabrics that The People had chosen.

Otter's thoughts were interrupted as Fox returned to the camp, dragging behind him a large pile of branches that he had harvested from an old fallen maple not far from the camp. Hawk broke the dry limbs into short sections and made a stack of them which reached nearly to his waist, a few steps from the fireplace area. The heavy limbs that were too thick to break, even when using two adjoining trees as a vise, he laid aside in a separate pile.

The remainder of the day passed quietly, with long games of French cards as well as gambling games using the dice made from marked deer ankle bones. Following the evening meal, Fox filled the copper skillet with dried beans, and covered them with water to soak overnight. He balanced the pan on a waist-high broken pine stump at the crest of the river bank, to reduce the likelihood that four-footed night prowlers would snack on the beans.

During the evening fire, Hawk placed the ends of several of the long, heavy limbs into the fire; those were the ones that had been too thick to break into short lengths. As their ends burned, he simply pushed them further into the fire. This eliminated any need to chop firewood.

After the family had talked long around the fire, the flames finally burned down to a small bed of glowing red coals. Hawk covered the coals with a thick layer of ashes and burned-out charcoal, to keep the embers alive overnight, and everyone turned in for a night of peaceful dreams.

The family was awakened early the next morning by loud raucous cawing directly in front of the shelter. As Fox raised the bottom edge of the front canvas wall to take a peek, his first view of the day was of two large ravens by the fireplace. Their shiny feathers matched the black coals that had remained from previous fires. As they closely inspected the cooking area, one raven paid particular attention to the long-necked bottle of green glass. The empty bottle made a hollow chunk-chunk sound each time she pecked at its spout with her beak.

Anxious to see whether they had upset the supply of beans that he had left out to soak overnight in the copper skillet, Fox emerged from the shelter. The two ravens flapped heavily into a nearby pine. Again the sky was overcast, the color of a bar of lead, but the temperature was comfortable.

With a length of firewood, Fox swept aside the layer of ashes and charcoal that Hawk had banked over the live coals before going to bed the night before. Then he tore a strip of birchbark into a few thin, narrow shreds. Dropping the bark onto the coals, he watched the shreds begin to curl from the heat. As he blew steadily on the coals, the bark burst into flame, providing another day of cooking heat and cheery warmth from the single spark that Hawk had struck with his flint and steel the previous morning.

By now, everyone was up and dressed. Hawk poured the swollen soaked beans into the cooking pot, added water, slices of dried squash, salt, and fat, and suspended the pot over the fire to cook. Soon he had tea water simmering in the copper skillet as well.

After the warming infusion of steaming maple twig tea, Otter took a small bark basket and headed down the slope of the river bank. The day before, she had located a small patch of ripe wintergreen berries not far from the camp. They had grown on the slope, hidden in the shade below the fallen trunk and tangled branches of a small pine that had broken off at knee height in a strong wind. Hawk and Fox had removed the trunk and branches for firewood, exposing the wintergreens to Otter's exploring eyes. Sun-loving blueberries grew over much of the open riverbank, but they would not be ripe for a couple more months. It was a treat to find these already-ripe wintergreen berries handy to the camp.

Otter's little rectangular basket had been formed by folding a single sheet of birchbark so that its white exterior side was on the outside of the basket. The two overlapping flaps at each end had been pierced in two places with an awl, and a length of sinew thread had been run through the holes and securely tied. The small, shallow basket had been chosen to hold the expected yield of the tiny berry patch.

As the little round berries began to accumulate in the bottom of the basket, their shiny red skins stood out in contrast against the dark tan of the interior side of the bark. Every now and then, Otter popped a couple of berries into her mouth rather than into the basket. They were firm and solid, and their interior, pure white in color, had a special tangy flavor unlike any other berry she knew.

After she had harvested all of the berries in the little patch, Otter also picked a good supply of wintergreen leaves. Back at camp, she spread them out on a panel of birchbark to dry. The dark green leaves, having the same tangy flavor as their fruit, were good for chewing when fresh or for brewing tea when dried.

During the breakfast of stew, wintergreen berries, and tea, the family again heard at intervals the steady tapping of a woodpecker, from some distance upriver. Jacques thought the berries were very boring, but his assessment of the stew was indicated by his wagging tail as he cleaned everyone's bowl after the meal.

In preparation for an exploratory trip upriver, before breakfast Hawk and Fox had removed the birchbark canoe from beneath the canvas shelter and carried it down the slope and into the water to soak. It floated offshore, moored to saplings on the bank by the two lines that were tied to the end thwarts. When its bark became well soaked and pliable, the canoe was ready for the trip.

Wading in the knee-deep shallows, Fox and Hawk loaded in paddles, *capotes*, weapons, Jacques, and a linen bag of food. They positioned two folded bedrolls on the floor, to shield their knees and feet from the ribs of the canoe. The two men were bare-footed and bare-legged, as was usual for canoe travel. Otter, however, as the prestigious wife of the trader, was granted the luxury of wearing her moccasins and leggings in the canoe on this voyage. Since Hawk had been assigned the task of keeping dry those leather garments (and their human contents), he cheerfully toted Otter on his back out to the canoe.

The conditions were excellent for paddling, with no headwind or waves, only a light current to paddle against, and very comfortable weather. It was at times like these that Otter and The People felt like singing as they paddled. Otter contemplated one of the strange quirks of Fox and Les Français : under these fine conditions, he was content to paddle in silence; yet he would belt out his *chansons* when he needed some distraction from hard conditions, boredom, or fearful situations.

As the canoe headed upriver and around the first broad curve, a rhythmic rat-tat-tat again broke the silence, as it had during the family's breakfast at the camp. Hawk, as *gouvernail* (stern paddler), guided the canoe silently toward the far shore. Before long, Otter pointed out a slight movement and a flash of color high on a dead birch halfway up the embankment. There, a redheaded woodpecker was busily seeking insects in the trunk of the old tree, which was already riddled with many holes from previous searches. As the bird worked, his claws held his black body vertically against the trunk of the tree, while his head, bright red on the upper area and pure white below, flashed forward and backward in a blur of movement.

The family paddled liesurely upstream until midday; then they took a meal break while afloat. From the tan linen sack came a smoked lake trout and dried apple slices, which were washed down with handfuls of water from the river. After a quiet downstream run back to the camp, the men unloaded in the shallows, and restored the canoe to its place under the rear of the tarp shelter.

As soon as they returned, a light rain began to fall. Snug under the shelter, Hawk used that opportunity to fashion a small bark case to hold his firesteel and fireflints together for quick access in his fire bag. With his sheath knife, Hawk split and carved from a piece of dried cedar a flat oval piece about as long as his palm and roughly half that distance in width. He then split it in two on its edge, forming two identical ovals, each about as thick as the tip of his little finger. Those pieces would be the top and bottom of his case. He also split out and carved five or six tiny cedar pegs, each with four flat sides and one tapered end.

Next, he cut a strip of birchbark about as wide as his palm and about as long as his forearm. This strip would become the wrap-around walls of the case. He tapered one end of the strip, and cut its tip into the shape of a barbed arrowhead as wide as the width of his thumb. Rolling the strip of bark into an oval shape, with the tan interior side of the bark on the outside of the roll, he made the roll the same size as the carved cedar end pieces. With his knife, he cut a slit through the rolled bark at the location of the barbs of the arrowhead-shaped tip. After forcing the arrowhead tip into the slit, the bark strip remained permanently locked in its rolled position.

Hawk then pushed one of the flat cedar ovals into one end of the bark roll, as the bottom of the case. He used Fox's iron awl, which was mounted with molten lead into a handle of deer antler, to bore four horizontal round holes through the bark walls and into the soft cedar bottom. He chose this awl, with its triangular cross-section, since an awl of this shape would not tend to stick in the hole in the bark and cause the bark to split, as sometimes happened when using an awl with a round cross section. Into each of these round holes he forced one of the square tapered pegs; these held the wooden bottom firmly in place within the rolled bark walls.

The other carved cedar oval piece would become the removable top of the case. Before inserting it into the open top of the bark walls, Hawk fitted it with a pull loop of deerskin thong, which he ran through two holes that he had bored with the awl through the wooden top. His little case was now finished, and Hawk was well satisfied.

In the meantime, after the light rain had stopped, Sunning Otter and Jacques, her ever-present shadow, explored further from the camp. Scanning the forest from a distance, Otter saw long stretches of dark pines with a few scattered maples, standing in a sea of rich green bracken ferns. When she looked more closely into and below the fronds of the ferns, she then saw the woods from Jacques' perspective: a forest of slender green fern stalks rising from a thick bed of pine needles and twigs, green and grey mosses, and scattered green-leafed plants. His world view was certainly more varied than hers in this case, so Otter explored further from his vantage point. As they wandered, she discovered a solitary group of eight lady slippers of a deep pink hue, growing in a single cluster in a opening in the ferns. Making sure that Jacques did not bumble into them in his usual manner, she quietly absorbed the scene, and finally turned back to report her discovery to the family.

Not a single glint of sunshine had pierced through the solid grey cloud cover during the entire day. After the family had eaten an evening meal of wild rice flavored with dried grapes, a few welcome shafts of sunlight from low in the western sky sifted through the needled tops of the pines. Fox sat on the crest of the bank, high above the river, with his back against a tall pine. The sun felt good on his face.

He unslung from his shoulder a tubular deerhide case that was about as long as his arm. As he untied the deerhide thong which secured the end closure flap, he noted the two tinklers which hung from short thongs below the flap. They were made from a pair of shiny black deer dew claws. From the lower open end of each cone protruded a spray of stiff hair from the underside of a deer's tail; originally white, the hair had been dyed a brilliant red hue. Fox compared those traditional dew claw tinklers with the ones that hung from the lower edge of Otter's belt bag. They also sported tufts of deer tail hair, but those tinklers had been fashioned from pieces of brass and copper that had been cut from trade kettles and rolled into cones.

From the deerhide case, he produced a traditional wooden flute of The People. It had been made from an arm-long section of a sumac limb, which had been split lengthwise, hollowed out, and rejoined with native glue and a couple of rounds of deerhide thong near each end. The flute had five round finger holes, drilled in a row through the upper surface, toward the lower end. In addition, two rectangular tone holes had been cut out from the upper surface, toward the upper end; the endmost one of those was covered by an adjustable block, carved from a piece of sumac into the form of a sunning otter. The block, positioned so that it faced toward the player, was bound to the body of the flute with several turns of a deerhide thong. The light tan color of the various binding thongs encircling the flute contrasted pleasantly against the rich reddish brown hue of the sumac wood.

Fox adjusted the position of the wooden block which covered one tone hole, so that it would produce the best sound. Then, placing his fingertips on the five holes, he breathed life into the flute. As the soft tones of the traditional songs of The People floated out over the river in the dusk, the calling of the daytime birds ceased, as if they had all stopped to listen.

Fox thoroughly enjoyed the flute songs of Otter's people, especially in the hush at the end of a day. The native flute, in both appearance and sound, reminded him of the similar instrument of his own people, the *flageolet*. It intrigued him that two such similar instruments had been independently developed on both sides of the ocean, ages before.

Young native men usually played their flute while courting, to attract the attention of a young woman of the village. Fox had not needed to resort to flute songs to attract Sunning Otter; the wealth of his supply of trade goods had been more impressive to her and her family than a thousand melodies.

After Fox had finished his playing for the evening and had replaced the flute in its leather case, Hawk drew out of his moosehide belt bag the tiny instrument which Fox had brought back for him with the latest canoeload of trade goods. Fox called it a *trompe*, but he said that Dutch people called it a *jeugd-tromp* (child's trumpet) and English people had derived from that name the terms "jew's-trump" and "jew's-harp".

Hawk held the thumb-long brass frame at its rounded end with his left thumb and forefinger. Raising it to his lips so that the two slender legs of the frame pointed toward the right, he plucked with his right forefinger the tip of the thin, narrow strip of black iron which projected beyond the yellow legs of the brass frame. The strange twanging sounds that were produced by the little instrument amused him; that particular sound had not existed anywhere in his woodland world before Fox had brought for him the *trompe*.

Only once had Hawk tried to accompany native flute songs with his twanging instrument. A single piercing glance from the flute player had been enough to convince him not to consider that again. But Fox thoroughly enjoyed Hawk's accompaniment whenever he sang the *chansons* of his people around the fire. Hawk had not yet decided what he thought of the odd taste that developed on his lips after holding the brass frame between them for some time; but a good swig of Fox's *eau-de-vie* always whisked the flavor away.

Although he was entertained by the twang of the little brass instrument, Hawk was deeply stirred by the traditional native instruments, whose sounds he had heard on ceremonial occasions all his life. He particularly liked hearing at a distance the resonating sounds that came from the deerskin head of a drum, which could be made from a hollowed log, a clay pot, or a hoop of thin bent wood. He found exciting the various pitches of rattles that were fashioned from a gourd, a turtle shell, a hollowed piece of wood, or a folded section of bark or rawhide. The thin buzzing tone that was produced by a notched wooden rasp when it was stroked by a stick made him smile.

That night, the rain was beginning early; so everyone had a second swig of brandy, as a substitute for the warmth of an evening fire, and turned in for the night. In the darkness, Otter and Fox each shared with their family a number of stories that they had heard many times as they were growing up. Although the specific stories of their two worlds were very different, they had many themes in common. Some of the legends were designed to explain how things in the world had come to be in their present form, while others attempted to explain why certain things happened. Many tales had been invented to teach appropriate behavior, while some were told simply for entertainment.

In her youth, Otter had heard tales about Manibozho and the Birch Tree, and others about Michibu the Great Hare, who was the Creator of Life. Fox still remembered the old stories about Le Nain Rouge (The Red Dwarf), as well as Le Lutin (The Goblin). Telling those legends reminded the two of them of their younger days, and also passed on the tales to the next generation.

One day, toward the end of their stay, Otter decided to replace a couple of frayed guylines which supported the poles at the front of the tarp shelter. She located a large coil of linen *corde*, cut off three long sections, and tied them together at one end. She then looped the joined ends over the forked top of one of the lean-to poles to hold it in position, and braided the three strands into a strong, solid cord. After installing the new line onto the shelter, she repeated the preparatory steps to fashion a second one. As she stood braiding the three strands of cord, she turned to admire her work on the first line. At that moment, she caught Jacques casually gnawing through the new product. Her shriek sent him scurrying for the cover of the woods, where he vowed never to do that again.

The final evening before departure was once again rainy and chilly, so the evening stories were again to be shared indoors, this time by lantern light. Using the tin *lanterne* to hold a burning candle inside the lean-to shelter was safer than using a brass *chandelier* (candle-stick), since there was no table on which to rest a candlestick. As Fox stooped to enter the shelter with the lantern, the slender beams of candlelight that shined out from every slit and hole in its tin walls and roof lit the scene inside.

At the back of the shelter lay the canoe: overturned and resting at an angle on one gunwale, it supported and concealed the low rear area of the angled canvas roof. The craft offered a solid, secure dome of cedar ribs and sheathing. At the left side of the shelter stood the venerable wooden trunk, with the storage box made from an old keg and miscellaneous pieces of equipment. The right side was stacked full of a variety of linen bags and birchbark containers, which held much of the foodstuffs and belongings of the family. Nestled into the middle area were the three warm woolen bedrolls, the two red ones flanking Otter's blue one.

After everyone had entered the shelter and its front canvas wall had been let down, each person crawled into his bedroll; the three then covered themselves with the bear and buffalo robes. Jacques located a comfortable spot between two of the covered bodies, on top of the robes. The aura inside the shelter was one of warm, dry security, as the rain pattered steadily onto the roof tarp. To bolster the sense of security, sheath knives and wheellock and flintlock weapons lay readily at hand, should any need arise for them during the night.

The lighted lantern stood on the floor tarp near Hawk's head. A bit of smoke and a slightly rancid odor drifted to his nostrils from the burning tallow candle. Through the tin walls, shafts of light beamed onto the ceiling in a pattern of bars radiating outward from a central orb. The design reminded Fox of a stained glass window that he had seen many times, in a grey stone wall of a church, long ago, back in Old France, before he was called Silver Fox. As the candle flame wavered inside the lantern, so too did the pattern of light dance on the ceiling, lulling half-closed eyes to sleep.

Fox awakened early for the final day at that camp. In the grey dawn, he kindled a new fire, feeding it twigs that were scattered around the area, all that remained of the former tall stack of firewood limbs. A single loon called in the distance; the faithful woodpecker tapped out his familiar rythms. As the jerkey stew began to simmer, a pair of large, pure white snow geese flew down the course of the river, along the route which the family would travel later that day. They flew so low that Fox could hear their beating wings whistling softly with each steady stroke.

Jacques emerged from underneath the front wall of the shelter. After gobbling down a couple pieces of jerkey from Fox, he found an unused end of an elk leg tendon that had been left over from the production of sinew threads. Hunkering down amid the ferns to play with it, he tossed his head from side to side.

When Otter and Hawk raised the canvas wall to greet the new day, a steaming pot of stew and a skillet of hot tea stood waiting in front of the shelter. They had breakfast without even emerging from their bedrolls.

As the family broke camp and loaded the canoe in preparation for departure, the solid grey cloud cover opened, revealing a clear azure sky and a warm glowing sun. That made it even more difficult to paddle away from the campsite of many good times.

On the downstream run of about two *lieues* or leagues (five miles) to Lac Supérieur, the prow of the bark canoe knifed easily through the shining surface of the quiet river. Near the river mouth, the downstream-bound family met an upstream-bound pair of geese escorting their five young goslings.

After the canoe left the river, it glided out onto the huge lake and eventually landed safely at the shore. A heavy bank of thick fog rolled in eerily off the surface of the lake. The grey mist completely obliterated from view the lake and the rivermouth, and postponed for a time any sight of the twentieth century, into which the family would soon emerge.

Chapter Seven

Sunning Otter nodded in satisfaction as she stowed the final piece of cargo in its place under the canvas lean-to. Then she stood back to survey her temporary home. To the right of the three blanket bedrolls, the canvas floor tarp was stacked with tan-colored linen bags and bales of various shapes and sizes, each securely closed with light brown trade cord or rope. Beside the bags of personal belongings were linen-wrapped bales containing outer layers of fabric or fabric items such as blankets or garments, with other trade items enclosed in the center.

To the left of the bedding, the canvas floor was covered with sheathed guns, hunting bags, tools, ropes, canoe paddles, a tumpline, three cased flutes, and a variety of containers of birchbark, hide, and wood. Outside, above the rolled-up canvas front wall, Fox's broad-brimmed black felt hat was perched on the tip of the center pole. Beneath it, the pierced tin lantern hung from a stub of limb projecting from the same pole.

A few steps from the shelter lay the cooking and eating area. On one side of the fire stood the old scarred wooden trunk, surrounded by a great variety of implements and containers. On the opposite side of the fire lay a pile of dry limbs for firewood. Beside these two areas, the buffalo and bear robes were spread out as a sitting place. The family would spend much time in this area during their stay, carrying out various cooking tasks, eating, and working on a number of craft projects.

The camp had been set up at the edge of a rather large clearing, beneath two towering white pines. The sandy clearing was strewn with a thick layer of reddish brown dried pine needles, accumulated over many years. A stand of mature pines, mostly red pines with a few white and jack pines and scattered maples, surrounded the clearing. Their trunks rose from a thick cover of bracken ferns, interspersed with raspberry bushes in the open sunlit areas.

The clearing and its surrounding forest lay on a high, wide point of land. On one side flowed the broad and quiet Rivière Tahquamenon, at this location about two *lieues* (five miles) upstream from Lac Supérieur. On the other side lay a deep ravine, with a silent dark brown stream flowing along its bottom and into the Tahquamenon at the end of the point.

While Hawk filled the gourd bottle and copper pot at the river and Fox brought in more firewood, Otter began preparing the morning meal. As she worked, she considered how many of the daily activities of The People, both female and male, centered around the quest for food and its preparation. Natural conditions beyond their control often resulted in meager successes in hunting, fishing, gathering, and gardening. Lean times were certainly not uncommon, with many periods of short rations and even starvation. Thus, the native people were thankful each time they had enough to eat.

Reminded of lean times, she thought back to Fox's first winter with them, when a number of her relatives had suspected that he was a spirit, since he did not develop a gaunt face

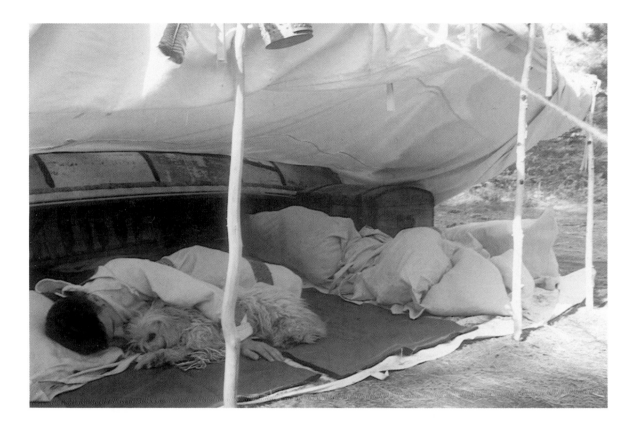

Upper: Linen bags and packs fill the shelter to the right of the three blanket bedrolls.
Lower: Two birchbark *makukon* and a storage box made from a keg lie in front of a variety of weapons and equipment.

Otter fills a gourd bottle at the junction of the small tributary stream and the placid Tahquamenon.

Hawk, a well-armed *Métis*, with a carbine over his shoulder, a pistol in its belt holster on his left hip, and a hunting bag with powder horn and powder measure at his right elbow.

Upper: Shelling dried corn with one side of a deer jawbone.
Lower: Starchy tubers of Jerusalem artichokes.

Upper: Native bowls of snapping turtle shell, basswood, gourd, and clay.
Lower: Cups of box turtle shell, gourd, and maple burl.

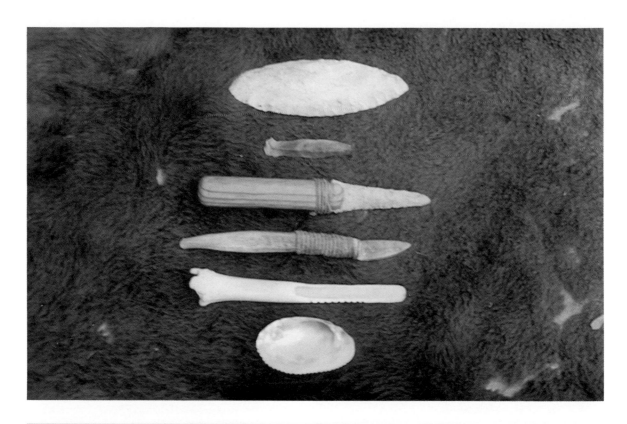

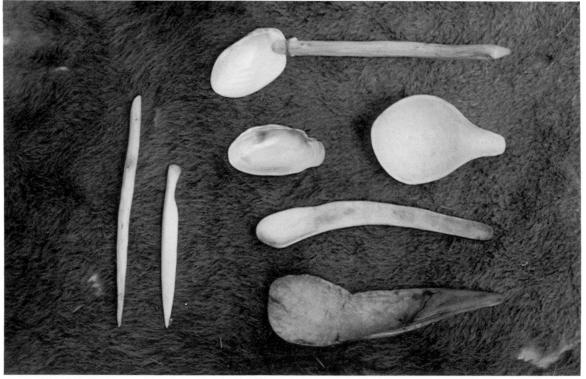

Upper: Native knives, top to bottom: hand-held flint blade, flint flake, hafted notched flint blade, blade of native copper mounted in antler, one-piece serrated knife of deer leg bone, and a serrated mussel shell.
Lower: Native spoons of mussel shell, gourd, moose antler tine, and a carved cedar root; picks or forks of bone and wood.

Upper: Bottles cooling beneath knee-high ferns: native versions(L) of gourd and unglazed clay, and European ones of glass and glazed clay.

Lower: Otter filling cornhusk wrappers with a mixture of cornmeal and raspberries. Three wrapped and tied cakes lie in the wooden dish.

Upper: Acorn squash, corn on the cob, and cornmeal cakes baking at the fire.
Lower: Cornhusk doll on a buffalo robe.

Upper: Trimming cattail stalks and roots with a serrated bone knife on an overturned wooden bowl.
Lower: Hawk shells hazelnuts with a stone mortar and pestle.

Daily practice increases Hawk's accuracy in throwing his tomahawk.

Upper: A leech and its captor at the canoe landing area.
Lower: En route downstream to harvest cattails.

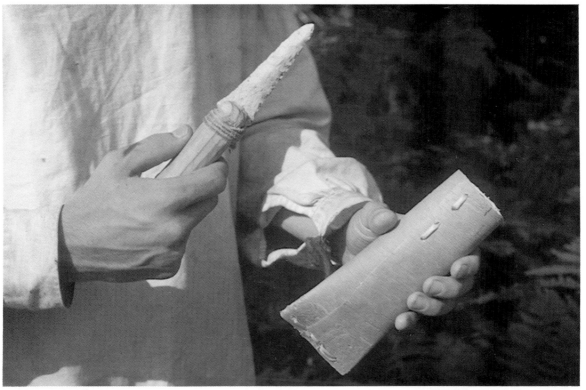

Upper: Otter stitching a birchbark sheath with black spruce roots; the sheath would protect the flint blade at her right leg.
Lower: Hawk also made a sheath, for the hafted flint knife.

Upper: A replacement lid of carved wood covers the copper pot, beside a small cast iron pot used for simmering tea.
Lower: European condiments in their containers of cowhorn, wood, glass, and tin.

Upper: Ceramic plates, mug, and jug; pewter porringer, mug, and spoon; iron knife and fork; and glass bottles and footed drinking glasses.
Lower: Typical French traveling fare of pea soup with salt and vinegar, biscuit, and brandy.

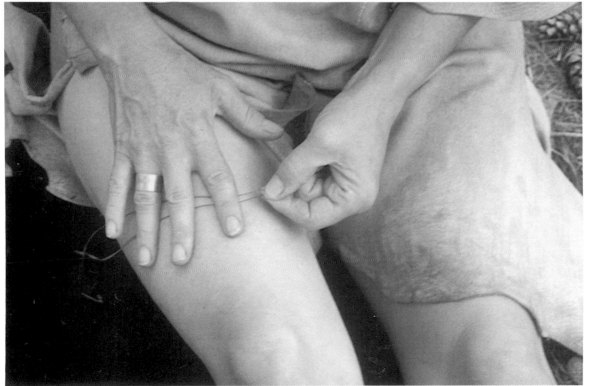

Upper: Hawk separating boiled inner basswood bark into its growth layers, by passing it through a hole carved in an elk shoulder blade. In front of him lie coiled rolls of boiled and unboiled bark.
Lower: Otter twists two separate strands of bark, before twisting the two together to create a cord.

Upper: Basswood cordage, L to R: untwisted thick, untwisted thin, and twisted versions.
Lower: Pot hook and birchbark ladle lashed with untwisted basswood bark cord.

Silver Fox harvests white pine moss for the cooking pot, using a basket of folded birchbark.

Upper: Preparing to depart.
Lower: Jacques has found a spot amid the cargo where he can observe the passing shoreline.

like the rest of them after weeks of meager supplies. They could not see that his cheeks, concealed beneath a full beard, had become just as hollow as theirs.

Otter's first task of the day was corn-shelling, the process of removing the dried kernels from the cobs. Beside a small pile of dried cobs on the buffalo robe, she spread out half of a deer hide. Sitting before the hide, she held in her right hand her shelling tool, a complete half of a deer jawbone, positioned so that its teeth faced downward. In her left hand she held a corn cob, and with her left thumb applied leverage to the jawbone to pry the kernels from the cob with the teeth of the jaw. By the time Hawk returned with the containers of water, Otter had produced a generous mound of kernels on the hide. She folded the piece of hide in half, and dumped its contents into the *marmite de cuivre*, the copper pot.

Next, she removed a few fresh Jerusalem artichoke tubers from a linen storage bag. She had earlier dug the tan-skinned knobby roots, which were about half the size of her palm. It had been a satisfying task to unearth the massed groups of tubers beneath the bases of leafy artichoke stalks that towered well above her head.

Spreading out the deer hide again, Otter placed on it a shallow carved basswood bowl, with its rounded bottom side facing upward. This would serve as her cutting surface. On it she placed one of the tubers, which she cut into thin slices using a shiny white mussel shell with a serrated cutting edge. Otter popped a couple of the raw slices into her mouth, and savored the light starchy flavor and crisp texture. She finished slicing all of the tubers, and poured them into the pot. These were followed by a handful of dried turkey slices, broken into bite-sized pieces.

To spice her soup, Otter added a few thin dried slices of wild ginger root, which she drew from a hand-sized drawstring pouch of deer hide. This same root was administered when necessary as a native antidote for indigestion, so it served as a double-purpose ingredient. She also tossed in a small palmful of dried corn silk, as a thickener. This she kept in a cylindrical container of thin rawhide that was about as long and wide as her hand. The light brown pouch had been made by stuffing a buffalo bladder full of dried grass, allowing it to dry into a firm thin container, and enlarging the natural opening with a knife slit. Finally, Otter poured into the kettle a little rendered bear fat from another buffalo bladder container. The thick liquid, dark tan in color, had a slightly pungent odor and flavor, which would add zest to the soup. It also provided some much-needed fat, since the turkey meat was very lean.

While traveling, Otter stored her supplies of foods and condiments in various portable containers of hide, bark, wood, and fabric. When she remained at a single site for an extended period, she stored much of her reserve supplies in underground pits. These holes, often lined with bark, grass, stones, or sod, kept the foods cool, dry, and safely hidden. She also cached extra food supplies in containers atop raised platforms of lashed poles, out of the reach of animal raiders.

The pot of *sagamite* or corn soup that she was preparing was one of the mainstays of the diet of The People, who made it with corn plus any meat or fish that might be available. The meat or fish often served more as a flavoring than as a main ingredient, especially when it was smoke-dried.

While Otter assembled the ingredients, Hawk inserted the straight end of the iron rod pot hanger into the sandy soil, kindled a small fire beside it with his flint and steel, and suspended the pot over the flames. As his contribution to the meal, Fox brewed tea. He located the gourd water bottle by its golden tan color beneath the knee-high green ferns, where it was kept cool in the shade. Holding the long slender neck, which served as the pouring spout for the ball-shaped gourd, he filled the small *marmite de fer* (cast iron pot) nearly to the top with river water. From a small linen sack he drew a few finger-length sections of dried raspberry bushes. These he added to the pot, which he covered with its cast iron lid, and nestled it against the fire. The three short legs of the pot raised it and allowed the fire and heat to reach underneath, heating the contents both from below and from the side.

While the pots of *sagamite* and tea simmered, Otter produced utensils from the old wooden chest for three place settings, and laid them out on the buffalo robe. For her husband, she chose all wooden items. The shallow oval bowl had been carved from a piece of bass-wood log. Its golden tan color contrasted with the dark reddish brown of the cup, which had been carved from a burl, a knobby growth that Eagle had chopped from the side of a maple tree. The spoon Fox had whittled from a twisted cedar root with his crooked knife. Beside it lay a slender pointed length of peeled willow sapling, which served as a pick or fork for eating pieces of meat.

Hawk had fashioned his entire meal setting from dried gourds. The round base of a large and a small gourd had been transformed into a deep bowl and a cup, after the dried seeds had been removed and the cut edges had been ground smooth with a piece of sandstone. The curved end of the narrow neck of a gourd had provided the proper shape for a spoon with a short handle.

Otter chose for herself a large snapping turtle shell as her shallow bowl, and a drinking cup made from the complete back shell of a box turtle. A slender curved tine from a moose antler, cut in half lengthwise and scooped out at the wider end, served as her spoon. Her meat pick was a flat section of deer leg bone which had been tapered to a long, graceful point at one end.

Fox had once described to Otter the linen *nappe* (tablecloth) and *serviettes* (napkins) which were sometimes laid out for meals at the major posts and mission centers. However, he was entirely content to utilize his sleeve or Jacques' long hair as a napkin. In addition, in native-style dining on the ground, robes of fur or hide, as well as mats woven from bulrushes, cattails, or strips of cedar or basswood inner bark, served as both a tablecloth and seats.

Hawk occasionally tended the soup, lifting the homemade pot lid of carved pine by its little brass rod loop and stirring the mixture with a long-handled spoon. The utensil had been made by carving two deep notches into one corner of a mussel shell, and lashing it at those notches with basswood inner bark cord into the split end of a length of willow sapling. When returning the lid, Hawk noted that it had become as blackened by the soot of many fires as the copper pot, which had once sported a gleaming reddish hue.

When the soup had simmered enough, Otter removed the pot from its holder above the flames, placed it on the ground beside the buffalo robe, and from there doled out generous portions. Leaving the cast iron pot standing in the coals, Fox scooped the brown brew of raspberry twig tea into the three cups with a short-handled gourd ladle.

After the meal, Jacques happily licked clean every dish, while the family savored a second round of steaming tea. Often, The People did not drink any other liquid at meals besides the broth of the soup, which was usually drunk after the meal. But Fox was accustomed to a separate beverage, taken during and after the meal, so Otter had adopted that French custom. Fox had also noted another major difference in the two worlds pertaining to the drinking of beverages. Visitors in France and New France were typically offered something to drink, while in the native world visitors were instead invited to eat.

With their tea, the family munched dried wild crabapples. These fruits, about as wide as a finger joint is long, had thin skins which ranged in color from a medium red to a deep, dark purplish red. When fresh, they had a very crisp and crunchy texture. However, these had been halved and dried, so they were rather spongy in texture. Fox thought that their moderately sour flavor was refreshing when washed down with raspberry tea. The couple of tiny seeds in each apple were pleasant to crunch, as well.

Although Jacques had licked the dishes clean, the interior of the pot still needed a little washing, to remove some persistent food from the deep corners where the dog's tongue could not reach. Those remnants would burn with the next use of the vessel, if they were not removed. While water heated in the pot, Otter pulled up a handful of horsetail rushes to use as a scrubber. She also gathered several fronds of bracken ferns, and folded them together into a washing pad, to be used with the addition of some sand.

While scrubbing and rinsing the copper pot, Otter asked about the dull grey coating that covered its interior. She had noted that most of the brass kettles that Fox brought did not have that coating on their interior. He explained that the *chaudronnier* (kettle maker) had applied that coating, called *étain* (tin), so that foods would not touch the copper metal. Copper reacted with foods much more quickly than brass, producing a poisonous green substance. Brass vessels could usually be kept safe by an occasional scouring with a moist paste of wood ashes or sand to clean away any buildup of the poison.

While Otter returned the cooking and eating utensils to the trunk, Fox banked the fire, raking a thick layer of ashes over the remaining embers with a length of firewood. This would preserve some of the hardwood coals, making it very simple to start the next fire.

Thunk. The razor-sharp edge of the black iron *petite hache* (tomahawk) bit deeply into the log target and held fast. Hawk strode up to the log, pulled the weapon free, and again paced off a throwing distance of seven normal steps. Standing in a slightly crouched position amid the knee-high ferns, he grasped the tan ash handle lightly in his right hand, and let the hatchet hang down beside his right leg. He then brought his right arm up and back, as if to throw a stone. In one smooth, flowing motion, while keeping his gaze fixed on the target, he took a step forward with his left foot while bringing the hatchet forward in a broad sweeping arc. At just the right moment, he released his grip on the handle. The weapon flew toward the target, making one complete revolution in the air before striking the log with its handle pointed straight down.

After considerable time and innumerable practice throws, Hawk had trod the fern-covered route between the target and the throwing location to a cleared path in the thick layer of pine needles on the forest floor. He had gained enough proficiency to look for a greater challenge, so he doubled the throwing distance. This caused the axe to make two complete revolutions in the air between his release and the target.

After practicing diligently at this distance for an extended period, he reduced the target size by aiming at a hand-sized piece of birchbark pegged to the log. With that target, he practiced at both the long and medium throwing distances. Hawk practiced off and on for much of the day, as he would do on each of the days ahead at that campsite. Although he was gaining in consistency and accuracy, he thought he was still not yet ready to clip a bluejay feather held in his mother's teeth at fourteen paces. His mother was likewise not yet ready for that test.

While Hawk perfected his throwing skills, his parents explored by canoe up the silent stream in the ravine beside the camp. At its mouth, where the slow current entered the Tahquamenon, the high sand banks rose steeply from the stream, with scattered pine cover. A short distance upstream, the watercourse made a sharp bend to the left, around the point of land on which the family's camp was set up. Here the banks became less steep, standing a bit further from the water. This allowed room for bushes, grasses, and scattered trillium to grow along the water's edge.

Years before, a pine tree had toppled from one bank, leaning over the stream in a nearly horizontal position. Its top had then grown upright, in a sharp bend, with its lower trunk lying in the stream in high-water seasons. Just enough room remained near the far shore for a canoe to squeeze beneath the branches of the top. Upstream from the elbow tree, the waterway eventually became too shallow for further travel. In addition, many submerged tree trunks and limbs obstructed the remaining depth, posing a threat to the bark craft. So the couple returned downstream, and paddled out onto the larger river to explore further.

Had they continued about ten miles upstream, they would have encountered clots of white foam on the river's surface, and would have heard a constant thunderous roar long before the huge falls came into view around a bend. The rock ledge that spanned the seventy pace width of the river caused its water to drop unobstructed about nine times Fox's height. The white turmoil at the base of the drop contrasted dramatically against the dark brown hue of the water. The Falls of the Tahquamenon was indeed a place where powerful spirits lived.

By late afternoon, everyone had returned to camp when their hunger revived. While Fox raked aside the banked ashes of the old fire and quickly started a new blaze using the exposed hot maple coals, Otter prepared a quick traveling-style meal. As wintergreen leaves simmered in water in the cast iron pot for tea, she prepared *rubaboo*. The main ingredient was pemmican, which consisted of slices of pounded dried meat preserved in fat which had been melted. Some fats, like those from deer, moose, and buffalo, congealed again after melting. Bear fat thickened somewhat, but it remained in a liquid state, as bear oil. Whether made with solid fat or thick liquid fat, pemmican was stored in sealed bags made of such materials as sewn buffalo hide or the complete skin of a porcupine.

Otter grasped the tin-coated copper skillet or *poele à frire* by its long black handle of forged iron, and rested it upon two small logs that straddled the little fire. After heating the pemmican, she added cornmeal, to provide bulk and dilute the grease, as well as dried blueberries to lighten the flavor.

In the meantime, Hawk laid out an oblong platter of basswood that was filled with bur oak acorns and a couple round cakes of maple sugar. The little hard cakes had been made by boiling down maple syrup and pouring it into mussel shell halves to solidify.

When raw, bur oak acorns had as extremely mild sweet nutty flavor, sometimes with a touch of bitter tang. After being boiled in the shell, the very light tan nutmeat turned a brownish tan, and the sweet nutty flavor became much stronger; any hint of bitterness disappeared. The meat of those that were baked or roasted in their shells on hot coals turned the same color, but the taste was more nutty, a little less sweet, and sometimes slightly bitter, compared to boiled ones.

After the *rubaboo* had cooked a bit, the family sat on the bear robe laid out on the ground, and hungrily consumed the mixture from the skillet. Each of them wielded a spoon made of a mussel shell on which a short handle had been carved at one end. In Fox's French culture, meals were usually eaten at a table, while sitting on raised chairs, stools, or benches. In contrast, The People ate from the ground, usually sitting on robes or mats. Fox had generally adopted this custom, although he sometimes sat atop the old trunk to eat or to do tasks.

Otter and Hawk sipped their tea from cups made of a single folded piece of birchbark, tied at each folded end with a narrow strip of basswood inner bark. Fox drank from a shallow pottery bowl of The People; he enjoyed the warmth that it radiated from the tea to his hands. In addition, the textured surface of the exterior had an interesting feel, having been worked by the potter with a wooden paddle wrapped with cord. Lifting the bowl to drink, he noted on the surface of the tea in the black bowl a clear reflection of the sky overhead and the dark tops of the pines.

The next morning, Fox and Jacques were the first to rise. While the dog munched a strip of jerky, Fox blew life back into the coals that he had uncovered. The softwood coals of pine had only retained a little warmth while covered with ashes throughout the night, but the hardwood ones of maple had remained as hot embers. A single puff of breath made them glow orange and cause strips of birchbark to burst into flame. By the time the rest of the family emerged from their beds, Fox had arrayed beside the robes a pot of hot corn meal mush flavored with dried strawberries, a birchbark dish of walnuts, and a gourd jug of maple sugar. The wide-mouthed opening at the end of the gourd's neck was capped with a dried buffalo bladder with a wide open end.

For the morning drink, dried grapes were soaking in water in a traditional pottery bottle of The People, beneath the standing ferns. The shade cast by the ferns tended to keep the liquid somewhat cool, but the vessel itself was also effective as a cooler. The liquid within the bottle seeped through the slightly porous walls of the round body and the short, wide-mouthed neck; this moistened the grey exterior, changing it to a blackish color. As the exterior moisture evaporated, it made the pottery very cool to the touch.

During the meal, the three people chatted softly, while Jacques listened attentively. Otter's people usually spoke little or not at all while eating. The custom of conversing during meals was another trait of French culture that Fox had introduced to Otter. The chat during this meal finally turned to the subject of the usual times for meals.

The typical eating pattern of The People, when in a camp or village, consisted of one meal rather early in the day, with a pot of food then available at the fire throughout the remainder of the day. Otter and Fox had altered this pattern slightly, having one meal in the early-to-mid morning and a second one near the end of the afternoon. This was the pattern followed by the majority of the native people who had settled in the mission settlements along the St. Lawrence among the French communities. Their mealtimes were generally about nine o'clock and four o'clock.

In comparison, the French along the St. Lawrence ate three or four times a day, depending on whether they were townspeople or farmers. The French inhabitants of the towns typically had a light breakfast at about seven or eight o'clock, followed by dinner at midday and supper around seven or eight o'clock. The latter two meals were of about equal size.

The farmers along the river, leading a more rigorous and active life, followed a different pattern. By the time they sat down to their hearty breakfast at about eight o'clock, they had already labored for three or four hours. At midday and again about four o'clock, they ate rather light, quick meals, often while giving the draft animals a rest. A hearty supper awaited them at about eight o'clock, at the close of a long work day. Fox's roots lay in the somewhat regimented world of the French, but in his new life with The People he had adopted many elements of their lifestyle, including their casual schedule of meal times.

After breakfast, Hawk wandered off to the tomahawk range, while the rest of the family set out on foot to explore away from the main river. About midday, everyone returned to the clearing, where they whiled away the afternoon on the robes with the pack of French playing cards. Fox had earlier noticed that the old birchbark ladle was getting rather dilapidated, so he eventually bowed out of the games to fashion a new one.

With a single chop of his tomahawk, he removed a small limb of finger thickness from a young maple that grew some distance from the clearing. Another chop removed a forearm-long segment from that limb. The dark grey bark, fresh and moist with sap, peeled off under the blade of his sheath knife with almost no effort. Fox completed the handle by cutting a slit about the length of a finger joint into one end and carving a notch completely around the exterior near that end.

With his scissors, he then cut a round disk of birchbark about as broad as his palm, and slit it once from the edge to the midpoint. Overlapping one edge of this slit over the opposite edge gave the disk a concave form, and created the scoop end of the ladle. The area of the overlapped slit edges was inserted into the slit in the end of the sapling handle, where pressure held it in place.

From a ball of twine made of narrow strips of basswood inner bark tied together, Fox cut off a forearm-long segment. With this narrow thin strip, he made a number of turns around the slit end of the handle in its carved notch, and knotted it firmly. This would hold the slit tightly together, and ensure its firm hold on the birchbark scoop. By the time Fox had completed the ladle, everyone was ready to prepare the evening meal.

The foods and beverages that Fox imported had introduced many new flavors, odors, and textures into the traditional woodland diet. Otter decided that this meal would be composed entirely of his imported ingredients. She set a pot of brown rice, dried beef, and water on the fire to simmer, and drew from the wooden trunk her linen bag of condiments. Uncorking a small bottle of light green glass shaped like a club, she poured a little of its grainy white contents into the kettle. Fox called this sand-like powder *sel* (salt). At first, Otter had disliked the bitter flavor that it gave to food. However, Fox loved salt in many dishes, so she had grown used to it in time. From a little round oak box with a fitted lid, she took out two tiny brownish-black balls. These she crushed between her stone mortar and pestle to make a tongue-burning powder that Fox named *poivre* (pepper). The pinch of crumbly dried green leaves that she drew from a round palm-sized tin box would add an interesting greenish pungency to the rice dish. Fox called this spice *marjolaine* (marjoram). Finally, she poured into the pot a small amount of light golden oil from a dark green *flacon*, a glass bottle that had four flat sides and a short flared neck. Fox had said this oil was squeezed from little fruits called *olives*. Later, when that imported oil supply would be depleted, she would refill the bottle with native oil from black walnuts, skimmed from the top of a pot after boiling the nuts in water.

As delicious smells began to waft from beneath the pot lid, Otter turned to making the fried cakes that Fox called *galette*. From a linen sack, she scooped a few handfuls of light brown whole wheat flour (*farine*) into a small brass kettle or *chaudière de laiton*. To this she added three spices. With her mortar and pestle, she pulverized three little brown spiked seeds that she kept in a small lidded wooden box. The odor of the freshly-crushed *giroffe* (cloves) gave a hint of the sweet zest that the spice would add to the dough. A small container made from a section of cowhorn with each end closed by a thin wooden stopper held her *muscade* (nutmeg). She removed the little wooden plug which closed a hole in one of the wooden ends, and sprinkled a small amount of the reddish brown powder into the mixture. It too gave off a deep, pungent smell. Tha last French spice that Otter added was a little *sucre* (white sugar), which The People sometimes called "French snow."

After adding water, mixing the dough, and forming palm-sized flat cakes, Otter scooped a dollop of *graisse* (pork grease) from a small keg, and melted it in the copper skillet. As she fried the cakes, she used a tool carved from a tree root with a sharp elbow bend to turn the browning treats.

Had it been the season for gathering wild bird eggs, or if Fox had brought one of the live *poulets* (chickens) that the French sometimes imported to their major posts and missions, she would have also blended an egg into the sweet dough. After the cakes had fried, a handful of French *cassonade* (brown sugar) was mixed into the hot frying grease to create a sweet topping, and the *galette* was ready.

Fox relished his serving of *riz et boeuf* (rice and beef) from a cream-colored ceramic porringer that looked like an oversized broad mug. As he ate, he contemplated what a strange voyage it must have been for the few calves and piglets that were occasionally transported by canoe from the settlements on the St. Lawrence into the interior regions, to be raised at various posts and missions.

Wielding a *cuillère* (spoon) made of pewter, Otter marveled at its glinting shine. She could hardly imagine the even greater sheen that Fox described on spoons made of a metal called *argent* (silver); he had said these were used by a very few of the wealthiest traders. As she ate the last morsels from her deep ceramic plate or *assiette*, she delighted in uncovering the singing bird that a potter in France had drawn with deep green glaze on the off-white vessel.

To serve the wine, Otter reached for the long-necked *cruche* or ceramic jug. She could appreciate that the dark brown glaze which covered all of its exterior made the surface very durable, but it also eliminated the cooling evaporation that took place so efficiently with the unglazed pottery bottles of her people. Otter poured red wine into two stemware glasses for Fox and herself, and into a slender mug of pewter for her son. As she and Fox raised high the thick footed glasses, she noted the bubbles and wavy lines in the light green glass. They reminded her of Fox's story of how drinking glasses and bottles were made of sand so hot that it melted. She never did understand the custom that her husband had taught her of lightly clinking their glasses together before drinking. But it seemed to please him, and she liked the delicate ringing sound the glasses made. No such sound had been heard in the woodland world before French goods had come to them.

The tinkling of wine glasses was not the only new sound that Fox's goods had brought to mealtimes in the forest. Hawk's pewter spoon made clinking and scraping tones against the inside of his pewter porringer or *écuelle à oreilles* (eared bowl). He held the shiny bowl by its single handle, a flat triangle of pewter that projected from the rim of the bowl. The ringing sound was not the only strange trait of this metal porringer. It kept its contents warm throughout the meal in most seasons, but chilled it rather quickly in cold weather. Because of this, Hawk preferred using instead the traditional bowls of wood, bark, gourd, or turtle shell during the winter.

The sun sank low in the west, and a slight chill fell onto the dinner scene. But the wine and the small fire had created a warm glow that made the change in temperature barely noticeable. Otter had learned to enjoy the new flavor of *vin* (wine). Of the beverages that Fox brought with his supplies, she preferred the red and white wines over the *eau-de-vie* (brandy). The flavor and effect of the wines was milder, even though Fox diluted the brandy with water.

While the family savored their dessert of *figues* (figs), *galette*, and water, Jacques applied his tongue thoroughly to the dishes and cooking pots. Another good day drew to a close.

In the dim early light of the new morning, Hawk quickly assembled a native breakfast that required no cooking. Fresh melon, smoked whitefish, hazelnuts, and dried grapes would provide solid nourishment as well as a great variety of flavors. Cool water sweetened with maple sugar would serve as the beverage. Only the hazelnuts required any preparation: as he lightly struck each one with the stone pestle on the stone mortar, its shell easily cracked open and the two halves fell away.

Shortly after the meal, everyone began preparations for making cordage. The most widely used cordage of The People was produced from the inner bark of basswood trees. Cords made from cedar or slippery elm inner bark or fibers from the stalk of the nettle were also commonly used. These cords, made in various weights and thicknesses that ranged from thread to rope, were used in a multitude of everyday tasks, as well as in the weaving of mats and bags. Otter had decided to show Fox how her people had made cordage for centuries before he had brought thread and cords to them with his other trade goods.

Long strips of bark, about two or three fingers wide and five or six paces long, had earlier been pulled from the trunk of a basswood tree, and soaked in water for several days. Then, the thin layer of inner bark had been pulled in a long strip from the thick rough outer bark, and wound into a coil.

Otter boiled the coil for several hours, during which its color turned from light tan to dark brown. The boiling loosened the growth layers within the bark from each other, so that they could be separated.

Hawk cut a section of bark about as long as his height from the boiled coil, which was still moderately stiff. Sitting on a bear robe, he held a large elk shoulder blade in an upright position between his moccasined feet. He then passed the cut piece of bark through a thumb-joint-wide hole that had been carved through the thin flat bone. He pulled the bark strip back and forth through the hole in the bone so that it was firmly worked against an edge of the hole. This softened the bark and made it separate into its thin growth layers.

With her fingernails, Otter first separated the paper-thin layers and then split them into narrow strands, which she tied together and gathered into a coil. This thin flat cordage was used for many tasks in which little strength was required, such as in binding the split end of a ladle handle to hold its birchbark scoop in position. The strength of the cord varied according to the width of the strip and the number of growth layers which were included in its thickness.

To produce much stronger two-ply cord, Otter first moistened two flat narrow strands by drawing them through her mouth. She then placed them on her bared right thigh, parallel to each other and separated by about a finger thickness. Holding their left ends together in her left hand, she twisted the two separate strands by applying a downward and forward motion with her right palm; this she did two or three times. Otter then caused the two twisted strands to twist together into a single cord with a downward and rearward motion of her right palm. Progressing along the two strands, she reached the end of each one; then a new strand was overlapped beside the end of each previous one, and the two ends were then rolled together with the palm.

Even stronger cordage would be produced by using thicker and wider strips of bark, as well as by twisting two of the two-ply cords together, or occasionally braiding together three such strands. The same rolling technique was used to produce cordage from cedar or slippery elm inner bark or fibers taken from rotted nettle stalks.

The various weights of *corde* and *ligne* that Fox imported were made of flax (linen) or hemp fibers. They functioned similarly to the native cordages which had been traditionally produced by The People. However, the main impetus for using his cordage was the elimination of the considerable labor that was involved in producing native versions.

In the late afternoon, after completing their cordage work, the family began preparing a hot native meal that needed no cooking containers. Near the edge of the fire, Hawk positioned two dark green acorn squash. He also laid a circle of ears of corn, end to end, around the perimeter of the bed of coals. The ears, still sheathed in their green husks, had been soaked a bit in water. The moisture would help to keep the husks from drying out too quickly and burning, and also add some steaming effect to the baking process. The corn was still quite young; it had been planted between the stumps of killed trees in the spring, at the traditional time when the leaves of the oaks had grown to the size of a squirrel's ear.

In a deep gourd bowl, Otter mixed together cornmeal, water, dried raspberries, and maple sugar. She also soaked a number of corn husks in a brass kettle full of water. Placing a flattened ball of the thick mixture in the middle of a water-soaked husk, she rolled and folded the firm green leaf into a flat packet about the size of her palm. The wrapper was held closed by a narrow strip of corn husk knotted around its midsection. Otter positioned each cake in the ashes and coals within the circle of corn cobs to bake.

As time passed, she occasionally rotated the squash and the ears of corn, and at one point turned over each of the cornmeal cakes. Eventually, the husks that encased both the cobs and the cakes dried and charred somewhat, but not until their contents had been cooked. The heat also blackened the skin of the squash, but did not burn the interior fleshy portion.

As the meal cooked, Fox relaxed on the bear robe and fashioned a little doll from a couple of spare corn husks. One leaf, split in two to its midpoint, formed the head, trunk, and legs of the miniature person. A shorter husk was laid across the trunk to form the arms, bound in position with a narrow cut strip of husk in an X pattern. He tied a wider cut strip around the junction of the split legs to represent a breechclout, and another narrower strip around the head as a headband. The ends of the latter strip were bent upward to represent two feathers. Fox no longer had young children of his own to whom he might give the doll, but making it brought back memories of earlier years when he did have little ones of doll age.

When the two squash were cooked enough to be indented by a squeeze, Hawk rolled them onto a wooden platter, and halved them with a copper knife. Scooping out the seeds from the interior cavity with a mussel shell spoon, he added maple sugar to the hollowed interior. Native cooks often used that sweetener in much the same manner that the French used salt.

As Otter brought out a handful of dried turkey and a native pottery jug of cool water, a sudden shower fell from a couple of passing clouds. The timing was perfect, at the end of the meal preparations; the family simply enjoyed their feast beneath the shelter, with its front wall rolled up.

While quietly eating her meal, Otter contemplated the effort that The People expended each year to grow crops of corn, beans, squash, and pumpkins. To produce clearings in the forest for gardening, they removed or burned the underbrush, and killed the larger trees by cutting a wide swath of bark from around each trunk. Then the soil was loosened with one-piece wooden hoes, or hoes that had a mounted head of stone, thick mussel shell, moose antler, or a shoulder blade bone. Digging and planting sticks were fashioned from wood as well as deer or elk antler tines mounted onto a limb handle. As the crops ripened during the summer, family members young and old stood watch over the garden plots, to keep animal marauders from claiming the products for themselves.

After the meal, Hawk discarded the corn cobs and husks, as well as the skin and seeds of the squash, in the woods a short distance from the camp. Other creatures of the forest, large and small, would now have their turn at the remains. By the end of the family's week-long stay at this campsite, odors from the refuse would be hardly noticeable. But when Fox traveled to native villages where numbers of people had been living for an extended period of time, he could often smell their garbage areas before he could see the village; the odors reminded him of the refuse in the streets and gutters of French villages. Some of the neater native settlments discarded their garbage in pits, occasionally covering them with soil.

Hawk and his father set off downstream, with Jacques watching the passing shoreline from the middle of the canoe. The craft skimmed along easily, since it carried no cargo. About a half-mile above the mouth of the river, the waterway broadened and its current became more sluggish. As they glided toward a large bed of cattails along the northern shore, they glimpsed a flash of black and reddish orange. A red-winged blackbird had sprung from his perch below the thumb-sized brown head of one of the tall green stalks. On a nearby floating log, a painted turtle left his sunning, and plopped into the quiet water. His ripples spread in widening circles, gently rocking the yellow-blossomed lily pads that floated on the surface. Edging the craft beside the cattails, Fox held onto some of the tall, sturdy plants to hold the canoe steady. Hawk tugged a number of them loose from the soft muddy bottom soil, and laid them on the floor of the canoe.

Meanwhile, Otter was also harvesting for the following day's cooking. She ambled among the white pines near the camp, gathering into a birchbark basket the wispy grey moss which grew upon their trunks. This was often used as a nourishing addition to the broth of meat or fish. Thanking the pines for their generosity, she returned to the camp. There, she poured two handfuls of dried beans into a pot of water to soak overnight.

The following morning, she prepared the cattails for cooking. The knife that she used had been fashioned from a section of deer leg bone, with both the blade and the handle of one continuous piece. The area of the sharp blade near the handle bore a serrated edge. Laying one of the long rushes upon an overturned wooden platter, Otter cut off and discarded the green upper stalk with her serrated blade, leaving the tender white base of the stalk. This crisp portion could be eaten raw or cooked. She also scraped the light brown peeling from the white tuberous root, which could be either boiled or roasted. Otter sliced the crisp stalk and starchy root into short pieces, which she tossed into the simmering pot of beans, along with some pine moss and a small amount of bear oil. This main dish was accompanied by dried cherries and cherry twig tea.

During the afternoon, Hawk and Otter each crafted a knife sheath from birchbark. Hawk made one to protect the flaked blade of tan flint that was mounted into the end of a sapling handle. Otter's case would sheathe the unhafted knife of white flint which had a long oval shape that narrowed to a point at each end.

Otter first soaked a coil of split roots of black spruce in the skillet filled with water. Hawk cut out of thick bark two square pieces whose dimensions were about the length of his hand. These he folded in half, with the dark tan inner surface facing outward. After the roots had become flexible, Otter pierced a row of holes along the side and one end of the rectangular folded piece of bark. Handing the iron awl to Hawk, she sewed the holes with a long strip of root in spiral stitches that encircled the edge of the bark. Hawk closed his seams with a series of in-and-out stitches. Both items would serve the family well in the years ahead.

Hawk then joined Fox, who was entertaining himself by making dental pictographs with maple leaves. After folding a large leaf into quarters, he bit with his teeth a design in the soft green leaf. When creating designs with a thin layer of birchbark, the teeth only indented the bark; with leaf pictographs, the teeth bit completely through the leaf. This created narrow slits that were visible when the leaf was unfolded to reveal the bitten pattern.

In the meantime, Otter wandered off to an open area on the high riverbank to harvest some wintergreen berries, since the raspberry crop was not yet ripe. Berry picking was one of her favorite tasks; she looked for ripe fruit at every stop the family made, whether the halt was for setting up camp or merely a traveling rest stop.

Since it would take rather long to roast the duck, Hawk began its preparation early. At Fox's request, he first washed the bird free of blood. Native cooks usually did not do that procedure, for they did not want to lose any of the blood or fat. Skewering the carcass lengthwise on the straight portion of the iron rod pot hanger, he mounted the bird over the fire across two low forked poles. In the copper pot he assembled a soup of wild rice, wild onions, and dried aster leaves. He also added a few dried pumpkin blossoms, as both a spice and a thickener.

As the duck roasted, Fox occasionally rotated it on the spit, while Jacques watched closely. Fox quietly explained to the dog that roasted or boiled dog was considered a great delicacy among The People. But he also reassured his canine companion that he would never end up as meal fare, since his long, thick coat was too valuable as an ever-handy napkin during cooking and eating times, preserving somewhat the appearance of Fox's shirt sleeves and leggings.

When the roast and soup were ready, Otter supplemented her harvest of wintergreen berries with some dried cranberries, and then placed the blackened duck on a wooden platter. Armed with an iron sheath knife and an ivory-handled iron fork, she carved off generous chunks of the bird. Sprinkled with plenty of salt, the slightly fat meat disappeared quickly under the pointed wooden and bone picks of her family. As they gorged themselves, Fox explained that the French had adopted iron and silver forks instead of sheath knife tips for dining only a few decades earlier. After eating the solid portion of the soup, the family drank its broth, in native style. However, they also followed that drink with a hot tea of steeped maple twigs sweetened with maple sugar.

During the cleanup after the meal, Hawk did not throw the duck bones onto the refuse pile at the edge of the forest. His people were very careful in their treatment of animal bones. In French settlements, refuse bones from meals were thrown to the dogs. The People believed that if they did the same, the forest creatures would learn how their brethren had been mistreated, and they would then become much harder to find and catch. To avoid this calamity, they discarded animal bones in a fire or underwater, or buried them, where dogs could not find them. Dogs were only allowed to gnaw the bones of those creatures that were easy to catch.

As the bed of maple coals began to die down toward evening, Hawk preserved one of them for the morning fire in a fire carrier that had been used by The People for many centuries. First, he placed a small glowing coal in one half of a hand-sized mussel shell which was partially filled with ashes. He then mounded the ember with ashes, so that it would hardly burn during the night, and covered it with the other half shell. The two halves were securely bound together with a couple of turns of deerhide thong, and the ember holder was placed safely inside a hide pouch for the night. Sometimes, a thin sherd from a broken clay pot was inserted as insulation above and below the coal, to prevent the shell from deteriorating due to the heat. On other occasions, the shell was filled with powdered semi-rotten wood or tree fungus, which barely burned yet kept the ember alive.

The next morning, Hawk requested one of his favorite foods, a meat that Fox called *lard*. This fat meat, taken from the side of a *cochon* (pig), had streaks of muscle meat through it. When smoked or salted, it would last indefinitely, making it an excellent food for French traders who traveled into the interior. Other than bear meat or buffalo hump, none of the generally lean wild meats approached this degree of energy-rich fattiness.

While thick slabs of sidemeat fried in the skillet, Fox brought out a round loaf of wheat bread *(pain)* and a linen bag of *raisins secs* that he had recently brought from the St. Lawrence with his new supplies. As he tore the loaf into fist-sized chunks, his mouth watered for a taste of the *beurre et fromage* (butter and cheese) that he had heard were produced at some of the interior posts and missions.

With her granite mortar and pestle, Otter ground up a small handful of special dark brown beans. She then poured the resulting coarse powder into the little water-filled iron pot, and placed it onto the flames. After the liquid had reached a boil, she removed the vessel from the heat, and let the powder settle to the bottom before serving the dark brown brew with a gourd ladle into three cups. Sweetened with a bit of *cassonade* (brown sugar), this beverage that Fox named *café* made an excellent drink with her bread. She had saved her piece for the end of the meal, as a separate course; this was a common custom among her people when they were served French bread.

While Hawk finished off the last of the sidepork from a pewter plate, Fox told his family that the *assiette* (plate), made of wood, pottery, or pewter, had been added to the dining table of the French only a few decades before. Previous to that, a flat square of bread had served as each person's plate or bowl, to be eaten after it was emptied.

After the morning meal, Hawk set a kettle of French *pois* (peas) over the fire to simmer in water until late afternoon. He would return at intervals from his tomahawk range to add sticks to the flames.

After Fox departed upstream, paddling alone, Otter and the dog bathed in the side stream where it joined the main river. As she waded in the warm shallows, she automatically watched the light-colored sandy bottom for leeches. Fox had found a black one the length of his hand at the canoe landing area the day before. At that time, he had told her a strange story.

He said that some Frenchmen willingly allowed leeches to be attached to their bodies. In the native and French worlds, a number of medical treatments were similar, such as some herbal remedies, the setting of broken bones, and certain treatments of wounds. However, the French custom of purposely letting blood out of people who had ailments, by cutting them or by attaching leeches, struck Otter as very strange. Native healers did not practice this technique, since they thought that it would weaken rather than strengthen the patient.

As a growing and active young man, Hawk was often hungry. By latter afternoon, the familiar pangs in his stomach urged him to finish the preparations for the final meal of the day, which would be a typical French traveling meal. To the pot of cooked pea soup he added olive oil from a green glass *bouteille* (bottle) that had a round body and a short neck; he also poured in a little *vinaigre* (vinegar) from a *flacon*, a green bottle with four flat sides. In addition, he spiced the dish with salt, pepper, and a bit of crumbled dried leaves of *pourpier* (purslane).

The soup was accompanied by *biscuits*, hard flattened palm-sized buns baked from wheat flour. These buns, made to last for many months, were broken into pieces and dropped into the pea soup to moisten and soften a bit, so they would not break anyone's teeth. During the meal, the pungent aroma of the vinegar reminded Fox how much he enjoyed that special flavor. To suit his tastes, Otter sometimes followed the French custom of adding vinegar when simmering tougher kinds of meat, to tenderize them.

French *pruneaux* (prunes) and *eau-de-vie* (brandy) mixed with water finished the meal. The brandy, transported into the interior in a small keg, had been transferred to the glass bottle with the aid of a birchbark funnel. Otter had learned after only one mishap how to distinguish with a single glance between the two square bottles of vinegar and brandy: the one that held the drinking liquid was somewhat deformed around its top, the way her head felt whenever she drank its contents without enough diluting water.

During the evening chat around the fire, the subject turned to the various native foods which had been adopted by the French. Fox marveled that all of the main plant foods of The People — corn, beans, squash, pumpkin, and wild rice — had been completely unknown in Europe before the 1500s. Corn had only begun to be raised in France in the 1630s.

The yellow light of the evening fire eventually died away, and the orange coals faded. However, the camp was still rather brightly lit. From high in the east, a full moon shined brightly in a cloudless sky. Its perfect silver reflection also gleamed on the unruffled surface of the river. The sight would be one to remember after they moved on from this campsite.

When Otter had first arrived at the site, she had gathered a little bundle of six short maple twigs. Each morning, she had discarded one of the sticks. This was a common method of keeping track of days for her people; it was often used to coordinate the arrival of various scattered parties at a predetermined rendezvous location. Otter had thrown away the last remaining twig that morning, signalling that the next morning would be their time of departure.

On the final day, the pleasant voyage down the Tahquamenon and onto the shores of Lac Supérieur was short, covering only about five miles. However, that same voyage spanned more than three centuries.

Note:

Many of the comparisons in this chapter between French and native customs of food preparation and dining are based on a detailed report which was penned for the *Jesuit Relations* of 1658 by a Jesuit missionary in New France.

Chapter Eight

Otter wanted to look her best, since she expected important visitors to arrive that day. She began by washing her hands and face at the lakeshore, using a fist-sized ball of *savon* (tallow soap). Fox had explained that his people created the magical substance by cooking together animal fat and water which had been poured through hardwood ashes. The off-white soap created a strange lather that made grease and dirt disappear from her skin, without even having to scrub it in the usual manner with sand or horsetail rushes.

Next, she unfastened the deerhide thong bindings from her hair. Otter usually gathered her long hair into a single club or a braid that hung from the back of her head; for special occasions, she dressed it with bear oil or goose grease, and wore it in two braids. The oil not only added sheen to her hair, it also killed lice. As she wielded her brush before forming the braids, Otter felt a sharp point jabbing her hand from the handle area. Looking closely, she discovered that when she had fashioned the one-piece brush from a dried porcupine tail, she had overlooked one short quill when cutting the sharp point from each of the quills.

To supplement her traditional hair brush, Silver Fox had given her two *peignes* (combs), for which she had made two moosehide cases. One of the trade combs, made from reddish brown boxwood, had long, moderately slender teeth along one side. The other comb had been fashioned from a hard off-white material that reminded Otter of antler. Fox had said that the comb had been sawn from a long, curved tusk that grew from each side of the mouth of a huge creature. If his story were true, the animal stood twice as tall as a man, and it had a very long nose that looked and moved like a large snake. The special feature of this comb was its second row of teeth: the usual ones on one side were moderately slender, while the teeth on the opposite side were very fine and closely spaced, to be used for combing lice from her hair. Fox had occasionally mentioned that combs were also sometimes made from a flattened section of cow horn. He had also pointed out that the iron-sawn teeth of trade combs, whether of ivory, wood, or cow horn, were much longer and narrower than those found on native combs of bone or wood.

After forming a long braid down each side of her head, Otter tied the end of each one with a short thong, using both of her hands as well as her teeth. Alongside her head above each braid were two vertical hair pipes, one of wild turkey leg bone and the other of rolled kettle brass. Each of these tubular ornaments, about the length and diameter of a finger, was held in place by a number of strands of hair running through the tube. Those strands had been incorporated into the braid below, so that the two decorative pipes on each side of her head were held in place above the braided area.

Otter wrapped each braid with the flat tanned pelt of an otter's tail. The glossy, dark brown tail, about as long as her arm, was just the right width to wrap around the braid; it tapered gradually in width to match the taper of her braid. A long thong of deer hide, tied

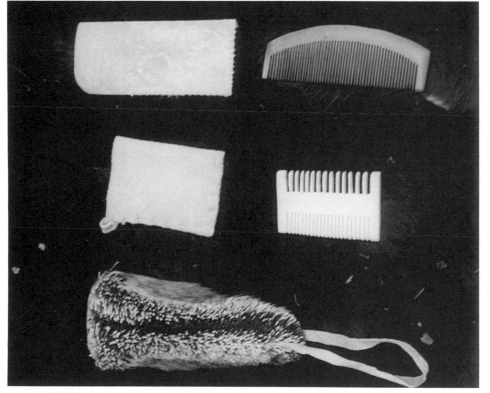

Upper: Otter wields a brush made from a dried porcupine tail.
Lower: Hairbrush, combs of ivory and boxwood, and two comb cases.

Otter dressed to greet visitors, wearing her full complement of ornaments.

The backside of her outfit offers an equally pleasant view.

Painted decorations and jewelry befitting a special occasion: armband, bracelets, finger ring, and ornaments at the ends of the braid thongs.

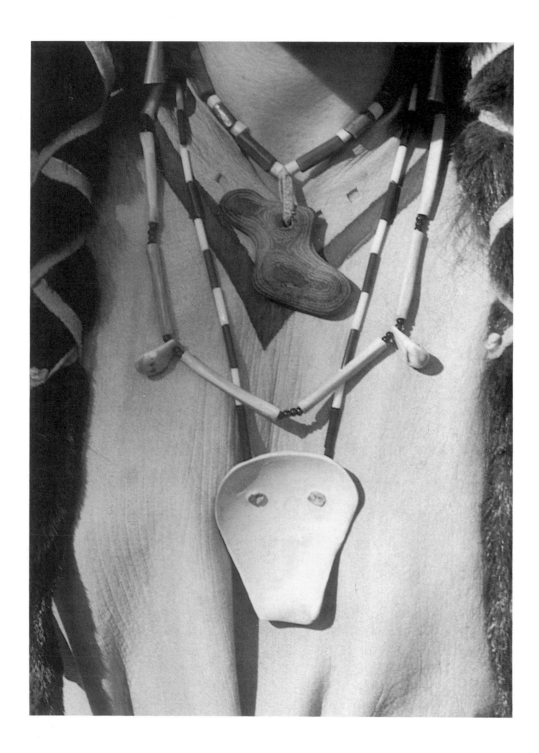

Three necklaces support pendants of banded slate and elk teeth as well as a gorget of conch shell.

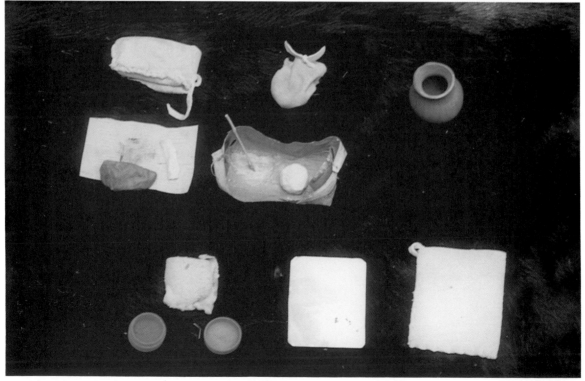

Upper: A tin mirror facilitates face painting.
Lower: Otter's paint kit, top to bottom and L to R: hematite stone and flint flake knife on birchbark, beneath their hide pouch; white clay in birchbark mixing dish, beneath hide sack; tiny clay pot of bear oil; lidded wooden box of vermilion, beneath its hide pouch; tin mirror beside moosehide case.

Upper: *Cassette* or traveling trunk.
Lower: Painting and drawing equipment in the lower compartment of the trunk.

Writing board and the removable tray containing writing paper, quill pens, bottles and paper packets of ink, and sticks of sealing wax.

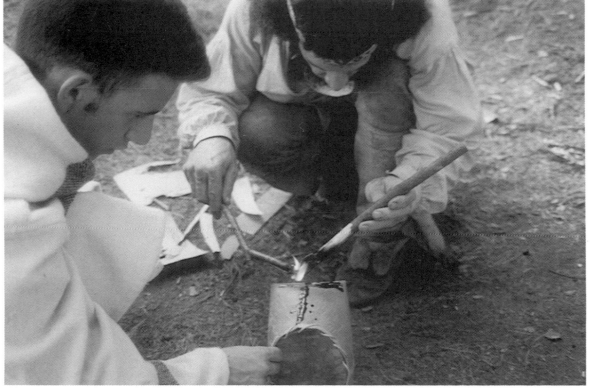

Upper: Fox sews a birchbark *makuk* with spruce roots.
Lower: Hawk assists him in sealing its seams with melted pitch.

Otter in her strap dress of deer hide. The two detached sleeves are joined together in front by a horizontal painted strap of moose hide.

Upper: A large boar's tusk pendant hangs from the juncture of the two sleeves in the middle of Otter's back.
Lower: Ember holder of a mussel shell lined with two pottery sherds and filled with ashes.

Ready for portaging, with two paddles lashed in position with a tumpline. The forehead strap of the tumpline hangs below the paddle shafts.

The weight of the canoe is shared by the tumpline strap across Fox's forehead and the paddle shaft on each of his shoulders.

at its midpoint around the top of the braid and the otter tail, was then wound in a series of four descending X patterns around the braid and its fur wrapper. About a hand's length above the tip of the tail, Otter's braid of hair ended; there, the two ends of the thong encircled the wrapped braid a final time and were knotted together. Decorating each end of the thong was a short tubular bead of bone, a round bead of blue glass, and at the end a cup-shaped bone tinkling cone. That hollow bone, taken from the ankle of a deer, was twice the length of a person's finger joint; it had been sawn open at the wider end and drilled for suspension with a single hole through the narrower closed end.

At the front of each shoulder of Otter's deerhide dress, near each of her braids, a single black dew claw of a deer hung from a short thong. This was the other traditional tinkling cone of The People, an item that looked much like a miniature front toe of a deer; it was taken from the rear of a deer's leg above the hoof. From the open base of each conical dew claw extended a bright splash of red. A clump of white hair from the underside of a deer's tail, the area that flashed white when the animal raised its tail and ran, had been dyed a vivid red color. The rich hues produced by natural native dyes, in a variety of reds, oranges, yellows, golds, browns, and black, were much admired by the French.

Otter's dress had been made from two deer hides, brain-tanned and then smoked to a light golden hue. The two hides were joined with stitches of sinew thread above her shoulders and upper arms and along her sides. The edges of the elbow-length sleeves and the knee-high hem of the dress were formed by the original edges of the hides. They had been left untrimmed, so that those edges undulated in very irregular curves, in the shape of the knife cuts that had removed the hide from the animal.

Besides the red and black tinkler at each shoulder, the dress bore other decorations as well. The base of the V-shaped neckline was outlined with five small diamond-shaped cutouts in the leather. The entire neckline was also decorated with a V-shaped stripe of dark brown paint. The stripe, about as wide as a finger, had been applied with dye produced by boiling the outer husks of black walnuts. A similar dark brown stripe, in the form of a curved inverted V, decorated the lower front half of the dress. The design, extending upward from each side seam beginning at about Otter's hand height, reached her waist with a sharp point.

The hem area also bore a stripe of dark brown paint on the front half of the dress. This narrower stripe, applied about a palm's width from the edge of the hem, undulated as it generally followed the broad curves of the hemline. In addition to the various decorations, each hide also bore two fingertip-sized holes, where the hunter's lead ball had entered and left the body of the deer.

Each of Otter's leggings was made of a rectangular piece of deer hide that had been folded in half in the long direction. A long row of in-and-out stitches of sinew thread had created within the folded hide a long tubular area that tapered to fit her leg exactly. The two long, loose edges created a doubled flap that gradually widened from a finger width at the upper end of the legging to a palm width at the bottom. These long-style leggings, worn primarily in colder weather, extended from Otter's ankle to her upper thigh. Women sometimes wore in warm weather short leggings which only reached to the knees; those were held up by a garter that encircled the leg just below the knee. At the top edge of each long legging, a thong was attached at the outer side of the thigh. This thong, tied to a narrow waist belt that Otter wore beneath her dress, held up the legging.

Additional support for each legging was provided by a garter tied around her leg just below the knee. Made of a strip of thick moose hide two fingers wide, the garter had been rolled over into a short loop at each of its ends; these were sewn with sinew thread. Through the two end loops ran a thong of deer hide, which was tied in a bow behind the knee to fasten the garter in position.

Otter's leggings were decorated with the same dark brown walnut husk dye that appeared on her dress. A finger-wide vertical stripe ran along the outer edge of the side flap, while a broader horizontal band along the bottom of the flap extended from its outer edge to the vertical sewn seam.

The two moosehide garters were entirely dyed dark brown, in contrast to the tan color of their deerhide binding thongs. In addition, a mink tail was sewn to the lower edge of each garter. The glossy, dark brown fur, about as wide as a finger and as long as a hand, hung down on the outer side of Otter's leg. In the center of each garter, at the front of her leg, gleamed a little square insert of kettle brass. The ends of the strip of sheet metal had been inserted into two vertical slits in the leather and folded over each other on the back side.

While sitting to tie on her garters, Otter also slipped on a pair of moccasin liners, to guard against the chill. Fashioned from blue woolen fabric and sewn with white wool yarn, the liners had been made in the same manner as her one-piece moccasins. A central seam extended from the tip of her toes up the midline of the top of her foot, while a second seam ran vertically up the midline of her heel. The two side flaps of fabric she tucked beneath the cuff of her legging.

Over the liners, she slipped on her moosehide moccasins, made in the same style as the woolen liners. They were ornamented with finger-wide stripes of dark brown dye, running along the three sides of each side flap and up the midline seam on the top of her foot. These moccasins, which she often wore without liners, could easily fit over a liner made from a single layer of lightweight wool. In winter, multiple layers of liners, consisting of woolen fabric, thin furs such as rabbit and muskrat, and stuffing of dried grass, cattail down, or deer hair, required much larger moccasins. Those winter versions had a very tall, one-piece cuff that covered the lower leg and was bound with long wrap-around thongs.

Standing upright, Otter tied on her narrow waist belt of moose hide; it was closed with a deerhide thong that passed through a sewn loop at each end of the belt. A finger-wide horizontal stripe of dark brown dye decorated most of its length. Each end of the stripe gradually narrowed to a sharp point near the thong-tied area at the front of her waist. Just before each end of the brown stripe began to narrow, it was ornamented with a shiny square insert of golden kettle brass, which was nearly as broad as the stripe.

Otter's sheath knife hung from the belt beside her right hip. Its iron blade and bolster were hidden within the narrow main portion of the sheath, which was painted around its entire perimeter with a slender stripe of brown dye. In addition, two widely spaced inverted

V designs, made of thin brown lines, decorated the middle area. The wide, rounded upper portion of the sheath flanked the tan wooden handle of the knife. This area was decorated with two tubular beads that were bound to the sheath in a vertical position, one on each side of the knife handle. The two brownish red beads, each about the length of a finger joint, had been formed by pounding a small chunk of native copper into a flat sheet, grinding its edges straight, and then rolling the sheet into a narrow tubular form.

With the introduction of French cooking vessels of copper and brass, ornaments such as tubular beads, tinkling cones, hair pipes, and flat pendants made of native copper were becoming scarce. There was no longer a need for The People to laboriously mine copper in the region of *Gitchi-Gumi* (Lake Superior). No more would they labor with heavy stone mauls to expose veins of pure copper running through quartzite bedrock, pound off pieces of the ore, and transport it southward. Now they simply cut up imported cooking vessels at their own camp, producing a supply of thin and perfectly even sheets of reddish copper and golden brass.

On Otter's left side, a hand-sized pouch of thick moose hide was suspended by two short leather loops from her belt. This pouch, which held her fire making kit, was closed by two wooden toggle buttons that each fit into a thong loop. The cover was decorated with a single keg-shaped glass bead which had a color pattern that fascinated Otter. The gently rounded sides bore narrow parallel stripes that alternated between blue and white; each end showed a series of concentric sawtooth circles or chevrons in blue, white, and red. In the pouch she stored her firesteel, fireflint, and two small round wooden boxes, whose lids protected a supply of charcloth and dried tinder.

Otter tucked the top of her long rectangular belt bag over and behind her waist belt, toward the left side of her front. In this manner, the vertical slit opening, which ran down the midline of the upper portion of the closed tubular bag, was held firmly shut. This kept her clasp knife and other possessions safely inside. The elaborate decorations on the thick moosehide bag made it one of Otter's most prized possessions.

The upper half of its front was dyed a rich dark brown, to contrast with the light tan smoked color of the lower half. In the middle of the brown area glistened a small rectangle of kettle brass, whose ends had been inserted into two slits and folded over on the interior side. Each long edge of the bag was decorated with two widely spaced tinkling cones of sheet brass. A spray of red-dyed deer tail hair projected from the open bottom end of each cone. The full length of the bottom seam of the bag was decorated with twelve smaller kettle brass tinklers. Each cone, hanging from a short thong, displayed a narrower spray of deer tail hair, which had been left in its original white color.

The closely spaced metal cones sometimes jangled softly against each other when Otter moved. As soon as Fox had begun to import cooking vessels of brass and copper, The People had started to replace their traditional tinkling cones of deer ankle bones and dew claws with ones fashioned from those two sheet metals. The new metal versions produced a very light tinkling sound when they tapped against each other, compared to the heavier clicking sounds that were produced by the native cones of bone and hoof material. Otter enjoyed the sounds of all of the various cones, so she incorporated each of them into her outfit.

For this special occasion, she decided to dress in all of her finery, including jewelry, headdress, and face paint. Otter stored her jewelry in a small pine box that Fox had given her as a gift. The wooden container, about as long as her forearm and as wide as her hand, was opened by sliding the thin top board out of its horizontal grooves near the top of the side boards. The thin wooden top which covered similar native boxes of carved solid wood was usually fastened to the shallow box by a thong bound around the box and lid; sometimes the top was made to swivel by attaching it to one end of the box with a wooden peg or a thong running through drilled holes.

From the box, Otter removed her jewelry, which had been fashioned from both traditional woodland items and new materials that had been brought by her husband. To adorn her right wrist, she chose a wide moosehide bracelet; it was tied closed with a deerhide thong that ran through a pair of holes pierced through each end. The hide bracelet, two fingers in width, was decorated with a block or step pattern of porcupine quills; some were dyed bright red, while others were left in their original white color. This bracelet was accompanied by another made from a slender iron rod that she had bent into a C shape, and a finger ring fashioned from a strip of brass cut from a kettle. Otter did not find particularly attractive the bracelets of iron wire or the finger rings of iron that Fox sometimes included in his stock of goods; she preferred the golden shine of brass ornaments.

On her left wrist, she also wore two bracelets. One consisted of alternating tubular beads of kettle brass and wing bones of a wild turkey. The bones, about half as wide as a fingertip in diameter, were cut into segments about as long as a finger joint. A second bracelet was made of a rectangular piece of sheet brass that had been rolled into a narrow rod and then bent to shape.

Above each elbow, Otter wore an armband. The one on her left arm consisted of a moosehide strap two fingers wide that was bound in place by a deerhide thong attached to its ends. It was decorated with a block or step pattern of porcupine quills dyed bright red, deep wine red, orange, and gold. From the lower edge of the armband, an oval pendant of pinkish tan mussel shell hung on the outside of her arm.

Her right armband consisted of a finger-wide curved strip of thin, flat bone. It had been cut from the shoulder blade of an elk and boiled until it softened a little; then it was bent into a semicircular shape. Each end had been drilled to receive the single binding thong; the area adjacent to each of those end holes was decorated with an X ground into the flat surface of the bone. From two holes near the midpoint of the armband, two pendants were suspended. One was a molar tooth of a black bear, hanging from a hole drilled through one of its roots. The second pendant was a little curved disk cut from a conch shell; that exotic whorled shell had been imported through inter-tribal trade from the Southern Sea (the Gulf Coast).

Otter's three necklaces were graduated in length, so that the items that made up each one would all be visible. The longest one, made of alternating dark blue and white tubular *rassade* (glass beads), suspended a palm-sized gorget of tan conch shell. The concave section of shell, cut from the broadly curved outer whorl of a conch, had a rounded upper edge, tapering sides, and a straight bottom edge. Each end of the sinew cord of the necklace ran through its own hole in the upper portion of the shell, where it was knotted after passing through a tiny circular button of deer hide. The form of the piece of shell and its two flat leather buttons implied an effigy face with a pair of eyes.

The second necklace consisted of sections of fox leg bones alternating with groups of four small round beads of dark blue glass. The fox bones, about a finger in length, had a diameter of about one-third of a finger tip. Two of the groups of blue beads near the bottom of the necklace also contained a rounded canine tooth of an elk, drilled through its single flat root.

The ends of the deerhide thong of the shortest necklace were tied in a bow behind Otter's neck so that the beads fit snugly against her neck. She had included three types of native tubular beads in this choker: four-sided tubes ground from red slate or catlinite, each about the length of a finger joint; round tubes of brownish red native copper about half that long; and short segments of wild turkey wing bone. The off-white bone beads alternated between the longer stone and copper beads to provide contrast. From the middle of the necklace, an effigy pendant of banded slate hung from a short deerhide loop. The shape of the stone, with a long-nosed head, an upright neck, and a horizontal body, had been formed naturally along the shoreline of a large lake, where Otter had discovered it. The addition of a suspension hole for the thong had provided an eye for the head, while the alternating layers of black and grayish tan of the slate provided dramatic coloration to the animal form. Otter had never divulged to Fox which protective spirit had appeared to her in her vision quest during her youth; but it was clear to him that the effigy pendant that she wore close to her throat represented that spirit to her.

From a brass wire loop running through each ear lobe, Otter had suspended on a sinew cord two rattlesnake vertebrae and nine small round beads of dark blue glass. Each of the little white vertebrae bristled with ten narrow bony projections. At the end of the cord was tied a slender raccoon incisor tooth, drilled through its long single root.

The headdress that Otter wore on special occasions was mounted upon a moosehide headband. The upper edge of the band was cut in a series of shallow scallops, and its front half was decorated with a horizontal strip of porcupine quillwork. The quills, bright red, deep wine red, orange, and white, had been flattened and spirally wrapped around a narrow strip of rawhide to create a pattern of alternating blocks of color. The strip was then attached with sinew thread to the headband.

At the back of the headdress stood an elegantly splayed tail of a ruffed grouse. The fan of eighteen tail feathers displayed its natural wavy pattern in hues of white, grey, and dark brown, with a solid area of dark brown near the tip of each feather. From the base of the fan of feathers, a long narrow ermine pelt hung down the middle of Otter's back to just below her waist. The soft fur, about three fingers wide, was white in all areas except the black tip of its slender tail. Between the eyes of the ermine was lashed a shiny black deer dew claw. From its open conical base hung two short thongs, each one suspending two tinkling cones of sheet brass. At about the midpoint of the ermine, a ball-shaped *grelot* (hawk bell) of gleaming brass was tied; it occasionally produced a hollow rattling sound when it was suddenly moved.

For her final preparations, Otter brought out her painting kit. From a small leather draw-string pouch, she produced a small hematite stone, a long slender flake of white flint, and a hand-sized piece of birchbark. Placing the soft reddish brown stone onto the bark, she sliced off one of its edges with the flake knife, producing a tiny pile of fine powdered pigment on the dark tan bark. After adding a bit of water and mixing it with her finger, Otter applied with her fingertip a large brownish red dot to each cheekbone area. She also decorated the center of her forehead with two short vertical lines, using a small lump of charcoal.

Then Otter removed from another pouch a small cake of white clay that she had gathered from the bottom of a nearby stream. She sliced from its side a little powder, which fell into a palm-sized dish of folded and tied birchbark. With a twig, she transferred a couple drops of bear oil from a tiny clay pot to the pigment, and mixed them together. To apply a fingertip dot of white to the part of her hair, just above her forehead, she checked her reflection in a *miroir* of tin. Every time she removed the shiny mirror from its flat moosehide case, she marveled at how easy it was to use that reflective surface compared to the surface of a river or a lake. Although the reflected image on her tin mirror was less clear than the image that she had once seen on a glass mirror, Fox preferred to trade non-breakable tin ones; they could be protected from scratches and dents with a thick moosehide case.

To paint the vertical lines on her chin, Otter removed the lid from a little round wooden box that she kept in a drawstring pouch of leather. Dipping a water-moistened twig into the fine powdered pigment, she created a vivid red hue that had a slightly brownish cast. Fox regularly carried a supply of this *vermillon* (vermilion) in his trade goods. The People found it very attractive, since it produced a brighter red color than any of the hues of hematite stone paint. They were also drawn to the powdered *azur* (blue pigment) that he imported, since very few native dyes could produce a blue color.

Fox was fascinated by the great variety of designs and color combinations that native men and women painted on their faces and bodies on ceremonial occasions, as well as when the men fought in battle. He had adopted the ceremonial practice himself since coming to live with them; however, he had chosen not to acquire any permanent tattoo designs. When he considered the dramatic patterns that were applied in native face painting, he thought that the simple reddening of cheeks and lips that was done by wealthy French men and women was very tame in comparison.

When Otter had finished donning her jewelry, Fox once again noted with approval that she did not wear a French crucifix, cross, medal, or religious ring, like some of her people did. He did not appreciate such reminders of the life he had left behind in the settlements on the St. Lawrence. He had noted that the few missionary priests who were in the interior regions gave those shiny brass religious items to any of The People who would learn to recite one of their prayers, sing a hymn, or memorize an answer to a simple religious question. Few of the native people were willing to adopt the teachings of the blackrobes and reject the ancient spiritual traditions of their ancestors. However, some of them took the oppportunity to exchange a little of their time and effort for a brass ornament, or for a long string of thick beads of cow horn or wood that the blackrobes called a *chapelet* (rosary). Such a string of black or red beads made an excellent headband, especially if it had a brass cross pendant at the end.

Fox was aware that most of Otter's people thought the teachings and demands of the priests were outlandish. The People had practiced since time immemorial a number of spiritual customs that had served them well. Their teachings had been passed down through the generations by spiritual leaders, teachers, and healers. Now the blackrobes insisted that those men and women, respected members of their communities, were evil and not to be believed.

Native traditions had taught the people to make offerings and appeals to a great variety of spirits, in hopes of good fortune in acquiring food, success in their various activities, good health, and safety. The missionaries wanted them to ignore all of their spirits, those powerful forces that controlled the fate of the native people. Instead of beseeching the spirits, they were told to pray to a man who had died with his arms and legs tied to a tree, as well as to that man's father, mother, and friends. Otter had been taught since her youth to develop an individual, personal relationship with the world of spirits, including her personal guardian spirit. The blackrobes wanted her instead to pray aloud, together with the rest of the villagers, as a group.

For many centuries, native tradition had encouraged the more successful and talented hunters to take more than one wife. This custom greatly increased the survival rate of women and children in a way of life that often included food shortages and starvation. The missionaries harangued them to have only one spouse. Native ways also taught that intimate relationships were both natural and healthy, even before marriage. The People thought that the blackrobes' celibacy was both abnormal and ludicrous. In those matters, the priests had a very different opinion.

Few of Otter's people could see any advantages to believing the strange messages of those strange men. On the contrary, they could clearly see that wherever the blackrobes traveled among them, many of The People sickened and died of strange illnesses that had never before been in their world. Many thought that the priests themselves were evil spirits.

Fox's thoughts about missionaries and their teachings were as negative as those of his adopted people. He could see the destructive ways in which the ideas of the priests were slowly beginning to erode some of the ancient traditional beliefs and customs of certain of his native relatives. The French clerics were starting to divide the people in their allegiances to each other and to ancient goals and principles. In addition, Fox had other personal reasons for rejecting the teachings of the missionaries. He had left the settled life of the St. Lawrence communities partly to escape the meddling and repression of the priests and other authority figures. He did not appreciate their presence in his new world of freedom.

The missionary priests railed at what they considered his sinful ways. However, they knew, as Fox also knew, that the survival of the economy of the French settlements depended upon the presence of Fox and the other French traders in the interior regions. Without them, the trade would fall into the hands of the hated English.

Otter's relatives were due to arrive shortly, for several days of gift exchanges, trading, and celebration. In preparation, Fox surveyed the stock of trade goods beneath the tarp shelter, and then decided to review his trading records in the *cassette*. The pine trunk, about as long and wide as his arm and as tall as his forearm, was considerably smaller than the trunk which carried the family's cooking equipment. It had been constructed for rigorous travel and wet conditions. The corners were strongly built in a series of interlocking square projections about as thick as the end of his thumb. The top and bottom board were each attached to the walls with glue and stout vertical wooden pegs. The two hinges, the hasp, and the mounting plates of the iron rod handle atop the lid were securely fastened with long tapered nails that were clinched on the interior of the trunk. Each of the items of black iron hardware had been forged to a graceful tapered form.

The closure mechanism consisted of a flat hinged hasp mounted on the lower front edge of the lid; its lower movable half had a wide vertical slot which fit over a rounded staple projecting from the front wall of the main portion of the trunk. A finger-long tapered wooden peg was inserted horizontally through the loop of the staple to hold the hasp in the closed position. When Fox removed the rounded peg and lifted the hasp, the peg remained attached to the hasp; it dangled from a thong loop that ran through a hole in the wide end of the peg and a loop of iron at the lower end of the hasp.

Raising the lid, he admired the clever way that the woodworker had made the lid of the trunk water-resistant. The interior edge of each wall board in the lid had been planed away to a considerable depth, and a matching raised lip had been formed along the interior edge of each wall board of the trunk. Thus, water entering the crack along the lower edge of the lid would be blocked by the raised lip. Many *cassettes* used for traveling were covered on the exterior with grained leather, such as cowhide or goatskin. But Fox preferred plain wooden trunks for canoe travel, since the exterior dried quickly after a wetting.

The topmost item stored inside the trunk was Fox's broad writing board; this he removed by placing two fingers of each hand in the wide hole drilled through the right and left ends of the board. Below was a removable tray, made of thin boards, which had finger-high walls. Within the tray, upright divider boards created three narrow storage compartments: two long ones along the left and forward sides, and a small square one between them in the left front corner. These compartments flanked on two sides the main storage area of the tray.

From the long compartment at the front, Fox chose out one of the graceful dark brown wing feathers of a wild goose. He trimmed the tip of its translucent quill into a tapered point with his clasp knife, to make a *plume* (pen). From the corner storage area, he removed a tiny round bottle of green glass from its wadded padding of blue woolen cloth, and extracted the cork stopper. After filling the bottle with water up to the base of its short neck, he poured a small amount of black powder from a folded paper packet into the vial, producing black *encre* (ink). The other little corked bottle in the corner compartment held dark brown ink, which he had acquired when Otter boiled walnut husks to make dye for coloring leather. Whenever he had no other inks, he mixed pulverized charred wood in water.

Fox was now prepared to record new transactions and update old ones, as payments of furs and hides would be handed over by his native customers. He next brought out his trading records, to review the various accounts. These records he kept on sheets of light tan *papier* (paper), which were stored in the main compartment of the tray. To write, he laid the sheets upon his thin writing board, which he placed on his lap or on any other handy raised surface.

The storage compartment along the left side of the tray contained a couple finger-long sticks of reddish brown *cire d'Espagne* (sealing wax). On those occasions when Fox sent a written message or letter, he folded the sheet of paper into a closed packet form and sealed it with a drip of melted wax on the outermost overlapping edge. This kept the paper securely folded, protecting the ink inside from becoming damp and smearing. Some traders who wore a brass *bague* (finger ring) with an engraved design on the flat face pressed the ring into the melted wax; this indicated that the writer had applied the wax seal himself after closing the letter. An unbroken seal verified to the receiver that noone had read or tampered with the written contents en route.

With the various items of his *écritoire* (writing set), Fox kept his business records, wrote a journal book and letters, and created maps of the areas of the interior in which he traveled. Many of the items for map making and for painting pictures of new discoveries were stored in the bottom of the *cassette*, beneath the tray of writing materials.

The tray had a broad finger hole drilled through its right and left walls; these enabled Fox to remove the tray to expose the lower half of the trunk. This area was divided by two thin boards into three long compartments, in which were stored his painting and drawing materials. He first reached for a round, hand-sized *boite de fer blanc* (tin box), and removed its lid. With four of the black iron tacks inside, he attached the four corners of a fresh sheet of paper to the writing board, so it would remain still even in a stiff breeze. Next, he chose from the shallow tin box the larger of the two *crayons* (pencils). The slender grey rod of lead, about as long as his finger, tapered gradually to a point at its drawing end. The broader end, half as thick as a finger tip, was useful for shading in areas of a map or a drawing. The first compartment also held a small wooden box with a sliding lid, which contained the paints. The various powdered pigments were each wrapped in a packet of paper.

The second long compartment in the trunk held a back shell of a small snapping turtle, as well as a supply of mussel half-shells. After filling the turtle shell with water, Fox brought out one of the mussel shells; he poured into it a little pigment powder from one of the folded paper packets. From the third compartment, he chose one of the larger brushes, and used it to transfer a small amount of water from the turtle shell to the pigment. With the brushes was also stored a small piece of sponge, for covering broad areas of the paper with color and for creating special effects.

Silver Fox painted and drew, in an untrained style, pictures of his discoveries about the lifeways of The People, as well as maps of their region. He felt that these would some day be of interest to his friends along the St. Lawrence. However, he was disturbed by stories that he heard about the efforts of another artist in the interior. He had heard of a missionary who painted vivid scenes to frighten The People. The priest depicted the horrible agonies they would supposedly suffer in *l'enfer* (hell) if they did not give up their old ways and follow his teachings.

Before Fox had arrived with his materials for drawing and painting, Otter was already accustomed to painting, on faces, bodies, and leather clothing. She quickly adopted his methods of creating artworks on paper, and reveled in it. While waiting for her relatives to arrive that day, she painted a watercolor of Fox's black felt hat perched atop the center pole of the lean-to. She particularly enjoyed portraying its colorful ornaments of dyed deer tail hair and a splayed mallard wing. Watching from a distance, Fox smiled at the sight of her intense concentration, surrounded by paint packets, brushes, water containers, and several mussel shell paint pots.

Although he was able to read and write moderately well, Fox could have kept his simple trading accounts of customers' names and their credits or debits with simple drawings. A number of other traders recorded their business dealings in that manner. The native people could relate to such pictoral writing, since they sometimes left simple messages for one another by means of symbols drawn on birchbark. Spiritual leaders also sometimes recorded sacred stories and ceremonies by making drawings on rolled scrolls of birchbark, or by engraving figures on wood. But those ceremonial writings served as memory aids rather than as detailed accounts.

The ability of Fox and other Frenchmen to communicate highly detailed accounts to each other over great distances by writing letters was a great marvel to The People. Fox had explained the secret of reading and writing to Otter, who was beginning to learn a bit of his written language. She had already learned to speak a certain amount of French in the process of teaching Fox her language.

Red-tailed Hawk left the campsite beneath the pines, joined his father and the dog at the lakeshore, and asked to use the *lunette* (telescope). Removing the brass instrument from a hand-sized moosehide pouch that hung from his belt, Fox extended its four tubular sections out to full length. Hawk loved to scan along distant shorelines with the magical instrument. He could sometimes see in great detail an approaching canoe an hour or more before it arrived at camp. This morning, he searched the open waters of Lac Huron for his relatives, scanning across the ten mile width of Anse du Tonnerre (Thunder Bay) to its northernmost point.

Leaving Hawk to his search, Fox and Jacques ambled out to the tip of Pointe des Rochers (Stony Point). Beyond the end of the long, slender spit of sand, waves broke over the barely submerged ridge of granite cobbles which extended well out into the lake. That unusual feature was a clear landmark for all canoe travelers who followed the coast of the large, deep bay.

Just inland from the base of the point, regiments of dark green horsetail rushes grew in irregular formations in the sand. Scattered among the rushes were a few wild irises, nearly ready to open their purple blossoms. Nearby, waist-high bushes served as handy supports for wild grape vines; in their shadows, a garter snake as long as Fox's arm tried to hide.

Sitting to empty the sand from his moccasins, Fox noticed that he had worn a hole the size of his thumb tip through the bottom of each one, at the ball of his foot. In addition, the entire bottom area had become thin, black, and smoothly polished from use. But he certainly did not wish for a pair of *souliers* (shoes) to replace them. Fox and many other Frenchmen had readily adopted moccasins, not only for living in the interior regions but also in the communities along the St. Lawrence; there, they were often made in native styles but of oxhide or cowhide.

For woodland life, native footwear was lighter, more comfortable, and quieter than European-style leather shoes. Moccasins could also be dried more easily beside a fire at the end of each day. Although moccasins wore out much more readily than shoes or boots, replacements could be quickly made by nearly everyone. Spare pairs, as well as hide and sinew threads for making new ones, were often carried as standard traveling gear. Since moose hide readily absorbed water, Fox periodically treated each family member's moccasins with bear oil, to make them somewhat water-resistant. When they did become damp, the leather conformed to the curved shape of each foot. To offset this, they switched each moccasin to the opposite foot every morning; this distributed the wear more evenly, and thus made them last longer. Whenever Fox thought about long-lasting footwear, he was reminded of his younger days in the St. Lawrence settlements. For outdoor work, he had worn *sabots,* wooden shoes that almost never needed replacing unless they were outgrown. However, wooden shoes were certainly no match for moccasins in any category except durability.

Fox wore liners of woolen cloth inside his moccasins to ward off the chill, like Otter did. However, he had recently worn out his moccasin-style ones sewn with yarn, so he used instead another type of native liners. He wrapped a long, thin strip of blue woolen fabric, about three fingers wide, numerous times around his foot and ankle. More layers of woolen strips could be added for colder weather, as well as strips of rabbit or muskrat fur. Those thin hides provided many layers of windings without adding a great deal of bulk. However, liners of woolen fabric dried faster than those made of pelts, and were warm even when wet. Hawk preferrred wearing French *bas* (stockings) instead of wrappings or moccasin-style liners. He liked the way those warm, tube-shaped trade items of woolen or linen cloth extended up beneath his leggings nearly to his knees.

Silver Fox and most other traders had also adopted *mitasses* (leggings) and a *brayet* (breechclout) instead of *culottes* (knee-length trousers). The three separate native articles made active movement much easier than when wearing one-piece trousers. In addition, leggings and moccasins could be quickly removed for loading or unloading a canoe offshore or wading across a stream. Since canoe travel often involved jumping into the water to drag the craft against strong currents, through shallows, or up rapids, Fox found it easiest to wear only a breechclout and a *chemise* (shirt) in the canoe. Even the shirt was left off in warm weather. When ashore, he donned his warm leather leggings and moccasins, which remained dry in the craft.

Fox chose to wear deerhide leggings rather than ones of fabric, due to the much greater durability of leather. He did stock some cloth leggings in his trade goods, as well as much fabric for the native women to fashion into leggings and breechclouts for both men and women. For his own clout, he chose fabric over leather: durability was not a factor in that garment, while the faster drying time of cloth made it preferable to leather, and it was warm even when wet.

In addition to wearing a number of items of native clothing, Fox had also learned from his adopted relatives to coat his body with animal fat, particularly bear oil. This layer of fat helped keep him warm in winter. When mixed with skunk oil during the summer, it also protected his skin from biting insects.

Fox's breechclout and the fastening thong at the top of each legging were held up by a narrow moosehide belt that he wore beneath his shirt. The forearm-wide strip of woolen cloth of the breechclout passed between his legs and over the belt at front and back, where each end hung down nearly to his knees. The lower edge of the front end was decorated with a narrow row of zigzag stitches in white yarn. He smiled as he remembered how Hawk used to gauge his growth by the height of the ends of his red wool clout: the ends, now above his knee caps, had once flapped well below those knees.

Like Otter, Fox wore brown-dyed moosehide garters tied below the knees to help support his deerhide leggings. The garters, as well as the palm-wide waist belt of moose hide that he wore over his shirt, had a loop sewn into each end; a deerhide thong was run through the end loops for tying.

Instead of wearing wide leather bands at the knees and waist like his father, Hawk wore a pair of garters and a wide sash woven of woolen yarn. For centuries, The People had finger-woven these items using yarn made of dark brown buffalo wool or dyed opossum hair. Now they simply unraveled trade blankets to acquire a supply of red, blue, and white sheep's wool yarn for weaving. Frenchmen had quickly adopted the native sash and garters, wearing both finger-woven versions and others made from a loom-woven strip of cloth. At the ends of Hawk's finger-woven sash, the individual strands of yarn hung free, creating a fringe about a forearm in length. The end fringes of his finger-woven garters were more elaborate: the strands of yarn extended beyond the woven area as six braids for a hand's length, and then hung as free strands about as long as a hand.

Each member of Fox's family owned a *chemise* (shirt) of linen; Hawk's had been bleached from its natural light tan color to an off-white, while those of his parents were dyed light blue. Otter sometimes wore hers beneath her leather dress for additional warmth in cold weather, or alone, without the dress, in warm seasons. After long use and many washings, Fox's shirt had faded considerably; its former light blue hue was now nearly off-white on the shoulders and the upper back area. Whenever Otter washed it, she wondered about the strange item called a *fer à repasser* (flatiron) that Fox had indicated was sometimes used on shirts at the major posts. As he described it, that piece of black iron with a handle was heated in the fire and passed over a washed *chemise*, to make it as flat and smooth as when it was first unloaded from a pack as a new garment.

The wide cut of his shirt sleeves allowed free and easy movement; at the wrists, the cuffs were tied closed with a length of linen tape runnning through two sewn holes. To allow free leg movement, the nearly knee-length hemline was slit upward for a hand's length beside each hip. Over time, the V neckline of Fox's shirt had torn considerably at its apex. He had repaired it by sewing the tear with a length of sinew thread. Since shirts required considerable tailoring skills, he traded large numbers of them each year as finished articles, instead of supplying fabric to be sewn into shirts.

Fox wore his sheath knife suspended by a neck strap, so that it would always be available, even when he wore no waist belt. The moosehide sheath was not tapered to match the curved shape of the knife blade. Instead, it tapered equally in width on both sides, ending in a squared-off tip about two fingers wide. The lower area of the sheath was dyed a deep rich brown in two wide bands, while the remainder was left in its golden tan smoked color.

Just above the sheath on his chest hung his coyote bone necklace and conch shell gorget. The segments of leg bone, each about two finger joints long, had a triangular or square cross section about half to two-thirds the width of a finger tip. Near the bottom of the necklace, a long incisor tooth from a black bear curved out gracefully from each side. From the long tan root of each tooth, the white enameled tip curved outward while it tapered to a slightly rounded point. The shell gorget attached to the bottom of the necklace, light tan in color, was about the size of Fox's palm. The oval concave section, cut from the outer whorl of a Gulf Coast conch, was suspended by a cord running through two widely spaced holes drilled a little above the midline.

Hawk's bone necklace and conch shell gorget were similar to those worn by his father. In addition, he wore a narrow thong choker which supported an oval pendant carved from catlinite or red slate. The rounded surface of the pendant bore a star pattern of carved lines radiating from its center.

In keeping with the customs of The People, Fox wore an ornament in a hole pierced through his nose septum and one ear. A small ring made from a slender copper rod hung from his nose and the lobe of his left ear. He avoided wearing any ornaments in his right ear, so that they would never be caught when he shot his carbine from the right shoulder. The men of Otter's people had traditionally worn ornaments of stone, bone, shell, or native copper suspended from their nose and ear lobes and rims, as well as feathers inserted through holes in their ear lobes. With the introduction of Fox's copper and brass wire, they sometimes also spiralled those decorative wires through a series of holes along the rim of the ear, creating the appearance of a coil of wire.

Hawk wore two different ear ornaments on brass wire loops from his left ear lobe. The shorter one consisted of two nested deer dew claws hanging from a string of eight little round glass beads, alternating in white and dark blue. His longer ear dangle contained four whitefish vertebrae, each one separated by a pair of small blue glass beads. Below these was tied a wheel-shaped chevron bead, which had an end pattern of sawtooth concentric circles in white, blue, and red. The glass bead was tied in position on its edge, so that the ornate end pattern and coloration were clearly visible. At the bottom of the ornament dangled a tinkling cone of kettle brass.

Around the camp, Fox usually wore a headband of rattlesnake skin. The band portion, dark tan in color, was decorated by the natural pattern of its scales: a long row of greyish brown ovals of finger tip size ran all along the midline. At the back of his head, the end of the tail pointed downward for a hand's length. Backed by a thick strip of moose hide, this portion bore its natural pattern of horizontal bars of alternating greyish brown and light tan. At the tip of the tail hung a stack of six tan-colored rattles; these created a high, thin rattling sound whenever Fox shook his head, just as they had when the snake had formerly shaken its tail.

When traveling in the canoe, Fox often exchanged his headband for a broad brimmed felt hat, to help shield his eyes from the sun's glare. His present *chapeau* (hat) of black felt was relatively new and somewhat clean. In contrast, his former one had been so greasy that he could produce a bowl of drinking water, when traveling in winter without a kettle, by melting snow in the hat over a fire.

At the junction of the broad brim and the crown of the hat, a string of whitefish vertebrae encircled the crown. Taken from whitefish that had been smoked to a golden color, most of the little spool-shaped bones had acquired a golden tan hue in the porous midsection area. The entire left side of the brim, raised and sewn to the crown, was colorfully decorated. Toward the rear of the raised portion, a splayed wing of a male mallard pointed its feathers upward and rearward. Brown feathers along both sides and the base of the wing framed nine flashy central feathers of irridescent greenish blue, each with a bar of black and another of white at the tip. Forward of the mallard wing, a pair of black dew claws of a deer hung from two short thongs. A spray of red-dyed deer tail hair projected from the open bottom of each cone.

Hawk wore a headband that was decorated in the traditional manner of The People. The front half of the wide moosehide band displayed a narrow rawhide strip wrapped with porcupine quills in hues of reddish brown, gold, and white. From the rear of the headband hung two tail feathers of a wild turkey, each one rotating freely on a deerhide loop. The forearm-long plumes bore their natural pattern of alternating wavy bars of brown and black across the width of the feather, with a wide black bar near the tip.

The base of each quill had been transformed into a loop upon which the feather could hang and rotate. One side of the hollow quill had been sliced away in a gradual taper to its tip, over the length of two finger joints. Then the thinned end portion was doubled back on itself, and its slender tip was inserted into the hollow center of the quill. The loop that was formed at the end of the quill was strengthened by a narrow strip of deer hide laid over the loop parallel to the quill. Then the area of the quill above its end loop was spirally bound with a slender deerhide thong for the length of a finger joint. Feathers equipped with such a looped end could be easily tied to long hair or to a headband.

Even though Silver Fox dressed and lived like his adopted native relatives, he was always immediately recognizable, due to his wavy dark hair and full dark beard. He did not use a *rasoir* (straight razor) to shave his face, like some traders and missionaries did. In contrast to Fox, The People had straight hair and only scant facial and body hair, which they usually plucked out. They had traditionally used for that task two mussel shells as tweezers; now they sometimes used instead a thin strip of sheet brass or copper folded over on itself.

Hawk wore his hair in a style that was quite typical of the men of his mother's people: it was cut and singed rather short over most of his head, with the hair above the forehead somewhat longer and held upright by bear oil or goose grease. Sometimes the men left only a strip of upright hair down the middle of the head, with a lock on top left long, or the sides were left long and tied behind the ears. Another style consisted of long hair with a long braid on each side of the head.

While waiting for their relatives to arrive, Hawk and Fox each fashioned a *makuk* of birchbark. The People made these deep boxes or pails in a variety of sizes, up to a maximum length and depth of about a forearm's length. The shape of most of these containers was similar, with a rectangular or square bottom, walls that slanted inward slightly, and an oval or round rim. Those that were to be regularly handled typically had a reinforcement strip lashed around the rim; boxes for storage often had no such strip.

Since the supply of birchbark had dried out after being harvested, Hawk soaked his piece for a short time in the lake. Then he cut it with scissors into a shape that reminded him of a miniature deer hide with an additional round projection in the middle of each of the two long sides. The bark was positioned so that its grain would run in the long direction, up the sides of the *makuk*; this reduced the likelihood of cracking while the container was being made and used. After heating the bark at the fire to make it more pliable, Hawk laid it down with its white side up. He then bent the wall and end portions upright, and lapped the end sections over each other in the middle of each end. When the bark cooled, it tended to retain its new shape.

Several coils of peeled and split roots of black spruce had been placed in the skillet to soak in warm water; this restored their flexibility. With an iron awl which had a triangular cross section, Hawk punched holes in the overlapping end sections of bark. These he sewed with a length of root in a series of in-and-out stitches, to create a vertical seam up the midline of each end wall of the container.

Next, he stitched the short rounded flap into place at the base of each end wall, using a harness stitch. For this procedure, the root was drawn to the midpoint of its length through the first awl hole. Then the ends of the root were passed through each successive hole, in opposite directions from each other. This created a series of end-to-end stitches, and a very strong and tight seam.

To complete his *makuk*, Hawk installed around the outside of its rim a strip of basswood inner bark which was as wide as a finger. This reinforcement strip was lashed in place with roots in a series of widely spaced spiral stitches that encircled both the strip and the rim. When installing the various root lashings in the container, Hawk finished off the end of each root by tucking it underneath an adjacent stitch or two on the interior, to hold it firmly in place.

In order to make his container waterproof, for use as a pail, Fox applied sealant pitch to the exterior side of each of the seams. With a little birchbark torch, he melted over the seam areas a finger-sized piece of pine pitch mixed with fat and pulverized charcoal. The melted sealant dripped onto the *makuk*, sealing the edges of the overlapped layers of bark as well as the holes of the root stitches. Glancing up from his task, Fox noted a box turtle ambling liesurely across the edge of the clearing.

On *makukon* that were used for long-term storage, a flat or convex birchbark lid was stitched to the rim area of the filled container. Those that were to be opened at intervals were fitted with a removable cover. The container in which Otter stored many of her cooking spices had such a lid. Two layers of bark had been cut into an oval shape a little larger than the rim of the *makuk*. These were positioned horizontally, with their white sides against each other, to counteract the curling tendency of each piece. A long strip of bark, two fingers wide, formed an oval slightly smaller than the inside of the rim; it was lashed in a vertical position to the underside of the doubled lid with split roots. This strip served as a flange to hold the lid onto the container.

Both the lid and the *makuk* bore decorations scraped into the surface in an ancient technique of The People. The bark, harvested in early spring or late fall, had come off the tree with a thin layer of reddish brown rind adhering to its interior surface. This side of the bark became the exterior surface of the container. After the *makuk* had been constructed, the surface of the bark was moistened. This allowed the thin dark-colored layer to be scraped off, exposing the tan bark in certain areas in a decorative pattern. Both sides of the container, as well as its lid, bore two long, curved stems with a row of slender projecting leaves along each side. In addition, a narrow line formed a series of scallops just below the reinforcement strip all around the rim.

In the region where Otter and Fox lived, as well as further to the north, The People usually did not craft baskets or containers of split strips of wood or slender saplings such as willow. White birches grew plentifully in their region, and sturdy containers of all sizes could be easily and quickly fashioned from their bark. On the other hand, French traders sometimes utilized for storage and transport strong baskets and hampers that were woven of strips of wood or young saplings. Fox had been surprised to learn from Otter about an unusual bonus of using storage containers made of birchbark intead of woven containers or kegs. Edible items stored in birchbark *makukon* tended to resist decay.

While Fox and Hawk stitched their bark containers, Otter paddled in the bay to the south of the point. The unruffled surface of the lake and the bright sun above allowed her to clearly see the bottom, even at a considerable depth. Through the light green tint of the water, she observed fields of large boulders lining the lake bottom at quite a distance out from the shore.

After beaching the canoe near the point, she silently followed the forest path toward the camp. Not far ahead of her, a deer stepped lightly into the clearing where Hawk often practiced throwing his tomahawk. Shortly, another deer joined the first, and the two glided without a sound through the woods to the edge of the big lake to drink.

Toward evening, as the sun approached the western treetops and a breeze wafted off the lake, the air began to chill. Fox slipped into his woolen *capote* and tied his wide *ceinture* (sash) around his waist. The semi-fitted coat had been fashioned of off-white fabric, rather thick and fuzzy, that had been woven with a single charcoal-colored stripe near each edge. The seamstress had arranged the cloth so that the dark stripe, half the width of a finger tip, decorated the mid-calf hem, both cuffs, the collar, and the front of the hood; in each instance, the stripe lay about a thumb's length from the edge. The shoulders and sleeves were tailored to Fox's dimensions, while the body of the coat simply overlapped in front for about a forearm's length. The wide lapels, overlapping beneath his chin, were held closed by a single toggle button at the collar. The button, made of a segment of peeled sapling about the size of a finger jcount, fit through a loop of deer hide. In winter, when he raised the long, pointed hood, its generous depth shielded his face from side winds.

The body of the *capote* was held closed by a colorful finger-woven *ceinture*. The sash, as wide as a hand is long, encircled Fox's waist once, and was tied in a knot on his left side. The woven ends hung halfway down to his knee, while a fringe of yarn strands reached the remaining distance to his knee. Native weavers had unraveled woolen blankets to produce a supply of spun yarn in hues of white, blue, and red. Those strands had been finger-woven into a design made up of rows of three adjacent V forms on Fox's wide sash; a VV pattern was sufficiently wide to fill Otter's narrower sash. Sometimes the native weavers incorporated a pattern of glass beads into the woven pattern, and ornamented the strands of end fringe with wrappings of dyed porcupine quills and copper or brass tinkling cones.

Otter often decorated her capote by wearing an armband with a dangling tail of a red fox on each upper arm. In winter, she wore for dressy occasions a pair of mittens fashioned from the same fabric as her off-white capote, with the narrow dark stripe running near the edge of the long cuff. When she removed the mittens, they remained close to her hands, dangling from the ends of a long thong that ran up inside each sleeve and across the top of her shoulders. For heavy work, similar woolen mittens were worn as liners for larger ones made of thick moose hide.

Fox traded considerable numbers of *capotes* to Otter's people each year, as well as a great deal of woolen fabric for making those coats. His own family wore white ones, which were effective as winter camouflage; however, he also stocked the hooded coats in other colors, including solid red and blue. In addition, he carried a number of decorative items to be applied to the native-made versions, such as *galon d'or, galon d'argent* (gold and silver braid), *frange d'or* (gold fringe), and *ruban* (ribbon).

The traditional native outerwear for winter consisted of a robe, a pair of tubular sleeves, and a hood, turban, or cap; these were all made of hides or pelts. One-piece robes were typically made from the pelt or hide of a bear, buffalo, elk, or deer, while multi-hide robes were often fashioned from beaver, otter, or marten pelts. Fox imported *couvertures, manches,* and *bonnets*, woolen versions of the native robe or blanket, sleeves, and cap, as well as bolts of woolen cloth for sewing those items. The hooded French *capote* was also a popular trade item, since it combined into one garment those four separate articles of clothing.

In addition, he sometimes carried in stock a *justaucorps,* a tailored knee-length coat which did not have a hood. This coat typically bore wide cuffs, a row of ornamental buttons down the full length of the front, and a decorative pocket on each side; it was often worn with a waist belt or sash.

After an evening of festivities with her relatives, Otter was awakened early by the honking of a north-bound line of geese. This day, she would wear her other leather dress, a shoulder strap dress with detached sleeves. Two brain-tanned, smoked deer hides formed the dress, which extended from her armpits to just below the knees. The top edge of each hide had been folded over twice, to create a flat band the width of a thumb. Then the two hides had been sewn down each side on the interior, with spiral stitches of elk sinew thread. A moose-hide strap two fingers wide extended over each shoulder; it was fastened with deerhide thongs to the double-folded top edge of the dress at front and back. The front end of each shoulder strap, hanging free, extended down to just below Otter's waist, as an ornament. The lower portion of this strap extension was decorated with three diamond-shaped cutouts down the midline, while the tip, cut into two lobes, bore four radiating stripes of dark brown walnut husk dye.

The flat folded band across the top of the front hide was decorated in three areas with sinew-sewn beads. In the center, a wheel-shaped bead of tan wood was flanked on each side by a horizontal tubular bead of dark blue glass. Near each arm, the band was adorned with a wheel-shaped chevron bead flanked by two white glass tubular beads in a horizontal position. The chevron bead was attached with its flat end facing outward, to clearly show the concentric sawtooth circles of blue, white, and red glass.

The hem area of the front hide was ornamented with narrow painted lines of brown walnut dye. The horizontal pattern consisted of two long parallel lines one finger thickness apart, with the area between the lines filled by a zigzag line. The straight painted decoration, generally about a hand's length above the hem, did not follow the irregular hemline; that bottom edge had been left in the curving form in which the hide had been originally sliced from the deer.

Since the morning air was a bit cool, Otter decided to wear her pair of deerhide sleeves as well. Each sleeve had been fashioned from a long rectangular piece of hide which was folded over in the long direction. The lower end of the sleeve was sewn near its doubled edge with a series of in-and-out sinew stitches, forming a tube the length of a hand. The rest of the sleeve was not sewn closed; instead, the hide that would have covered the inside of her elbow and upper arm was cut away in a gradual diagonal, to allow free and easy movement as well as unrestricted bending of the elbow. Each sleeve ended just below the shoulder, leaving the top of Otter's shoulders bare.

At her back, the flat expanse of the two sleeve pieces lay like a two-piece cape; the two segments were joined to each other at their upper corner by a thong. From the ends of the thong hung a crescent-shaped tusk of a French *sanglier* (boar). The finger-long tusk, light tan in color, generated considerable discussion whenever native people saw it for the first time. Such an amazing tooth had never grown in their woodland world. The lower pointed end of each sleeve piece at her back was also ornamented, with five diamond-shaped cutouts near the edges of the point.

Across her front at the collarbone level, a moosehide strap two fingers wide joined the two sleeves together. A dark brown painted design filled the midline of the strap along its full length. The pattern was similar to the motif that decorated the hemline area of the dress, with a zigzag line filling the area between two long parallel lines. However, on the sleeves strap, each of the lower triangular areas that were outlined by the zigzag line were colored solidly in brown. The cuff of each sleeve was also ornamented, with a row of end-to-end tubular *rassade* (glass beads) that alternated between white and dark blue.

Women of The People often created strap dresses and pairs of detached sleeves from deer hides, like Otter did. They also sometimes made cloth versions, using the various fabrics of linen and wool that Fox imported.

Since arriving at the campsite, Fox had gathered a little pebble each morning and added it to his skunkskin fire bag. When seven pebbles had accumulated, he knew that the next morning would be the time to depart.

Under a bright cloudless sky, the family broke camp, packed, and prepared to travel. They would have to carry their belongings and the canoe overland to a nearby waterway to continue their journey. To prepare the canoe for portaging, Fox uncoiled a *collier à porter* (carrying strap). This native device consisted of a wide central band that fit over the forehead of the carrier and two long straps, attached to the ends of the band, which were tied to the object being carried. The central band of Fox's *collier*, cut from a thick elk hide, was as long as his arm; it tapered gradually from a width of three fingers at its center to two fingers at each end. Through a fingertip-sized hole at each end was tied a flat strap. Braided from three long segments of dark tan trade cord, each strap was three paces in length.

Fox laid two paddles atop the center thwart and the thwart forward of the center, with their blade ends pointed toward the bow. The grips of the paddles were positioned about a forearm's length apart, while the blades lay adjacent to each other. The portage strap or tumpline was draped over the center thwart so that its central elkhide band hung down between the paddle shafts in a U form that nearly reached the ribs on the floor. After lashing the shafts firmly to the center thwart with the two braided straps of the tumpline, Fox ran the straps a short distance outward toward each gunwale. There, each strap encircled the place where a long tapered indentation had been carved into each edge of the thwart. The strap was then nestled against the sharp shoulder which lay beside each indentation, where it was knotted in place. This anchored the lashings, so the paddle shafts would not slide out of place along the thwart while the canoe was being carried. The long straps then extended to the forward thwart, where they lashed the two paddle blades to that thwart. The canoe was now ready for portaging.

Facing the midsection of the craft, Fox crouched and lifted its near wall over his knees, while keeping the stern end on the ground. He then reached across with one hand to grasp the far gunwale. In one motion, he pulled the canoe upside down and raised it over his head, while he stood and turned to face the raised bow end. After resting the shafts of the lashed paddles on his shoulders, he placed the elkhide band of the tumpline across his forehead; this lifted some of the weight from his shoulders. Resting his hands on the paddles in front of him caused the bow end to lower somewhat and the stern to rise.

Fox carried the canoe in that angled position along the forest trail, with the rest of the family preceding him, laden with linen bags and wooden trunks. Jacques tripped lightly ahead, leading his family over the divide between the seventeenth and the twentieth centuries.

Note:

The discussion of the teachings and methods of missionary priests, as well as their low rate of native conversions and their severe criticisms of the morality of traders, is based on numerous early religious documents. Particularly important sources are the many accounts in the *Jesuit Relations*, especially those of 1645, 1679, and 1694.

Chapter Nine

Fox piloted the canoe from the surging open waters of Lac Huron into a long, narrow inlet, where the bucking craft immediately quieted. As he and Sunning Otter paddled further up the placid waterway, a muskrat crossed in front of them. Swimming with only its nose and eyes above the surface, the dark brown animal quietly dived when it reached the grassy shallows near the far shore. Around the first bend, a blue heron that had been standing silently in the reeds flapped away in slow motion.

Following the broad curves of the slender inlet, the canoe traveled parallel to the shoreline of the big lake for about two miles. Then the waterway, which lay more than a mile from the lake, curved lakeward for nearly a mile. At its far end, where the inlet broadened to resemble a small lake, less than a quarter-mile of low, flat land separated it from Lac Huron. This narrow neck of earth was the only connection between the mainland and the large oval which was separated by the inlet. Fox christened that nearly detached piece of ground Presque Isle (Almost an Island).

When the couple stepped out into the shallows to safely beach the craft at the end of the inlet, Jacques leaped over the gunwales and happily splashed ashore. As the trio crossed the narrow neck of stone-covered ground, they could see glistening flashes of sunlight in the shallows of the big lake, among the thin patches of reeds offshore. As they neared the edge of the bay, splashing sounds reminded them of a small rapids in a stream. At the water's edge, Jacques could hardly decide where to run and bark first. Hundreds of spawning carp swam and basked in the warm shallows, each one showing its brown and gold upper back and dorsal fin above the water. At intervals, small groups all along the shoreline broke into action; as they formed swirling, splashing circles, the clear water was whipped to a muddy tan color. High overhead, three hawks glided in broad circular patterns, watching for a potential meal.

As the canoe glided back down the inlet with hardly a sound, a deer bounded from the water back into the safety of the underbrush. A little further, a group of three mallards paddled silently into a cove. From his position at the stern of the canoe, Fox admired Otter's strong paddle strokes at the bow. With each rhythmic pull, the high prow of the craft surged forward, cutting the placid surface of the water.

Ever since he had first arrived to live among The People, Otter had been his wife, partner, and friend. As he had learned to live and thrive in the native world, she had been his closest companion, assisting him in many important ways in both his daily life and his work. Like other native wives, Otter ran their household, gathered firewood, preserved foods, and prepared meals. She also made the various items of woodland clothing that he had adopted: moccasins and liners, leggings, garters, breechclout, belts, and woven sash. When traveling, she served as his paddling partner as well as his guide on the waterways and overland paths, while he memorized the routes that she had traveled all her life.

Sunning Otter maintains many of the traditions of her people, while embracing new items and ideas from the French culture.

Silver Fox straddles two worlds, the French one in which he was raised and the native world which he has adopted.

A profusion of trillium blossoms decorates the forest floor near the shores of Lac Huron.

Fox valued just as much her assistance as a translator and language teacher, as he learned to communicate with The People and other trading allies of the French. She also acted as a cultural ambassador, guiding him while he mastered the social customs of native life. He smiled as he remembered one particular incident in his education program.

Shortly after he has begun living with her people, Otter had quietly advised him to get rid of his *mouchoir*, or at least to leave it knotted around his neck. She had explained that whenever he blew his nose into that square of fine linen and tucked it away inside his shirt, her relatives and friends laughed at him. They thought it was ludicrous that he would so carefully save his nose waste, rather than blowing it onto the ground like they did.

As a trade ambassador, Otter had provided an important linkage between Fox and a wide network of her relatives and friends, who then became his customers. The long-established relationships between her family and those individuals created bonds of trust and good will between trader and clients. This was important, since his customers often needed to make purchases on credit, against their future successes in hunting and trapping. Fox was very aware of the many important contributions that Otter regularly made toward the success of both his business and his new life among The People.

Some of Otter's people traveled far beyond their home region to serve customers of their own, trading with other native groups that lived deeper in the interior. Certain of these native traders peddled goods which they received in trade from Fox, while others traveled out to the St. Lawrence settlements with him each year to acquire their own goods themselves. Many native groups had no direct contact with Fox's people; they were willing to pay to the native trading allies of the French great prices in hides and furs for rarities of European cloth and metal. These far-flung groups welcomed the opportunity to acquire from Otter's people even their broken iron tools, patched copper and brass cooking vessels, and semi-worn items of fabric clothing. The greater the distances that those foreign items were transported into the interior, the rarer and more valuable they became.

Fox had heard stories about native trading networks such as these which had operated across vast areas of the interior for centuries before he and other French traders had arrived in the New World. Various native groups had particular items which they could produce in their home regions that were rare or unavailable in other areas. For instance, rich furs and supplies of meat and fish that were harvested in the cold northern regions were traded for cultivated food crops and tobacco that flourished further to the south, in more temperate climates where furs were of lesser quality. Supplies of native copper or high quality flint for tools were quarried locally by some groups, while others excelled at weaving or pottery production. Otter had told him that her people had been particularly active in long-distance trading for many generations. They had woven great numbers of mats from dyed rushes, which they had exchanged for pigments, shells, pottery vessels, and sashes of buffalo wool yarn. Since the introduction of European items of metal, glass, and cloth, a great deal of the inter-tribal trade handled these new articles instead of native-made ones.

As Fox and Otter paddled further down the narrow inlet, they discussed other changes that had occurred since he had begun to trade among The People. His European goods had replaced many items which had formerly been fashioned by native craftworkers. Those replacements involved both positive and negative aspects. A great amount of labor was no longer necessary in a number of craft areas, allowing time and energy to be expended on other aspects of life. However, this easing of labor was not necessarily only a positive event. Many handwork tasks had brought contentment, satisfaction, and a sense of carrying on the ancient traditions of previous generations. Those feelings were lost when foreign items were purchased instead of creating homemade articles.

Fox was aware that some traditional crafts were being entirely eliminated by the introduction of his trade goods. The gradual replacement of pottery vessels with containers of copper and brass, as well as the switch from stone tools to ones of iron, reduced the prestige of those who had spent much of their lives becoming expert potters and flint knappers.

Other crafts were only partially changed. Otter had observed that many weavers of nets for fishing and hunting had stopped producing their own cordage from basswood inner bark or nettle stalk fibers. Instead, they fashioned their nets from linen trade cord. Other weavers who created mats, bags, sashes, and garters often utilized native yarns and cords in combination with the new materials of unraveled blanket yarn and trade cord.

Some of the changes that took place in traditional crafts caused an upsurge of interest in new areas of handwork. Craftsmen who had flaked flint and pecked and ground other stones into implements found that there was no longer much demand for their products. However, the importation of iron knives, awls for drilling, and files encouraged another type of stoneworking: the carving of soft stone, especially catlinite or red slate, into ornaments and smoking pipes. Leather workers began to find that fewer hides needed to be tanned, as cloth replaced leather for many garments. But the newly-introduced fabrics, scissors, needles, and threads generated a great deal of interest in sewing and decorating clothing.

Fox was aware that certain crafts, such as woodworking, were greatly enhanced by the introduction of his trade items. With the more efficient iron tools, larger and more elaborate wooden articles could be produced with less labor and time. Builders of birchbark and dugout canoes found that the new iron tools facilitated their work considerably. This helped them supply the increasing numbers of canoes which were needed, as more and more trading voyages were carried out.

When Fox had first arrived to live among The People, the traditional metal workers had labored with nuggets of native copper; these had been laboriously mined and transported from the copper regions of the north. His European goods now provided a ready supply of thin and even sheets of copper and brass, cut from cooking containers, as well as brass and iron salvaged from broken firearms and tools. Using iron knives, scissors, chisels, punches, and files, native craftsmen now produced a wide array of metal objects that had formerly been fashioned from forest materials such as wood, bone, antler, and shell. This in turn reduced the demand for the products of the craft workers who had formerly used those native materials. It was clear to Fox that virtually all of Otter's people were affected by the new items that he brought into their lives, often in ways that were not apparent upon first glance.

Otter pointed out that some of the changes that had been wrought by his trade affected The People in areas that were far more important than their handcrafts. In former times, their lives had centered around a balance between hunting, fishing, gathering, and gardening. That balance had now been considerably altered, especially for the men. A much greater emphasis was now placed upon the accumulation of furs and hides to be used in trade. This encouraged them to invest more time and effort in hunting and trapping, so that they made longer, more frequent, and more distant trips from their families. Technological changes also affected the work of many of the hunters. As French firearms gradually replaced the traditional bow and lance, the prestige of the most expert archers and spear throwers waned in favor of those who mastered the new noisy weapons.

The greatest focus was placed upon harvesting beaver pelts. However, the hunters also sought the furs of otter, marten, mink, muskrat, ermine, fisher, bobcat, lynx, panther, bear, wolverine, fox, coyote, wolf, skunk, and raccoon. They also accumulated the hides of deer, elk, moose, and buffalo in considerable numbers.

In addition to increasing their emphasis on hunting and trapping, Otter's male relatives and friends had also expanded in length and duration their voyages to carry out inter-tribal trade. Some of the native traders also made the trip all the way to the French settlements on the St. Lawrence each summer; they led entire convoys of canoes to carry out the accumulated pelts and hides and return with a new stock of foreign goods.

Otter's female friends and relatives had also increased their efforts in response to the trade. As hunting and trading voyages increased dramatically, the need for dried provisions to be consumed by the travelers also rose. The women who lived far enough south to raise substantial gardens harvested and dried larger crops. Those living to the north beyond the gardening regions prepared greater amounts of meat, fish, fat, and foods such as fruits and wild rice that they gathered.

Besides the increasing numbers of native travelers that required provisions, each year more Frenchmen also lived in or traveled into the interior regions. These included traders and their canoe crews, missionary priests, and a few soldiers. They exchanged European goods for supplies of native provisions, strips of birchbark for shelters, and many of the birchbark canoes in which they traveled.

Otter could clearly see that the focus of The People had switched to producing for the trade large supplies of furs, foods, and canoes; she also noted a great increase in their trading voyages. These alterations in their lifestyle were beginning to lead to changes in the social order and power structure of her people.

Traditionally, their society had been based upon individuals acting, for the most part, according to their own initiatives; the people were led only by the suggestions and persuasiveness of experienced leaders. The independence and freedom of individuals in this system differed greatly from French society, which was based upon obedience and a leader-follower hierarchy.

In addition, The People had developed great degrees of flexibility and adaptability, by living for thousands of years in a natural environment where success was never assured in their endeavors of hunting, fishing, gathering, and gardening. Their attitudes contrasted strongly with the carefully planned ventures of Frenchmen, who had lived for eons with the relative security of domesticated plants and animals.

As their economic lives became more and more centered around acquiring European goods, native leaders began to feel increasingly pressured to live by French standards and to comply with French demands. Over time, Otter had noted that certain younger individuals who cooperated with the French and their new ideas had gradually become powerful leaders, replacing older, more experienced men who lived in the old ways. These new leaders could be kept under a certain degree of French control by the lure of the trade, as well as by threats of the trade being witheld.

Warfare had been traditionally carried out by The People in small war parties, based on the willingness of each individual within the party to participate. Now, large campaigns involving hundreds of warriors and great fleets of canoes were becoming more common, led by Frenchmen and fueled by the economics of the trade.

Traditional native ways of living were beginning to change, in both large and small aspects. Otter understood that the very presence of her husband and his trade goods was contributing in various ways to those changes. However, she was also aware that Fox preferred the native life to the one in which he had been raised; he had very willingly left his French world to live in her world. Ironically, by living with The People, he was changing them.

When Otter and Fox had paddled up the inlet, they had encountered in one location the strong odor of skunk. On their return trip, they landed on a point on the inside of a bend in the waterway to investigate the situation. As they beached the craft, a few spawning carp in the reeds finned noisily away, while a red-winged blackbird flew from its perch on a dried cattail stalk.

Along the bank stood mixed stands of cedars, poplars, and a few white birches. A young garter snake lay sunning atop the grass near the water. About six paces inland, Otter discovered a heavily-used deer trail skirting the water's edge, deeply worked with hoof prints and dotted with occasional piles of pellet-shaped brown droppings. Further in from the water, red and jack pines towered over young tamaracks which were sprouting new needles.
In a grassy clearing, she came upon blooming irises, violets, forget-me-nots, and wild strawberries. Near the edge of the sun-drenched clearing lay a pile of large, bear-sized droppings, reminding her that she was not the only berry harvester in those woods.

Further along the bank, Fox located the source of the pungent odor which had led them to the point. On the grassy bank, a skunk lay dead, close to the entrance of its underground den amid the roots of cedars. Having died very recently, the skunk was in better condition than the one that hung as a fire bag from Fox's belt; the tail on his bag had been singed at many a campfire as Fox had tended to cooking chores.

As Fox and Otter discussed the demise of the white-striped animal that lay beside its home, the conversation gradually turned to the funeral customs of each of their worlds. In the French world, Fox explained, when deceased people were buried, they remained buried. He had never grown accustomed to the funeral rituals of The People. Their dead were first laid in graves or upon scaffolds of lashed poles, until the flesh had disappeared. Eventually, the bones were cleaned and wrapped in woven mats or sheets of birchbark, in preparation for their final burial. Every certain number of years, a Feast of the Dead was held. The remains of all those individuals who had passed away since the previous Feast were gathered and reburied together, with great ceremony, in a mass grave. To Fox, the thought of handling the skeleton of a loved one was very disconcerting; but Otter had been exposed to that custom all her life, and she understood that by those rituals her people honored their departed ones.

The ways of life of the French and the ways of The People seemed to create two entirely different worlds. Their homes, clothing, ways of acquiring food, modes of transportation, weapons and styles of warfare, and entertainments all differed radically. Likewise, many of the customs, beliefs, and attitudes of each of the two groups were very much unlike those of the other, sometimes almost direct opposites.

However, many of the basic attributes of human beings were quite similar the world over, irregardless of the cultural surroundings. In addition, most of the French traders who chose to live in the interior regions were very receptive to adopting native ways. Fox and Otter shared many human traits and ideals, and both were open-minded about borrowing the good traits of each other's world. They had achieved a balance between their two cultures, melding together many of the best features of both worlds. If only French governors, military commanders, and priests would not interfere, the future of their descendants and of all The People would be a bright and fruitful one.

Index

The following listings are not intended to function as a detailed index, but merely as a guide to the primary subjects which are considered in each chapter. The subjects are listed in the order in which they first appear in each chapter.

Chapter Four
    Canoes
    Shelter
    Games
    Bedding
    Spirituality
    Modes of Transportation
    Cooking
    Songs

Chapter Five
    Hide Tanning
    Hides and Fabrics

Chapter Six
    Fire Starting
    Leatherworking
    Sinew Thread Production
    Sewing Fabric
    Hides and Fabrics
    Berry Picking
    Bark Case Construction
    Music
    Stories
    Guyline Braiding

Chapter Seven
    Cooking and Eating
    Tomahawk Throwing
    Barkworking
    Cordage Production
    Refuse
    Food Gathering
    Dental Pictographs

Chapter Eight
 Grooming
 Clothing and Ornaments
 Face and Body Painting
 Spirituality
 Writing, Reading, and Art
 Barkworking
 Outerwear
 Portaging

Chapter Nine
 Otter's Roles
 Native Traders
 Impact of Trade
 Burial Rituals

The Author

Tim Kent is an independent scholar and lecturer living in Ossineke, Michigan. He is shown above (left) with his son Ben and dog Toby upon arrival in 1995 at Fort Chipewyan, Alberta, at the northwestern end of the mainline fur trade route. The Kent family, including his wife Doree and son Kevin, paddled the route from Montreal to Fort Chip in a series of annual segments.

Of the 725 direct French and French Canadian ancestors that Tim has researched (originating from over 120 communities in France), many were involved in the fur trade of North America, from about 1618 to at least 1758. They were engaged in the occupations of fur trade company manager, clerk, trader, interpreter, guide, voyageur, merchant/outfitter/fur buyer, investor, laborer, tradesman (cutler, gunsmith, post carpenter, etc.), birchbark canoe builder, and trans-Atlantic shipping merchant. In addition, other ancestors served as soldiers in Canada, in the Carignan-Salières Regiment during the 1660s and the Troupes de la Marine in the 1680s and 1690s. Biographies of these individuals are in preparation for publication.

Tim has nearly completed a detailed study of some five hundred dugout canoes across the U.S. and Canada, ranging from the southern tip of Texas to Nova Scotia to the Yukon. This research will result in a major publication on these craft.

Numerous museums, schools, and organizations have enjoyed the family presentations and slide shows concerning the living history experiences of the Kent family.